SUMMONING THE BONES

Inviting The Goddesses In

Larisa Hunter
Sheal Mullin-Berube
Sarah Strickland

TLS

ISBN13: 978-1-959350-35-4

Set in: Georgia 31pt, In the Wood 13/14/19pt, Esther 32pt, Geneva 11pt

©The Three Little Sisters
USA/Canada

CONTENTS

"I THINK YOUR BONES WERE MADE IN AN ELSEWHERE PLACE. HOW ELSE DOES ANYONE EXPLAIN THIS INCONCEIVABLE STRENGTH THAT MAKES YOU.

THE WAY YOU LOOK INTO DANGER'S MOUTH AND SEE NO CEMETERY OR DEATH. INSTEAD, CARVE YOUR NAME INTO IT'S TEETH WITH A SWITCHBLADE, DEFEAT IT SO EFFORTLESSLY AND THROW YOUR HEAD BACK AND LAUGH.

PARADOX GIRL, MIGHTY WOMAN, YOU ARE THE THING THAT TERRIFIES THEM. BOTH MONSTER AND MAIDEN, BOTH CURE AND POISON, ALL OF THESE THINGS AND AT THE SAME TIME HUMAN.

DEFINED BY NO MAN, YOU ARE YOUR OWN STORY, BLAZING THROUGH THE WORLD, TURNING HISTORY INTO HER STORY. AND WHEN THEY DARE TO TELL YOU ABOUT ALL THE THINGS YOU CANNOT BE, YOU SMILE AND TELL THEM:

"I AM BOTH WAR AND WOMAN AND YOU CANNOT STOP ME."

--An Ode to Fearless Women
Nikita Gill

INTRODUCTION

WHY IS THIS BOOK CALLED SUMMONING THE BONES?

In this volume we look at the more spiritual side of following and living with the gods. We wrote this book as a companion to the first one to include the more esoteric elements of our path and to further expand on why certain goddesses were included in the book. To call the goddess implies that we have some ability to control the comings and goings of goddess, but it is more that we are summoned to them. They come and go as they please. It should be stated now that what the three of us believe is different but has some overlaps, the first being that the goddess do not come when you demand, they come when they see fit. The gods for us are living, breathing, sentient beings who are alive in our homes. We express the belief that they become part of our world by bringing them into our lives through worship and daily devotions.

LARISA

For me there is a tipping point in which you decide that this path will be not just the one you walk down but the one that transforms your very nature. This point is when you transition into a living breathing heathen that models the worldview into every aspect of your life, this usually allows for one to begin living with the gods instead of only appealing to them at specific points of the year. There is nothing wrong with only contacting the gods/ancestors when you choose to do that, but it does at some point if you make specific logical steps on the road move from occasional to regular to living quite quickly and seamlessly. Sometimes you are unaware that you casually shifted so far into the path that the gods are just there. I do caution those who walk down this path, that occasionally the doorway that is open in which the gods are welcomed in, is generally a doorway not easily closed. It often involves you giving way to the gods living with you which does reduce some level of privacy in your home, it creates room and space for the spiritual which can be consuming at times. They are often loud and particular about your way of living, so it's a relationship that is not for the faint.

If you do go down this road and have them in your home, the best way to ensure a working and healthy relationship that is mutual and full of understood boundaries is to agree to these in concert with them. I know all this sounds a wee bit crazy and fictional, but you can have conversations with them and get feelings as to what will and won't be acceptable. The way we structured this book is to assume that you believe in the living gods like we do, that you want to have a closer relationship with them and so invite them into your space with open arms. This book will do just that, and you can use it as a jump point to further your spiritual relationships and kinship with the gods.

The book is designed as if you are calling to them as you would a friend, you create a world for them to inhabit, you set a place for them, you allow yourself to be vulnerable to that which they might demand of you. I will say and it's a hard truth for which some seem not so eager to stipulate, these gods are not always kind. They do care, and they are loving, but these are not some all-loving mother goddesses in the way that some would have you believe. They will call you out on your imperfections. Each of them has deep and traumatic scars that reflect the suffering and joy that they have endured. They understand pain, trauma, tragedy, and the real true nature of that which women must keep silent. There is something so deeply profound about the love and acceptance they give, but they also have no issue calling you out on your bullshit.

They do not see the need to constantly make you feel good, they will be brutal, honest, make you confront things that you may or may not be ready for. They do this not to be cruel, but to truly heal and be whole, often requires a complete tear down of what we are and a rebuilding slowly to a more secure place. They are the dread sisters who often hold in them the power of life and death, they are the mistresses who walk in the darkness carrying secrets of the lords to whom they serve, they are the women who are often dismissed, the ugly ones, the disfigured and defamed, to be with them is to be with the most marginal of people. There is something so meaningful in this sisterhood.

I truly never understood how profound they would be until I allowed my whole being to be given over to them, once I committed myself to them and what they wanted from me, I was given truly wonderful gifts. Most of these have been the ability to finally heal from my own trauma to be made whole and to accept what and who I am. These gifts are most treasured by me, as I was often lost in a sea of emotion from which I could find no shore. This is more just an accessory book to the first Riding The Bones it is the items we left out, our breadcrumbs for those willing to dive into dread sisterhood, it is the second step along the way.

What Makes a Goddess?

Through the lore and archaeological records, most of the gods inside the Nordic regions are not always assigned a strict gender or role. Some are gender fluid or hermaphroditic in nature, some have more subtle almost non-binary attributes to them. Some are strictly placed in more feminine or womanly houses in that these places would be for better or worse be confined to women or those that were viewed as women to be the most skilled in this area. We will look at the example of birth in Old Norse Society to buttress our point of the women's only sections of life. "Only women were present.... Runes and songs were offered as age-old remedies for difficult births, performed by a healing woman" [pg 80. Women in Old Norse Society, Jenny Jochens].

In this same book it defines the divisions of work into categories of indoor and outdoor, women controlled the interior work of the estate/property, "fyrir innan stokk: literally, "within the threshold". This does not mean however they did only what work was within the four walls of the house, it means they were mostly kept out of activities that required a large amount of labor for example, planting and preparing soil. This did not apply if you were lower or slave class.

Often slave women would be expected to do the same work as a man, often grueling amounts of labor as they had no real rights. Regardless of the status of the person though, the goddess can be seen from the high born to the low in what rites/rituals they had sway over, the domestic work that they showed favor to and the protective/ magical nature to which women were ascribed to base on the magical links to the goddess that exist.

There is no real methodology in which the goddess become goddess. Many of them don't have an elaborate backstory with a huge moment of deification, they just seem to be 'there' the entire time and seem to be ageless, constant, and unwavering. Many of them are married to powerful gods, some are married to powerful giants. Some of the seemingly sweeping roles over certain aspects like Freyja who has sway over the battle-dead, Valkyries, and often referred to as the 'priestess of the gods' implying her great knowledge of 'magic'.

A second example is Frigga who is responsible for the household, motherhood, prophecy or at least the weaving of, and to some degree marriage although this is mostly that she has 13 handmaids which all take roles that are within the same 'realm'. Some have specific roles like Sif who is the representation of wheat and Ran who is the mother of the waves and responsible for the ocean or at least is the one who receives the dead at sea. Regardless of the status or gravity of their roles they all deserve the same amount of respect. In fact, in my opinion, they deserve some greater understanding for they bear much of the burdens that women often don't discuss.

This does not mean that women face more burdens or that all the burdens they bare are so terrible they can't be dealt with. These are more nuanced. Many of them are responsible for the marital happiness of the husbands they are joined to, many faced issues of infidelity, bastard children, chronic abandonment, and death of lovers/husbands etc. They are not innocent either, some of them have been free with their beds and often participated in actively wooing lovers that would be particularly irritating to their husbands.

With gods its complicated and one should not really look to them to solve relationship issues as they don't' really conform to any real strict rules when it comes to that and don't really advocate for this despite what some people like to think about the role of the Nordic women being all pure as the driven snow and only responsible for children is clearly far from accurate. These women birthed gods, watched the universe unfold, buried their lovers/husbands/children, suffered deep humiliation/rape/abuse, they were banished/revered worshiped/avoided and remain the most elusive in terms of sources that can be definitively pointed to for us to have a full picture of what they really thought/felt/did in the myths.

Whatever scant evidence is found is often nuanced and needs advanced scouring to uncover. There are many continual narratives that seem to branch across all the Nordic gods as pointed out in several works by Maria Kvilhaug. The mythological stories are written in a style that is not meant to be read literal but to be understood in deep and meaningful ways. The same is true for Celtic gods. This region was even harder to peg down in terms of historical sources on any god/goddess and so the same issue is found.

You have goddess that sound almost like clones of Nordic ones such as The Morrígan who is similar in many ways to Hel and the Norn's and then goddess like Brigid who are linked to magic like Freyja. There are gods that cross such similar boundaries like Wotan that you can't really tell them apart from Odin. This is true to across several cultures in the region, the crosses barriers of language/region and often bare such striking similarities you would swear they are the same. There are however nuanced differences that make them different, and that difference creates a different way in which we approach them.

Welcome To The Sisterhood

-The summoning cards are an expansion of our original Riding The Bones Deck. The cards symbolize each goddess (covered in this edition) as well as cross over cards that were mixed into our original deck-

Hail the blest Gods! See the rainbow of Asgard,
Bifrost, the bridge to the Aesir´s abode!
Hail to the far-seeing watcher and guardian,
Faithful defender of radiant road.
Hail to you, Heimdall, our elder and ancestor!
Hymns we will sing to the High Ones and you.
Come, let us call to the Megin once more,
Rig, tell the Regin their folk still is true.

Say, shall we give now in grateful devotion
Blots to the Aesir, and offerings divine:
Bread from the cornfield and fish from the ocean,
Mead from the beehive and gold from the mine.
All our lives shall be one dedication,
All our efforts to them shall belong.
Dear to the Gods is the soul´s adoration,
Near to their hearts are our prayers and song.
--© 2006 Michaela Macha

Inviting Nordic Goddess

The Norse goddess do not need that much ceremony to invite them. There is a big difference between heathen practice and pagan practice in that the setting is not as important as the level of respect you give. There is no need, unless you wish to open a 'circle' or sacred circle of any kind. You can if you wish but honestly they don't need these. In fact most of them are just going to prance across any boundary likely with a sour face and a snide eye roll that will make you think they uttered "really?".

These are goddess, good luck confining them. I would also recommend you do extensive research before combining them with other gods or adding more external elementals, these goddess sometimes don't want to work with certain gods. Ensuring that they have similar functions, personalities, responsibilities might help in persuading friendships. Some of us do practice a more eclectic pantheon faith in which we are comfortable including multitudes of gods from various paths, however some heathens are not.

There is no real right and wrong here, its what you feel your faith dictates and what the gods wish to do. They cannot be ordered around, so if relationships are not formed between practitioner and god/goddess or god/goddess from path a/b and practitioner, there is little you can do to force the situation. You may need to have flexibility in how you practice or carve out space for multiple deities in your home.

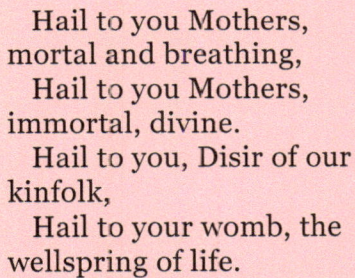

Hail to you Mothers,
mortal and breathing,
   Hail to you Mothers,
immortal, divine.
   Hail to you, Disir of our
kinfolk,
   Hail to your womb, the
wellspring of life.
   --© Michaela Macha

ANGRBODA

PRONUNCIATIONS:	Angrboða (Old Norse: [ˈɑŋgẓˌboða]
MEANING OF NAME:	"The one who brings grief", "harm-bidder", "foreboding"
SACRED DAYS:	None known
RACE:	Jotun/giant
GENDER:	Believed to be female
FUTHARK:	Perthro, Hagalaz, Isa
SEASON:	Late winter
RESPONSIBLE FOR:	In the mythology her responsibilities are mostly linked to her relationship with Loki but contemporaries point out that she could be responsible for the marginalized or disfigured and is linked to 'outside dwellers'. Most notable feature: she is described as a hag with very wild appearance, most notably she is always dressed in furs.
COMMON ASSOCIATIONS:	Sorrow, wolves, Hel, the Midgard Serpent, Fenrir, warriors
ANIMAL:	Wolf
COLOR:	Black, russet red
PLANET/ STAR:	Jupiter, Andromeda Constellation

She prefers meat offerings and things made from or of wood, fur type offerings would be also appropriate. These should be ethically procured or substituted for artificial furs.

For vegans, she would be fine also with forest greens or things like Fiddle Heads/Fiddle Greens also known as Ostrich ferns, which grow in wild environments very well.

HARROW/
ALTAR SETUP:

Using fur or faux fur build a flat pad for which you can place a plate or bowl. She prefers wooden items if possible but any bowl will do. In this you should place 1-2 herbs from the root variety. This could be anything from nutmeg to ginger root anything that has long and deep roots that have a strong smell to them.

If you can and are comfortable doing so, cooking a small section of meat to leave for her is appropriate or raw meat if you can leave this in a place where animals do not have access to it. If you are not able to use meat, then placing the fiddle head fern or similar woodland cuttings would be appropriate. [See Section on Disposal of Offerings]

DEVOTIONAL
IDEAS:

For Angroboda, devotional acts could include helping those who have physical needs or are marginalized. Assisting in acts of civil disobedience, standing up for justice, representing the rights of all is part of her power. Working to clean up public land would also be an amazing act of service for her, donating to wolf conservation efforts and working to reduce environmental damages.

*"A witch dwells to the east of Midgard, in the forest called Ironwood: in that wood dwell the troll-women, who are known as Ironwood-Women. The old witch bears many giants for sons, and all in the shape of wolves; and from this source are these wolves sprung. The saying runs thus: from this race shall come one that shall be mightiest of all, he that is named Moon-Hound; he shall be filled with the flesh of all those men that die, and he shall swallow the moon, and sprinkle with blood the heavens and all the lair; thereof-shall the sun lose her shining, and the winds in that day shall be unquiet and roar on every side."--*GYLFAGINNING 12 [BRODEUR'S (1999:XI-XX)]

POEM OR PRAYER

In Iron-Wood's
wasteland,
   Wild wolves she
whelps;
   Her brood is bringing
   Both balance and bale.

   Hati is harrying
   Mani to move,
   Sköll in the sky
   Is pursuing the sun;

For night and day,
They never may dally;
Time cannot tarry,
Flees ever so fast.
To Byleist's brother,
Breaker of bonds,
   Three boundaries she
bore,
   Three barriers birthed:
   Limit of Life,
   Hel holds what she has;
   Only what ends
   Has value and worth.

Edge of the Earth,
Serpent encircles us;
Borders and bounds
Define who we are.

End of Everything,
Fenris will fall,
A new age from ashes
Beginning again.

Both grief and gain
Are the gifts she begets,
The Járnviðja jotun,
The   Womb   of   the
Wood.
   --© Michaela Macha

There are no real stories of her in the myths, what is known about her is only through the one or two poems that describe a woman who lives in the ironwood, who birthed wolves. There is not much about her after that. We don't know where she came from as with most of the lore on giants, it seems they lived either parallel or separate from the gods and so do not have much lore dedicated to them. In contemporary literature, there is a book called The Witches Heart by Genevieve Gornichec which retells a variation of her life based loosely on the lore.

In this book she has an apt description of her abode:

"Angrboda made her home on the far eastern side of Ironwood, where the trees clung precariously to the steep mountains bordering Jotenheim. She stumbled upon a clearing near the base of one such mountain where she found an outcropping of rocks that led into a cave quite large enough to stand in."

[The Witches Heart by G. Gornichec.]

She further describes that she arrived here without any real garments or items and thus had to make her own clothing from furs and flax. This is interesting because it could be possible that she could be associated with those who are perhaps poor or without a house. We will begin with finding a sense of calm. Breathe in through your nose, feeling the air fill your lungs, then breathe out slowly through your mouth, letting your worries float away. Breathe in a sense of calm, breathe out your tensions.

Breathe in, and feel your heart beats steadily, breathe out and know that you are safe. You find yourself standing in lush grass before the largest tree you have ever seen. The trunk stretches up, branching majestically out well beyond your ability to see, strong, vibrant, filled with life. It is Yggdrasil, the world tree, and you approach the great trunk, peering at the deeply textured bark, at the contrasting light and shadow and find that the shadow before you is not simply the play of light on bark, but a deep opening into the tree itself. Stepping forward, you find that there is a hollow inside the tree with living steps curving down towards the great roots, and curving up to great heights.

You set your foot on the steps leading up, and begin making your way towards the upper reaches of the great tree. As you proceed, you encounter several landings that lead out of the tree, but you ignore them – those are journeys for another day. High in the tree, you come to a landing which is lit with a light of living green, and you step off the staircase and move through the passage to emerge into a field of tall grass which ripples in the gentle breeze. Looking around, you see structures in the distance, but your eyes are drawn to the left, where the morning light shines down on a large forest which stretches into the distance, dark and vibrant. You begin to walk towards it, feeling the grass brush against you as you walk.

A hawk circles high above you, and in the distance a stag raises his head to watch as you pass. You continue towards the woods which grow taller as you approach until you can see nothing to the east but tall trunks draped with vines and darkness. A faint path stretches into the shadows under the looming trees, a tall rock marking its place. This is the Ironwood, where few are welcome without the permission of Angrboda. She has invited you however, and you see that the rock has a hollowed out section with several Thurisaz runes attached to leather cords. There is something carved on the side of the stone beside the bowl.

"Wear the mark of the Jotun, the strength and protection of Thurisaz while you are within the Wood. Stray not from the pathway however, for the Wood is alive the protection is only for the areas for which you have permission to travel." You choose one of the pendants and slip it over your head to rest against your chest. You step forward onto the pathway and the first thing you notice is the darkness. The path itself casts a faint glow, but it does little to lift the shadows beneath the trees. You can hear movement around you in the darkness, but you stay on the path, winding through the forest which seems to breathe.

The trail twists beneath the tall night-shrouded trees, folding back on itself, maze-like as you travel – it is disorientating, but the pale light leads you forward until you come to a clearing. Stepping into the clearing, the first thing you notice is a house. It is small and primitive looking – as if it had grown out of the forest itself rather than being built. Moving closer you see a woman dressed in leather and fur. She has long black hair and a fierce beauty about her. This is Angrboda, Leader of the Ironwood Clans, and she beckons you closer. You approach her and take a few moments to speak with her. After Angrboda dismisses you, step back onto the pathway and begin following it once more.

It seems much shorter and straighter as you walk, and you find yourself on the edge of the wood fairly quickly. The sun is bright as you step free of the tree-line, and it warms your skin – a sharp contrast to the chill of the Ironwood. Taking one more glance at the looming forest, you head west towards Yggdrasil which is clearly visible before you. Upon reaching the trunk, you once again find yourself stepping into a shadowed alcove. Moving towards the living staircase, you begin to walk downwards, passing several landings until you come to the one you'd started at. You exit the tree and slowly become aware of your physical body once more. You feel your heart beating, the rise and fall of your chest as your lungs fill with air before releasing it once more. You continue to breathe deeply and slowly until you feel grounded once more in your body, you open your eyes and sit up. Welcome back.

> "At the front of it all is the Wolf Chieftess herself, Angrboda. The wise women of the Jotnar, and a myriad of giants and giantesses that populate the edges of Norse Mythology, and it is the Ironwood to which Angrboda calls home." **I.M Knosp, Wylder Homes Project**

OFFERING TO ANGRBODA

Gather with you a piece of raw meat (if you are vegan you can substitute this with a meatless alternative), dark honey, a piece of molasses bread, and two compo-stable bowls. Find a secluded place, perhaps near a bog or in a dark wood, if you can't find a place like that, gather up sticks from a craft store and build a small circle of sticks. In the bowl place the raw meat or meatless alternative, a drop of honey, a piece of bread, in the other bowl, place your piece for eating of the bread and honey (do not eat any of the meat or meatless alternative).

Recite the verse below:
    Angrboðaln Iron-Wood's wasteland,
    Wild wolves she whelps;
    Her brood is bringing
    Both balance and bale.
    Breaker of bonds,
    Three boundaries she bore.
    -(Short Form) © Michaela Macha
[Leave out your offering for only three nights, cover if needed, bury everything but the raw meat, dispose of the meat safely in a proper green bin or other, that will have to be properly decomposed.]

Angrboda Card

Standard Depiction: Angroboda is a wife/mistress of Loki whom is said to be the mother of Hel, the Midgard Serpent and Fenris (a giant wolf), she is the Queen of the Ironwood, described as a hag, she is most linked to the source of 'dark' magic and prophecy.

Meaning: Come inside, this place is waiting, I the great terrible witch of the woods, welcome you in, if you dare. You are about to face yourself, clearly, Angroboda sees inside you, nothing you want to hide remains hidden from her, you must earn your place here, it is not for the faint of heart.

Upright card: The fire burns and she lights your way, you walk protected by the great ironwood witch.

Reversed card: Beware, your enemies are near, steal yourself, the wolves that seek to devour you howl closely, run now, hide, for my children are hungry.

Object: Opal, a wooden sphere or rounded piece of petrified wood.

Baba Yaga

Pronunciations:	Baba Jaga/ Baba Yaga
Meaning of name:	Unclear, she is described as one of three sisters who is a supernatural being.
Sacred Day/Month:	The Month of September
Race:	Depending on the translation of her story she is described as a ogress, a giant, or semi human.
Gender:	Female
Futhark:	Perthro, Laguz
Season:	Winter
Responsible for:	The forest/wildlife
Common Associations:	Wildlife, the forest, death, snakes, birds, possible early Earth Goddess
Animal:	Snakes, birds, animals of the forest, pelicans
Color:	Multicolored, she is often depicted in typical Slavic dress which varies from greens to reds and all colors in between.
Planet/Star:	Moon
Suggested offerings:	Stew, forest clippings, acorns, pine comb
Harrow/Altar setup:	A suggested base is something made from wood and or some natural element thats made from local materials. She likes local vegetables and meats and has a love of all things from rural Slavic regions.
Devotional Ideas:	Work at a soup kitchen, help a woman go 'camping', peaceful protests
Most Notable Feature:	Her shape is deformed, she is described as hideous with a large grotesque nose. Most notably she is associated with her hut which stands on chicken legs.

Poem or Prayer

Oger of the wood,
Baba, I come to you with open heart,
I leave this gift for you as a token of my thanks,
May I be granted safe passage through your wood,
May your cabin be a place of solitude for me,
Dear mother of the forest,
I graciously ask for your blessings

Outside of the classical tale of Baba Yaga [https://storiestogrowby. org/story/baba-yaga/] the book, Baba Yaga: The Ambiguous Mother and Witch of Russian Folklore by Di Andreas Johns offers this about her.

> "Baba Yaga is the guardian who lives at the gateway to the land of the dead. Her hut faces toward the land of the dead and therefore the hero(ine) must make the hut turn around with a magical phrase; he or she cannot simply walk around to the other side [sic she has two roles] guardian of the land of the dead, mistress of the animals."

In this work, Johns also notes that there are similar markers of Baba Yaga that may refer to early understandings of female power as she is sometimes described as having access to the ability to bring up the sun. She is also linked to fertility and motherhood as although a very unusual description implies. She is described as wanting to 'fry children' but scholars believe this was describing the method of ensuring babies remained warm by wrapping them and placing in a warmed oven with the door open to allow a place for them to remain safe. She is linked to weather although not directly, she is often described as carrying a large stick from which she road to bring about wind, rain, hurricanes and thunderstorms. This stick was also used to stir her cauldron which was filled with victims of Yaga.

MEDITATION TO BABA YAGA

Find a quiet place to sit. Steal yourself, as you go to face the witch in the wood, you walk along a narrow path. The winds are calm and peaceful, the sun is shining, you feel the warmth of it on your skin, you come to a wooden bridge. You cross to find a small little wooden house, made of feathers and twigs, you walk through the open door. A little old woman looks right at you. Careful there, dear one you might end up in the straw she smiles, laughing she offers you a chair. Maybe old Baba is in a good mood today, what have you brought me, you open your hand, there is an object there.

You see it clearly, know it, remember it, "ahhh", she says, snatching it in her hand, well let me see there, what will I make of you. She takes the object and tosses it into the cauldron, it bubbles and boils, and in a large puff of smoke, Baba looks, "Ahh, I see here what you need", she reaches into the cauldron, and out comes the gift, she gives it to you. Lucky you are today, that old Baba is in a good mood, she flings open the windows and snaps her fingers. The house vanishes, you are alone in the wood, you wander back, thankful that you are not eaten. Back in your house, you give thanks for the object, what this is, only you know, may you find it comforting.

OFFERING TO BABA YAGA

Grab a plate with a piece of dark honey bread (or a honey based bread/seeded bread), a beet, a small bit of broth (please heat to safe eating temperature). Find a quiet place; recite the following:

Little Old Woman that lives in the woods,
I prepared you a feast,
I ask you for your wisdom, which I gratefully accept. Listen to
you I will little mother, for I come here with love and respect
for you, and your ways.
This place I shall make for you, a chair for you to sit, a pillow
for your back, a pillow for your head, and baba
I promise to be truthful in my speech and not ignore the
wisdom of the grandmothers to whom I listen for now!

Eat the bread, drink the broth, and prepare a small area of your house, with a chair if possible, but if not, just a simple place with two pillows and tell everyone not to sit there for at least nine days, so that Baba can find some needed rest. It is also common for people to build a miniature of her home and place it inside or outside. A small bird house can be converted into a Baba house with some creative D.I.Y.

"Baba Yaga's wide range is attributed to her deep, old roots: in her earliest forms, Baba Yaga might been the Slavic deity Mokosh, or "moist mother earth,"who eats the bones of the dead."
-BABA YAGA, BURNS PARIS TO THE GROUND. WREN AWRY. 2015.

Baba Yaga Card

Standard Depiction: The name of Baba Yaga is composed of two elements. Baba means "grandmother" or "old woman" in most Slavic languages. There are two versions of the origin of this name. Yaga is probably a diminutive of the feminine name Jadwiga, in turn, is a Slavicized form of the Germanic Hedwig.

The other is the name comes from the old Russian verb yagat which means to abuse, to find fault. Baba Yaga is usually shown as an ugly old woman and quite unclean. Baba Yaga is often represented as little, ugly, with a huge and distorted nose and long teeth.

However, Baba Yaga knows something that women of all times and ages have been desperately trying to learn: the secret of turning from old into young in a blink of an eye. Baba Yaga knows a recipe of a special potion that helps her to turn young. Unfortunately she has been known to use this skill not to arrange her single private life, but to misguide and deceit strangers. She is also rumored to have only one leg, which is sometimes explained by her relation to a snake.

Meaning: Cackling, I am waiting for you, my precious, knock on my door if you dare. Baba Yaga aids the heroes and heroines, by giving advice, finding weapons and making tasks easier, as long as you enter her hut without fear.

Upright card: Listen to your elders, they have the truth you need, you will walk in wisdom with all the tools my cauldron can turn up, take them with my blessing.

Reversed card: Ignore me and be my supper.

Object: Peacock Marble, Blue Marble, Chicken Bone.

FREJYA

Pronunciations:	Freyja (/ˈfreɪə/; Old Norse: [ˈfrœyjɑ], "(the) Lady")
Meaning of name:	"Lady"
Sacred Day/Month:	Friday
Race:	Vanir/Adopted Æsir
Gender:	Female
Futhark:	Fehu
Season:	Spring/Summer
Responsible for:	Half of the dead, Valkyries, Seiðr
Common Associations:	Falcons, magic, sex, cats, beauty, war, fertility, abundance
Animal:	Cats, falcons
Color:	Red
Planet/Star:	The Big Dipper
Suggested offerings:	Cinnamon, apple mead, wine (red), mead, high quality chocolate, organic fruits such as strawberries and cherries, high quality wine, Goldschläger, erotic poetry; high quality honey, bread, pork
Harrow/Altar setup:	Freyja should always have something on the harrow made of feathers and possibly also leather objects and gold as myths about her often relay that she is potentially linked to the thrice burnt goddess Gullveig or "gold lust". Honey, corn cakes, strawberries, mead or mulled apple wine. Figures or photos of cats, amber, jewelry (especially necklaces) are also good.
Devotional Ideas:	All acts of please, whether with a partner or alone; support sex positive charities, influencer, organizations; study seidhr/witchcraft; work on being sex positive and/or overcoming any sexual trauma; honoring graves of those fallen in battle; supporting charities, organizations that support veterans

| Most Notable Feature: | Noted for her striking beauty and red hair, closely linked to her necklace Brisingamen. Odin asked Loki to steal the necklace, which he did. Figuring that she was discovered, she went to Odin to ask him about the necklace. |

Kevin Crossley-Holland writes,

"Where is my necklace?" Repeated Freya.

She stormed at Odin; she took his rigid arm and pressed herself against him; she wept showers of gold...

"You'll never see it again," said the Terrible One, Father of Battle, "unless you agree to one condition. There is only one thing that will satisfy me. You must stir up hatred. You must stir up war. Find two kings in Midgard and set them at each other's throats; ensure that they meet only on the battlefield, each of them supported by 20 vassal kings."

The Father of Battle looked grimly at the Goddess. "And you must use such charms as given new life to the corpses. As soon as each warrior is chopped down, bathed in blood, he must stand up unharmed and fight again." [THE NORSE MYTHS, CHAPTER 13. CROSSLEY-HOLLAND, 1981]

POEM OR PRAYER

From Freya´s hand you receive the cup of passion -
Once your lips have touched the rim, her fire sets you in flames.
Sweetly the drop flows down the throat, and you´ve fallen to her.
Freya´s favor carries you off as the flow in your mouth runs through you.
Climbing highest peaks of lust, you plunge into sorrow´s valley;
Give Freya yourself with body and soul, even though the last sip is bitter.
--© German Original: Michael Schütz

MEDITATION

Sit and calm yourself for you are to meet the goddess Freyja this night. Take a deep breathe, you find yourself in a green field, lush and warm, the laughter of children pass by your ears. Before you is a wooden palace, flanked with feathers, the building seems white, but shining and sparkly. The door guarded by two women who are dressed like swans, their cloaks made entirely of feathers, they grant you access. You walk through the rooms, feel the cold stone on your feet, a large set of doors appear, there on the handles are carved the head of two cats, another guardian stands to the right.

Opening the door, you find yourself in front of the most beautiful goddess, she sits on a golden chair, her hair in a woven braid, a bright red stone hangs around her neck, she looks fierce but kind. She offers you a seat, welcome, I am Freyja, priestess of the gods, what is it you seek. Humbly, you tell her, she smiles, pulling out of her cloak a set of bones, she tosses them, her eyes seem to carry some flicker to them, as if they are on fire. Here see your fate if you dare, she says, looking you see your answer, she stands, and takes your hand, walking you to the window, she points outside.

You see the sun rising, the warmth of the day, and as you look back there Freyja stands dressed in full armor, the palace fades. She seems to whisper something to you, and then a horse appears, she jumps on the saddle and off she rides, towards the setting sun. You find yourself in the present, feeling warmed and bright, what she told you is for you alone, remember her words, and head them.

Offerings To Freyja

Find a quite place, bring with you a red stone of some kind, or amber stones, bring a lump of honey smeared on corn cake/bread, a strawberry and some wine/cider.

Lady Freyja,
Priestess of the gods, I bid you accept my offering and be welcome in my home.

Recite the following:
Freyja
Lady, for all the love in my life, I give thanks.
For joy and pleasure, I give thanks.
For the beauty in all that I see, even when I have to look really hard to find it, I give thanks.
For the gifts of a wild heart and quiet strength, I give thanks.
For hard lessons in self-worth and dignity, I give thanks.
For your guidance on this day and every other, I give thanks.
-© Maris Pái

It is possible if you piece together hints about Freya that she is and acts as a priestess or völva of the gods due to the fact that she can 'shape shift' by doning a ritual cloak (something that was done physically by völva's, they didn't actually change into an animal but instead doned ritual wear to 'ritualisticaly' shift them into a different form. [See section on: Adorning The Body]

" Bird-hamir or feather cloaks that enable the wearers to take the form of, or become, birds are widespread in Germanic mythology and legend. The term hamir can be translated as various terms such as skin, cloak, costume, coat or form"

Freyja Card

Standard Depiction: Freyja is the twin sister of Frey and a goddess who came from a group of gods called the Vanir which were known to be linked to nature and magic, they were traded to the gods as hostages but became beloved to their captures and rose to be given ownership over important tasks. Freyja was given the role as priestess of the gods, and would be responsible for a group of Valkyries that served to 'ride over battles' choosing half of those who died to live with her in her hall. She is said to a glowing necklace, symbolizing her link to the fire of creation and links to the natural elements.

Meaning: Come sit by my fire, I embrace you, my ladies will aid you, my sword is yours, my hands are waiting, shall we go now and lay waste to the world and revel in the burning.

Upright card: Protected by the magic of the gods, you stand fiercely before your enemies, nothing will now harm you, prepare yourself for the battle, all omens lean victory in your favor.

Reversed card: Your battles will not be as victorious, you will be wounded and burned, for a time, until you grow dragon scales for which to protect yourself.

Object: Red marble, red stone (any), amber bead, amber marble.

FRIGGA

Pronunciations:	Frea, Frig, Frija, Fria, Frea, Frig
Meaning of name:	"Beloved"
Sacred Day/Month:	Friday
Race:	AEsir/Asynjur. Frigga's father who's name is Fjorgyn is often associated with Erda or Earth. In the Edda, her father is described as being both male and female and the father of Frigga and mother of Thor respectively. Trollrun, A Discourse on Trolldom and Runes in the Northern Tradition N. De Mattos Risvold.

In the same book, the author eludes to Frigga's connection with groves and sacred structures, as she was Queen of family units, the home, the physical boundaries, this makes great amounts of sense as if Jord is related to her, that power of being the 'earth' goddess would be strongest in her as well.

It is as if she is the polar opposite to Thor (who in some stories is her brother, in others her son) in that Thor is this raging, weather related force, concerned with order, and she is this airy/foggy maternal force, concerned with tangible structure of the home. Both are order in one sense or another.

Gender:	Female
Futhark:	Berkano, Perthro, Othala
Season:	Fall/Winter
Responsible for:	The home, family, mothers, wife's
Common Associations:	Wet-lands, butterflies, pussy-willows, spinning, marriage, prophecy, clairvoyance, domestic arts, keys, motherhood
Animal:	Cats, falcons, heron and the Frigga Fritillary Boloria Frigga

Color:	Red, blue, silver, ivory, white
Planet/Star:	The Big Dipper
Suggested offerings:	Cinnamon, apple mead, wine (red), mead, high quality chocolate, organic fruits such as strawberries and cherries, high quality wine, Goldschläger, erotic poetry; high quality honey, bread, pork
Most Notable Feature:	Large blue cape that symbolizes the sky.
Herbs/Stones/Incense:	Mistletoe, yellow bedstraw, mily white quartz, blue agate
Suggested offerings:	Flax seed, handmade items (things made with fiber are preferred, but hand embroidered items or other things that involve physical labor to create are good). mead, pastries (she likes things with chocolate or slightly salty items like gingerbread or gingersnaps), milk (whole or unpasteurized is great!
Planet/Star:	Frigga (minor planet designation: 77 Frigga) is a large, M-type, possibly metallic main-belt asteroid.
Harrow/Altar setup:	Frigga's harrow should have something spun on it. This can be raw wool, manufactured wool or other yarn. She generally likes painted china dishes but any dish will do. Items that she likes are cups (horn cups are a great option but a simple cup or tea cup would also be fitting), a drop spindle, mini spinning wheel or spinning wheel charm, divinatory tools (runes, bones etc), Berkano rune.
Devotional Acts:	Keep your house clean and make sure everything is in working order, donate or volunteer to charities that help and/or protect children and mothers, help care for a new, expectant or grieving mother (cooking or cleaning for her)

Poem or Prayer

Lady Frigga,
Queen of Asgard,
Keeper of Secrets,
This offering I make for you
--Larisa Hunter

Larisa: My favorite story of Frigga is the one in which she gets Odin to show favor to the tribe she picks. She does this in the most deliciously clever way, by changing the direction of his bed.

"The text mentions an island Scandanan, the home of the Winnili. Their ruler was a woman called Gambara, with her sons Ybor and Agio. The leaders of the Vandals, Ambri and Assi, asked them to pay them tribute, but they refused, saying they would fight them. Ambri and Assi then went to Godan, and asked him for victory over the Winnili. Godan replied that he would give the victory to whomever he saw first at sunrise. At the same time, Gambara and her sons asked Frea, Godan's wife, for victory. Frea advised that the women of the Winnili should tie their hair in front of their faces like beards and join their men for battle.

At sunrise, Frea turned her husband's bed so that he was facing east, and woke him. Godan saw the women of the Winnili, their hair tied in front of their faces, and asked "Who are these long-beards?", And Frea replied, since you named them, give them victory, and he did. From this day, the Winnili were called Langobardi, "longbeards"." [it should be noted that this is Frigga despite the difference in spelling]. It shows her cunning and also her commitment to those who come and ask her for help." [Origo Gentis Langobardorum 1878]

Meditation

Take a deep breath and slowly let it out, feel yourself breathing in, clean light air, and as you breathe out, feel all your negative thoughts float away. Breathe in and out, in and out again, feel your body, begin to relax, under you, feel the sturdy floor. Supporting your weight, comfortable and calm, you hear nothing but the music, feel nothing but the floor.

You are aware of the others around you, hear the soft sounds of each breath. You are perfectly safe, surrounded by friends, your body becomes heavier and heavier, and you begin to drift away. You find yourself at the bottom of a great ash tree, its roots are tough and hard, worn and slightly decaying. The roots appear like stone, strong and hard, and yet delicate. There is a slight breeze in the air, and from a distance. You hear the tree creaking, the leaves above moving, the great tree shakes a little, and a doorway appears. You grip the handle of the door and softly open it, you walk into the tree, unafraid.

You are now in the center of the tree, you can smell the damp wood around you. Feel the cold ground beneath you, the tree seems to be lit, and you can see the inside clearly, the tree, seems to be infinitely big, and there are doorways and staircases twisting and turning to all various directions. There is one that calls to you, there is one door that is illuminated; it is shinning and bright.

You walk towards the door, and notice it has a latch carved with a spinning wheel. You open the door, you walk unafraid, into a small room, the door closes behind you and melts back into the tree, you glance back, only to find the doorway is now gone. You are in a small little house, with comfortable seats, there is a fire burning in the hearth, and a big pot stewing gently on the fire. You have a sense that you are not alone, you glance around and there in the corner, is a grand spinning wheel.

Lit by one candle, there sits Frigga. You walk towards her, and she offers you a seat, "Have you walked far my child?" You answer. As you look into her eyes, you see the many lives she has lived, in her are the sands of time. Her face, weathered and her hands calloused by work, she is the mother of all. Her brilliant silver hair, is tied back in a beautiful braid, she is ageless and timeless. She stares at you, with a mother's love, she turns to her spinning wheel, and begins to spin. She says to you, look into the wheel, you begin to stare at the moving wheel, as it spins, round and round. You become caught up in the rhythm, you see images coming to you.

She says; "See what it is you need, look into the wheel." You stare into the center, trying not to be sick from the movement, in that one moment, just when you think you are going to lose yourself, the wheel halts'. She allows you to regain some composure, she reaches forward and removes the wool from the spinning wheel. She cuts a piece, places it in a pouch, she hands you the pouch. When you open it, she says "this is what you need, this is my gift to you, use it wisely." When you look at the gift, you notice it is not thread, nor yarn.

You take this gift, and close the pouch, you thank her for this gift, if you wish to say anything to Frigg or ask her anything, you may do so at this time. She is wise and very knowledgeable. If you have nothing to ask, walk and sit beside the fire. Frigga says it is time for you to go. She opens a door to the next room, and calls in a guide; she says "this will be your guide back to the entrance of the world tree".

You thank her again, and follow your guide. You walk through a green lush field, your guide walks you to the edge of a rainbow, and says that this road will take you home. You thank your guide, and wander down the rainbow bridge, you feel yourself getting lighter now. Back in the room where you started, you feel your body becoming more and more aware. More and more alert, you begin to take a deep breath in, feeling yourself beginning to wake, and when you are ready you open your eyes.

Offering to Frigga

Bring a bar of chocolate, a ¼ cup of flax, a pinch of sea salt, a small amount of Lady Grey tea, two cups. Find a place that you feel comfortable in, Sit with the tea in front of you, calm your spirit and mind, and recite the following;

Twist me, twist me, Frigga, into your distaff,
Spin me, Spin me, Frigga, into your wheel.
Mold me, mold me, Frigga, into some wool.
Fix me, fix me, Frigga,
Into the web of wyrd.
--Larisa Hunter

Drink some of the tea, then pour the rest in the empty cup. Take a bite of the chocolate, and place the rest inside the tea, eat one or two kernels of flax and drop the rest in the cup, eat a tiny bit of salt, and drop the rest in the cup. Leave the cup in a central place in the home (cover if you have pets) for 9 days, on the 9th, take the cup and pour it in a safe location in the ground, if you don't have an outdoor location, you can place the offering inside a potted plant.

Frigga appreciates offerings of bog situated plants such as pussy willows and reeds. If you live near bogs or wetlands any flora or fauna would be appreciated. For ocean adjacent dwellers, offerings such as natural washed up seaweeds or natural plants would also suffice. She likes things that are or have been touched by water if at all possible. For land locked dwellers offerings of any natural plant that is nearby is perfectly acceptable. She also appreciates culinary herbs like thyme, rosemary etc or any 'household' craft made or food product.

> "*Frigg apparently possessed a similar birdform, since in an early kenning she is called 'mistress of the hawk's plumage'--* (Skáldskaparmál 1, 18)" [The Lost Beliefs of Northern Europe, Hilda Ellis Davidson"

FRIGGA CARD

Standard Depiction: Frigga is the wife of Odin, she is considered to be the Queen of the gods, and is said to know the fate of all, but she speaks it not. She is the mother of many gods, responsible for the home, spinning, weaving, and motherly tasks.

Meaning: Come sit by me, and listen to my voice, I am the mother, the queen of the gods, and I am the one who weaves your fate.

Frigga depicts that all things are as they should be, your fate is woven, your destiny is set, she cautions you to prepare yourself for the challenges you will face.

Upright card: Sit at my feet, all will be revealed, the answers you seek are here.

Reversed card: You must wander longer, the path is not yet done, wander a bit more, my door will remain open until you return.

Objects: Flax seed [contained], a miniature cup (plastic), a mini wooden spoon, butterfly marble.

HEL

PRONUNCIATIONS:	Hella, Hel, Hell
MEANING OF NAME:	"Concealed place; underworld". Her name is identical to location she rules.
SACRED DAY/MONTH:	None. Halloween is not sacred to her but could be a good 'time' to reach her.
RACE:	Half iron wood giant. Daughter of Loki and Angrboda, Hel is described as being 'half dark' or 'half rotting' and is considered to be half or mostly giant as both Angrboda and Loki are from the giant line. Angrboda dwells in a realm that only female giants reside in called Ironwood. Little is known about the other women who live there. In this regard, giants or jotunn are more associated with places than the are a specific 'being' often the word is also used to describe; monsters, trolls, and other various creatures that don't fit into other categories like; elves, wights, fairies, etc. "Not necessarily notably large and may be described as exceedingly beautiful or as alarmingly grotesque"
GENDER:	Female
FUTHARK:	Hagalaz
SEASON:	Winter/Late Fall

RESPONSIBLE FOR:

Caring for the dead. Although most of the myths depict her as the Queen of the underworld whom takes those who died in 'straw beds' which generally meant those who died of natural causes, however in modern interpretations and research it shows that she might have been linked to accepting all the dead regardless of station.

She is often contested as she does not appear in some passages, but many scholars have concluded that she might have appeared in various forms and under different names that make her as part of the scope of belief in female figures that were responsible for death and dying. Most notable feature: often most people associate her with her skeletal and bony figure.

It is stated in both modern and ancient myths that she is either half corpse/half living (like the figures of Santa Murte) or blue in tone. This could be referring the state of decomposition in which blood pooling appears to turn the skin a bluish color.

COMMON ASSOCIATIONS:

Skulls, graves, funerals, the underworld in general

ANIMAL:

Foxes, ravens/crows, vultures

COLOR:

Black, blue, gray

PLANET/STAR:

Planet 949 Hel (prov. Designation: A921 EM or 1921 JK) is a dark background asteroid from the outer regions of the asteroid belt, approximately 63 kilometers (39 miles) in diameter. Pegasus, located along the Milky Way. Represents the 'wagon' used to transport the dead.

SUGGESTED OFFERINGS: (Let offerings rot on altar) traditional funeral foods, mead, water, apples, foods your ancestors enjoyed in life, tea, dark bitter chocolate 90% coco or higher, dried herbs/flowers that are 'winter bloomers' (snowdrops, black tulips).

MOST NOTABLE FEATURE: Her skeletal form. In some sources it mentions that Hel is half black which may be mistranslated, its more likely it meant half blue which is the color of skin as it initially appears after death. Some artists have depicted her as having visible bones protruding from her skin or her skin being very loosely attached to her bone as if in various stages of decomposition.

HERBS/STONES/INCENSE: Onyx or Bloodstone are great for her as is 'dried' flower herbs (ensure that you know what is safe to burn before burning it). For herbs use dried cinnamon, nutmeg, harvest spices or earthly spices like coriander

HARROW/ALTAR SETUP: Her table should have on it some photos of deceased family members if possible or loved ones/pets. Various small skeletons/skeletal figures are appropriate. She likes beeswax candles and does not care about the color too much. She likes wooden objects like spoons and bowls preferably painted or decorated with symbols of her. Steer clear of sage bundles with Hel and instead go for dried wild flowers or natural burning sticks that do not have sage in them. Wood burning offerings are very appreciated and she does approve of trolldom objects as gifts.

DEVOTIONAL ACTS: Caring for the grave sites of deceased ancestors, tending to ancestral altars, working through grief after a loss, working through fear of death, create an end of life plan (will, living will, funeral arrangements, etc), volunteer at a hospice center, become an organ/blood donor

"Hel he cast into Niflheim, and gave to her power over nine worlds, to apportion all abodes among those that were sent to her: that is, men dead of sickness or of old age. She has great possessions there; her walls are exceeding high and her gates great.

Her hall is called Sleet-Cold; her dish, Hunger; Famine is her knife; Idler, her thrall; Sloven, her maidservant; Pit of Stumbling, her threshold, by which one enters; Disease, her bed; Gleaming Bale, her bed-hangings. She is half blue-black and half flesh-color (by which she is easily recognized), and very lowering and fierce."

-Gylfaginning XXXIV

POEM OR PRAYER

Hail to you, Hela, Grandmother Death.
Silent your wisdom, yours my last breath.
Reading our wyrd in cobwebs and lace,
Ancestors´ hostess, grant us your grace.
Hail to you, Hela, stiller of strife.
Half fair, half rotten, mirror of life.
Cool is your comfort, equal for all.
Highways and alleys end in your hall.
Hail to you, Hela, Lady of Dust.
All wyrd will ever go as it must.
Carving our way on the edge of a knife,
Éljúðnir´s Mistress, teach us of life.
--© Michaela Macha

There are no real myths that encapsulate Hel in a real strong way, however, if you are one of those types that does not mind going outside the myths and into the folklore, you will find a good story or two in which a 'grandmother' of death type is somewhat helpful in making our discovery of her real.

Godmother Death by A. H. Wratislaw is a good one to read as it's a variation of Godfather Death by J. Grimm. Minus the overly Christian stuff, its conceptually good. Most of what we know of her comes from external resources and personal exploration/theory. You could say the best story of her though was not really one told in the myths but was articulated in the story The Worlds According to Loki by Mike Kassle. The book is no longer in print, but this is a excerpt of a few good passages that define her.

"I decided to pay a call on my third child, Hela, Goddess of the Dead. I took a deep gulp, assumed my vulture form and winged towards the bleak world known as Niflheim. I flew into that cold, dark realm, flying over many rivers until I came at last to the icy river known as Gjoll. A bridge spanned that frigid stream and an ominous form stood on the far bank... The ghastly figure on the other side regarded me silently as I crossed the bridge. As I neared, I could make out the ghostly, sorrowful features of Modgud, she who is the guardian of the entrance to Hela's domain...." *Page 100*

"As I entered, they all turned towards me, and I found myself staring into the bloated faces of the drowned, the ravaged faces of the diseased, the pain-crazed faces of those who had been tortured to death, the rat-gnawed faces of those who had died imprisoned, and many more jolly folk besides. In the center of the hall, on a raised throne of stone, sat my daughter, Lady Hela, Goddess of Death, sipping blood from an iron chalice....Her head and top half of her body were those of a lovely, if somewhat stern and gloomy, young lady, but the rest of her flesh was the greenish-black flesh of a putrefying corpse. Maggots climbed in and out of her decaying meat."
--*Page 101*

"There is much in what you say, Father. I, too, have no love for Odin. 'Twas he who condemned me to this foul place to play babysitter to the dead. Then, he has the nerve to keep the greatest, of the slain for himself, leaving me to preside over an army of walking corpses."...For the first time in the history of the nine worlds, the Death Goddess smiled. It was not a pretty sight.
--*Page 117, 119, 121*
[The Worlds According to Loki, Vampyre Mike Kassel]

MEDITATION

Take a deep breath, Slowly breath in, clean soft air. Breathing out all negative thoughts and feelings. Feel your body becoming heavy like a stone, solid like a rock, firmly planted on the ground. You feel attached to the floor; see your body tethered like a rope to an anchor, you are here and yet able to move, your bindings do not keep you bound, and you find you are easily able to walk about. Feel everyone around you, and keep them close to you as you drift away.

You see before you a mighty ash tree, strong and tall, you feel wind blowing through the leaves, and hear what sounds like a distant ocean. You feel life around you, and yet there is nothing there, except for the tree. Its bark harsh and rough, but yet soft and inviting, you find yourself wanting to climb up, but instead feel yourself pulled softly toward the back of the tree. As you move around the tree, you see a black ocean in front of you can only slightly make out the water, not really sure if it is water, or something else.

You pensively walk slowly toward the bank. A boat appears, in it there is a figure steering the boat towards you, the boat stops, get in, he says, all are welcome. You take his hand, and as you do, you feel the bony fingers of a skeletal figure underneath the robe, you start to think about getting off, but it's too late, you are aboard the ship of the lost, as you look around the boat, you notice many others on the ship, they cannot see you, but you can see them. "Don't worry about them," says the ferryman, "they are just along for the ride."

In a brief flash, you happen to see the face or not so much of a face of your captain, the ferryman, looks at you, "I have something that I believe belongs to you", he says, as you carefully reach forward, the ferryman hands you a piece of parchment. I would suggest you not open that here, he smiles. The boat travels on for a while, and finally reaches a patch of fog covered waters, as the boat travels through, but you hear odd sounds about you, people, tons of people, walking and waiting, talking and laughing. It is a bit unsettling in the mist, where you cannot see, but still, you are not afraid and trust that this journey is one that is safe and required. The boat docks, on a small narrow platform, where two women stand, they reach down and hold out their hands for you, and you unafraid let them help you up, the two women appear in black robes, their faces covered, and they wear gloves, we are the guardians of the water entrance to Hel they say, come with us, and do not stray from the path, should you separate from us we are not responsible for what happens to you.

You are here at your own risk, they say with a slight hissing sound, you follow the two up a dark ramp, down several hallways, it seems that you are inside labyrinth. There are several passageways, but you don't dare walk off the path on your own, they take you to a solid black door; it seems made of cast iron, with rivets and little carved in skulls, they look at you and say, we cannot follow you further, the rest of the journey is for you, walk carefully and unafraid.

You enter the doorway, and find yourself in a hallway, a hallway full of mirrors, you see yourself in all aspects, and follow the path forward, a voice suddenly echoes in the room. Don't look too deeply in the mirror, look only once, and see a rune, keep this rune in your mind and quickly move forward through the doorway, you look carefully and quickly into the mirror, and see a rune, remember it.

You walk through the final door, and there to meet you is another servant of Hel, before you enter the chamber of the goddess, I must see your pass, once you arrive, you see a fierce looking lady waiting at the shore. You hand her the parchment, she unrolls it, reads it, and leans in to whispers a question into your ear. Answer her. If she accepts your answer, you will be taken forward, if not you will have to wait outside, if you are kept outside, you may offer the mistress of the gate an offering to get in. You are now in the inner chamber of Hel, do not be afraid, for she will show you her true form.

She looks at you, and with all your resolve you look back, "I have been waiting for you", she smiles, You see the true form of Hel, as light cascades upon her skeletal face, she is there in her form, of Hel the bony. Her face is half-rotten, loose skin hangs off each corner. You try not to be horrified at her, and find yourself somehow at peace with her form. Not fearful of her and not afraid you stare into her one good eye, "I have many things to say, but I have a feeling that you may have a question for me."

It is time to ask Hel anything you may wish to ask, she is not to be feared, ask her what you want to know. She reaches out and hands you a small bag, "a gift for you" she says, half smiling, "use it well", After some time has passed, Hel looks at you and says, it is a good thing that you have a way out, not many who come here do.

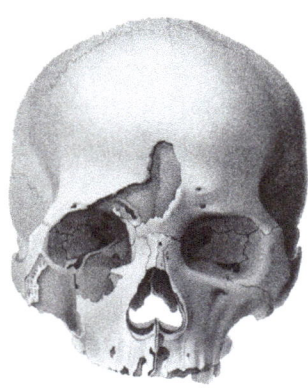

OFFERING TO HEL

Gather a bar of dark chocolate, highest cocoa content possible, a small glass and a shot of the darkest rum. Go into a quiet place, Take a deep breath, recite the poem below:

Lady Hel,
I come before you, laid bare,
I ask for you to accept the offering I leave to you,
Guardian of the dead,
Mistress of the Underworld,
She that walks in the darkened places,
I bid you welcome and honor you with this gift.

Hel is represented by three cards inside Riding The Bones, to reflect her different aspects. The meaning of these is contained within our free download for the deck, located on our site.

SIF

PRONUNCIATIONS:	SIF or SIv
MEANING OF NAME:	"Relation by marriage"
SACRED DAY/MONTH:	Thursday (Thor s Day)
RACE:	AEsir
GENDER:	Female
FUTHARK:	Fehu (because of the fact that this rune is often linked to the value of wheat or grain)
SEASON:	Autumn
RESPONSIBLE FOR:	Most associated with wheat because of her hair. In the lore, Sif's hair is often metaphorically linked to the shaft of wheat. "Thor's marriage with Sif of the golden hair, about which we hear little in the myths, seems to be a memory of the ancient symbol of divine marriage between sky god and earth goddess, when he comes to earth in the thunderstorm and the storm brings the rain which makes the fields fertile. In this way Thor, as well as Odin, may be seen to continue the cult of the sky god which was known in the Bronze Age.[25]" Scholar H. R. Ellis Davidson
COMMON ASSOCIATIONS:	Wheat, harvest, fertility, the earth, family, fidelity, cups, swans
ANIMAL:	Field mouse
COLOR:	Yellow, gold, green, brown
PLANET/STAR:	Sif Mons is a shield volcano in Eistla Regio on Venus. It has a diameter of 300 kilometers (190 mi) and a height of 2.0 kilometers (1.2 mi).[1] It is named after the Norse goddess Sif.

<u>SUGGESTED OFFERINGS:</u>	Golden mead, beer made from [hops, wheat, barley], bread [hearty or rustic] produce that you have grown, high quality breads/baked goods, water, honey
<u>MOST NOTABLE FEATURE:</u>	Golden hair
<u>HERBS/STONES/INCENSE:</u>	Rowan berries, wheat, sun stone, carnelian
<u>HARROW/ALTAR SETUP:</u>	Sif should have some element of natural wheat if possible but dried wheat will do in a pinch. She enjoys tables with lots of golden colored fabrics, a Mjolnir would be appropriate for her husband, bits of sun stone or carnelian would be appreciated. Additional items like wedding rings, swan figures, cups, fertility symbols or symbols of abundance (cornucopias would be awesome)
<u>DEVOTIONAL ACTS:</u>	Work to foster healthy relationships with children; spouses; partners; extended family etc, learn to garden (especially crops), cultivate firth (good will) between feuding family, self care. Donate your hair to a cancer patient.
<u>OGHAM (CROSS OVER GODDESS)</u>	Rowan- Grimm connects Eddic references to Sif's golden hair (gold is referred to as Sifjar haddr; Sif's hair) with the herb name haddr Sifjar (Polytrichum aureum) [verification needed]. Grimm says that Thor's mother was the earth, and not his wife, yet "we do find the simple Sif standing for earth." Grimm adds that he is inconclusive regarding Sif and that, "we ought to have fuller details about Sif, and these are wholly wanting in our mythology. Nowhere amongst us is the mystic relation of the seed-corn of Demeter, whose poignant grief for her daughter threatens to bring famine on mankind (Hymn to Cer. 305–306), nor anything like it, recorded."[22]

It is possible that Sif is an earthly fertility goddess. In Old Norse Stories by Sarah Powers Bradish published in 1900, it mentions that Thor and Sif were "expecting a fruitful season and had promised the peasants an abundant harvest"

Image by Antonieta Saavedra
(Commercial Use Permitted)

POEM OR PRAYER

Sif´s Seasons
From springtime´s barley sowing,
Ears shining like the sun
Deck bald fields with their glowing,
A headdress newly spun.
The rain descends in summer
Midst Thunder´s rumbling clap
As gently as the hammer
Into the young bride´s lap.
With autumn come the thieves
To cut the golden hair,
Our folk again receives
A harvest rich and fair.
As winter fields lie fallow,
We cherish every sheaf:
We bake and brew and hallow
The golden gifts of Sif.
--© Michaela Macha (lyrics, tune, voice)

The most appropriate story of Sif is how she lost her hair and got a replacement made out of pure gold. This story has a lot of humiliation for Thor written in it, and one can't help think that a wife's hair has more symbolism to it, perhaps linking her hair to the concept of his seed (literal and figurative). https://www.storynory.com/sif-and-her-golden-hair/

MEDITATION

It is time now, to meet the goddess Sif.

Take a deep breath, and slowly let it out. Feel yourself breathing in, clean light air, and as you breathe out, feel all your negative thoughts float away. Breathe in and out, in and out again. Feel your body, begin to relax, under you, the feel of the sturdy floor. Supporting your weight, comfortable and calm, hear nothing but the music, feel nothing but the floor. You are aware of the others around you. You hear the soft sounds of each breath. You are perfectly safe, surrounded by friends, Your body becomes heavier and heavier, and you begin to drift away. You sense now, that you are in the middle of a gigantic wheat field, its stalks tall as the eye can see, in fact, the stalks are so tall that you cannot tell where you are in the field, or how in fact to get out.

The wind blows softly, and the wheat softly bends, you hear what sounds like a soft whisper, it seems to echo your name. You follow the sound of the voice, and the field of wheat seems to bend a path for you to walk along. You follow the path, through the wheat and find yourself at a large building, it has many doors. Each door, is carved with a hammer, and each has the rune of Thor and a rune of Sif. You pick one of the many doors, it opens at the slightest touch of your hand, you enter, cautiously but unafraid. The inner hall is decorated with furs and antlers, fine linens hang on the walls, and burning torches light your way. You make your way along the passage that lead into what seems like a central point.

There is a smell of sage and pine and wheat, in fact the smell is not quite defined, or quite clear, but is seems familiar and comforting. You feel drawn to the smell, and follow it. In a large circular room sits a lady by the fire, her golden hair spilling onto the marble floor, in her hands, she holds shafts of wheat. She is a beautiful woman, with soft, porcelain skin, and Gentle eyes. The lines of her face are that of a mother and a wife, carved from the many troubles of her life, and of the many joyous moments that she has spent over the years. She is of indeterminate age, like the other goddess, she is timeless.

At her hip, are keys, you take note that one is made from bone, she appears wearing a comfortable robe, with leather adornments, around her neck is a Thor's hammer colored in red. She beckons you forward, and offers you a seat on an antler covered chair, "Greetings", she smiles at you, "I am the lady Sif, wife of Thor, mistress of his hall and home, I bid you welcome". She leans forward and reaches for her sickle, and tosses it onto the floor, a fair distance from your feet.

She waves her hands, and the sickle begins to spin, the metal sickle, flashes with light from the fire, and you begin to follow the mesmerizing movement of the sickle, she says, "look into the center and see what will come of your harvest", you look in and see a rune. Remember it. She hands you a shaft of wheat, "I give to you my hair, that you may be filled with the promise of a good harvest."
You take the gift. If you wish to say anything to Sif or ask her anything, you may do so at this time, she is wise and very knowledgeable. If you have nothing to ask, walk and sit beside the fire.

Just before you are ready to leave, Sif picks up her sickle, looks at you and cuts one lock of your hair, when it falls onto the ground, it becomes a stalk of wheat, she picks up the stalk and tosses it into the fire, she says to you: "thus fulfilled is your wish, your sacrifice renewed, as my hair stolen and returned, so all things are to you." She tells you now, it is time to go and takes you to the front door of the hall, you cannot tell if it is the same door to which you entered, but it is a door none the less. When you exit, you see the field of wheat, demolished, every stalk torn or strewn across the field, you look behind you, Sif smiles; she says "harvest has come", she closes the door and leaves you outside.

You walk over the demolished field, back to where you came, you can see clearly now, a defined road back to the rainbow bridge. You follow the path, and get ready to embark down the bridge, you walk down the smooth colored bridge, back to the realm of Midgard, you find yourself feeling back in the here and now. Back in the room that you started in, you slowly return to present, breathing in and out, you slowly open your eyes. We ask now for those who wish to for you to share with us the rune that was given to you.

OFFERINGS FOR SIF

A glass of honey wine or mead, a corn cake (corn bread), flax bread. Go to a place where there is a lot of sunlight, preferably fall, bring with you a basket with at least three apples, some herbs of your choosing, a small lump of honey, and a compost-able container of some kind. There in this place recite the following:

Sif,
Goddess of the grain,
She who's hair is made of gold,
Body of the harvest,
I offer you these gifts,
And wish you welcome
Wife of Thor, I welcome you,
I offer these gifts, and thank you for the bounty of my table

[Place your offerings in the container, leave it out and spend a few minutes basking in the glow of the season, take a bite of one of the apples in thanks to the goddess of the harvest.]

The herb Polytrichum Aureum has been seen as a possible representation of Sif's hair. The herb is commonly called haircap moss or hair moss.

SIF CARD

Standard Depiction: Sif was the wife of Thor, she is said to be a daughter of the Ironwood a place which is linked to mysterious female witches. Her hair was stolen by Loki, and replaced with forged strands of gold. She is linked to the concepts of harvest and renewal.

Meaning: I am that which signifies the sacrifice of self, my hair the golden wheat cut short by those who forsake the land, and toss my sacrifice asunder. To see Sif means you understand the sacrifices you must make to move on in your life.

Upright card: Your sacrifice is well received and your burden is lightened.

Reversed card: There is still more that needs to be sacrificed, but you will be able to manage these without hardships, I send you the hammer of my husband to protect your home and hearth.

Objects: a lock of your own hair, a stalk of grain, a corn doll, gold marble

"Ran has a net, in which she catches those who venture out upon the sea. AEger and Ran have nine daughters, the waves. With her hand She is able to hold the Ships fast. It was a prevailing opinion among the ancient Norsemen that they who perished at sea came to Ran." [NORSE MYTHOLYG. R.B. ANDERSON.1879]

RAN

PRONUNCIATIONS:	Rán (Old Norse: [ˈrɒːn])
MEANING OF NAME:	"Theft, robbery"
SACRED DAY/MONTH:	None known
RACE:	Giant/Jotunn
GENDER:	Female
FUTHARK:	Laguz
SEASON:	None, as she is a natural element that holds year round
RESPONSIBLE FOR:	The ocean and waves
COMMON ASSOCIATIONS:	Waves, water, seashells, nets, death at sea
ANIMAL:	Ocean dwelling animals/mammals
COLOR:	Ocean blue

PLANET/STAR:	The Eridanus Constellation, Epsilon Eridani
SUGGESTED OFFERINGS:	Sea water, kelp or seaweed, foamy ales
MOST NOTABLE FEATURE:	Her net, which is closely linked to the death at sea
HERBS/STONES/INCENSE:	Costal herbs like; rosemary, coriander, thyme, basil, chives, lavender, marjoram, sea kale, common sage (not white sage). Stones l like Lapaz, sea glass, jasper, agate, serpentine are good or any stone that is generated by water meeting the land. As Larisa lives in Hawaii this is generally lava rock and its not advised to move it, for the lava is considered a sacred element of the goddess Pele and should not be moved or altered.
HARROW/ALTAR SETUP:	Ran's altar should be one that is made with a lot of natural procured shells, bits of rope, mermaid figurines, pearls, altar cloths in her colors covered by netting, shells, gold jewelry or coins, figurines or pictures of ships.
DEVOTIONAL ACTS:	Volunteer for ocean or beach cleanup days

POEM OR PRAYER

Ran, mother of waves, Goddess of salt waters, she who takes the souls lost among the billowing mounds of foam.

May you find this offering welcoming, may you provide safe harbor for those seeking you.

Remind us that the ocean is the womb from which we sprung,

May we find peace among the waters to which you rule.

To your daughters who swell, swirl, bubble and spin, I give this offering to them, in honor of the mother of the billowy mounds.

May it be received by the great mother goddess of the deep blue seas.

--Larisa Hunter

Ran is yet another one that is missing in terms of the myths around her. She is only mentioned as mothering the 9 waves and as the mother of Heimdall. Not much else is said about her. Dinning with Ran was a common saying when someone was about to sale in hopes of not getting caught in her net. Often sailors would carry gold coins for her to tempt her off from them.

You can see elements of her in the original story of The Little Mermaid as when she leapt to her death, she turned into sea foam and floated out into the waves. This is similar to Ran's common links to both mermaids to the 'types' of waves that existed.

- Bára (or Drǫfn) - Foam Fleck, Comber
- Blóðughadda - Bloody Hair
- Bylgja - Billow
- Dúfa - Pitching Wave
- Hefring - Rising Wave
- Himinglæva - Transparent Wave
- Hrǫnn - Welling Wave
- Kólga - Cool Wave
- Unnr (or Uðr) - Frothing Wave

A modern interpretation of her story is found here, this best sums up Ran.

"The sea the great big beautiful sea is my domain. I have swam hidden in the kelp and seaweed forests. Aegir my husband and god of the sea said once that he built Aegirheim for me. But his greatest gift to me were our nine daughters, one embodying one of the nine kinds of waves.

In the great hall, I welcome the souls of the fallen and drowned, as any good hostess should. But for those who in preparation for meeting a watery end, brought with them some trinket or other gleaming pieces of gold I include, no let me amend, invite them to join the grand feast.

Most of you mortals will never see the blue green spires or the mother of pearl floors. Only in Aegirheim do I walk among the corridors allowing my long seaweed strewn hair to trail in my wake. I am not malevolent, as one such sailor commented, a long time ago. More than once my sharp pointy teeth, and clawing hands have released a living person, not yet meant to perish, from the grasp of our underwater forests.

Equally they have torn away flesh freeing the trapped soul of one who has died. So next time I swim near the surface and smile at you, do not assume that I mean you harm. I may just be wishing you a good day, or appreciating your unique presence upon my waters. But then again, I may be awaiting you to join us in the halls of Aegirheim. Either way be sure to be prepared, all it takes is a small piece of gold to ensure a warm welcome."
https://themythdetective.com/index.php/ran/

If possible do this by an ocean or body of water or some kind of water, a bowl of water will do

You see yourself on a beach, the waters are blue and calm. You step out in the waves and the water rises up to form the shape of Ran. She touches your face, and grants you the ability to breathe underwater. Taking your hand she lovingly says, come with me, swim in my ocean. With her hand in yours, you step out, and feel yourself immersed in the clear warm ocean waters, she takes you deep down into a coral reef. Reaches in and hands you a pearl, a gift she says, to guide you on your way, the pearl glows, alighting the dark ocean floor. Still she drags you further down, until you reach her mighty throne. There at the darkest, deepest depth of the sea. You sit with her, as she brushes your hair, she sings to you sacred songs, and whispers in your ear. You feel safe here, comforted here, she tells you what it is your heart needs to hear. As the day dawns, she lifts you from the ocean, and walks you to the shore, around your neck she strings a single shell, a reminder of the things you have learned, and from this place you leave feeling rested and happy.

Offering to Ran

Find a lump of sea salt, a small dish, a shell if possible, if possible head to a beach or at least put a dish nearby with sand in it. A small bowl of water. Recite the following:
"In the deep sea-caves
By the sounding shore,
In the dashing waves
When the wild storms roar, in her cold green bowers.
In the northern fiords, she lurks and she glowers, she grasps and she hoards, and she spreads her strong net for her prey."
- James Baldwin, "The Story of Siegfried", 1899

Into the bowl of water, place the sea salt and sprinkle of sand, take the shell and dunk it in the water/salt mix. Leave the shell out to dry, and keep in a central palace for as long as you like. Note: Ran loves anything from the ocean, however its best if this is cultivated with minimal impact, found objects are ok as long as you ask her if you can take objects from the beach. She also loves a good stout beer or dark ambers with lots of foam.

"Gymir's spray-cold spæ-wife often brings the twisted-rope-bear [ship] into Ægir's jaws [under the waves] where the wave breaks.[16]
But sea-crest-Sleipnir [ship], spray-driven, tears his breast, covered with red paint, out of white Ran's"
-Fragment of a work by the 11th century Icelandic skald Hofgarða-Refr Gestsson

Image--Rán uses her net to pull a seafarer into the depths in an illustration by Johannes Gehrts, 1901

RAN CARD

Standard Depiction: Ran is considered to be the Queen of the ocean, wife of Aegir, she rules the sea. She is said to be the mother of mermaids and has named the waves. Ran was called by sailors before each departure to ask for safe passage, she was considered to be the one who would guide those who died at sea into the afterlife. She can appear as a mermaid or as a blue looking giant woman who has deep gray eyes, sometimes she has scales like a fish and gills to breathe and sometimes she appears as an average woman.

Meaning: The waters of life surround you, the sing to you, offering you peace and guidance but yet there is danger in the depths, glide carefully through the dark places.

Upright card: The waves wash over you, and you receive the blessings of their healing waters, the calm waters offer you rest, take time, see the benefit of stillness, float safely in the waves of Ran.

Reversed card: The tide is growing, the sea is rough, it is time to seek out harbor before you find yourself caught in my net.

Object: sea marble, artificial pearl, found ocean object.

THE CELTIC GODDESSES

THE MAKING OF AN IRISH GODDES

Ceres went to hell
with no sense of time
When she looked back
all that she could see was
the arteries of silver in the
rock,
the diligence of rivers always
at one level,
wheat at one height,
leaves of a single colour,
the same distance in the
usual light;
aseasonless, unscarred earth.

But I need time –
my flesh and that history –
to make the same descent.

In my body,
neither young now nor
fertile,
and with the marks of
childbirth
still on it,
in my gestures –
the way I pin my hair to hide
the stitched, healed blemish
of a scar –
must be an accurate
inscription of that agony:
the failed harvests,
the fields rotting to the
horizon,
the children devoured by
their mothers
whose souls, they would
have said,
went straight to hell,
followed by their own.

There is no other way:
myth is the wound we leave
in the time we have
which in my case is this
March evening
at the foothills of the Dublin
mountains,
across which the lights have
changed all day,
holding up my hand,
sickle-shaped, to my eyes
to pick out
my own daughter from
all the other children in the
distance;
her back turned towards me.

BRIGID AS A GODDESS (SAINT BRIGIT)

PRONUNCIATIONS:	Brigid or Brigit (/ˈbrɪdʒɪd, ˈbriːɪd/ BRIJ-id, BREE-id, Irish: [ˈbʲɾʲɪjɪdʲ, ˈbʲɾʲiːdʲ] Brigantia, Brid, Bride, Briginda, Brigdu
MEANING OF NAME:	"Exalted One."
SACRED DAY/MONTH:	February 1st
RACE:	The Tuatha Dé Danann (Irish: [ˈt̪ˠuə(hə) dʲeː ˈd̪ˠan̪ˠən̪ˠ], meaning "the folk of the goddess Danu"), also known by the earlier name Tuath Dé ("tribe of the gods")
GENDER:	Female
RESPONSIBLE FOR:	Goddess of Healers, Poets, Smiths, Childbirth, and Inspiration; Goddess of Fire and Hearth and a patron of warfare or Briga. Her soldiers were called Brigands.
COMMON ASSOCIATIONS:	Poetry, wisdom, healing, protection, smithing
ANIMAL:	Domesticated animals of all kinds, but in particular lambs and ewes
COLOR:	Gold, white, yellow or orange
PLANET/STAR:	None
SUGGESTED OFFERINGS:	Sage, milk, honey, seeds, filtered water
MOST NOTABLE FEATURE:	Firey red or gold hair
HERBS/STONES/INCENSE:	Brass, silver, carnelian, agate, copper, amethyst, red jasper, and rock crystals.

Brigid is the daughter of the Dagda, one of the more universal deities of the pagan Gaelic world. She is said to lean over every cradle. The lore and customs have continued to this day regarding Brighid, more vividly than all the other Gaelic deities combined. In the Middle Ages, Brigid is in many stories. In one she is the wife of Bres, the half-Fomorian ruler of the Tuatha Dé Danann. Their son, Ruadan, wounded the smith god Giobhniu at the second battle of Magh Tuireadh but he himself was slain in the combat.

Brigid then went to the battlefield to mourn her son. This was said to be the first caoine (keening), or lament, heard in Ireland. Until recent time, it was a tradition to hire women to caoine at every graveside. In another story, Brighid was the wife of Tuireann and had three sons: Brian, Iuchar and Ircharba. In the tale, The Sons of Tuirean, these three killed the god Cian, father of Lugh Lámhfhada when he was in the form of a pig.

She was transformed by the Church of St. Brigid into St. Brigid about 453 C.E. Saint Brighid is known as the patroness of farm work and cattle, and protector of the household from fire and calamity. To this day, one of her most common names in Gaelic is Muime Chriosd, "Foster-Mother of Christ." St. Brigid was said to be the daughter of Dubthach, a Druid who brought her from Ireland to be raised on the Isle of Iona, sometimes called "The Druid's Isle."

❧

[Author's Note: "A fascinating link to the traditions of the saint Brigid is the fact that a woman called Darlughdacha appears in St. Brigid's community in Kildare as her close companion, sharing Brigid's bed. Darlughdacha, who became abbess of Kildare on Brigid's death, means 'daughter of Lugh' and the 'saints' lists' also give her feast day as 1st February. Mary Condren thinks that Darlughdacha might even be the original name for the goddess Brigid, presumably as Brigid (Exalted One) is a title rather than a name."]

❧

"...And I was putting another word to it, for her, fair Foster-Mother of Christ, when she looked at me and said, "I am older than Brighid of the Mantle...I put songs and music on the wind before ever the bells of the chapels were rung in the West or heard in the East.

I am Brighid-nam-Bratta, but I am also Brighid-Muirghin-na-tuinne, and Brighid-sluagh, Brighid-nan-sitheachseang, Brighid-Binne-Bheule-lhuchd -nan-trusganan-uaine, and I am older than Aone and am as old as Luan. And in Tir-na-h'oige my name is Suibhal-bheann; in Tir-fo-thuinn it is Cú-gorm; and in Tir-na-h'oise it is Sireadh-thall. And I have been a breath in your heart. And the day has its feet to it that will see me coming into the hearts of men and women like a flame upon dry grass, like a flame of wind in a great wood..."

Is tu gleus na Mnatha Sithe,
Is tu beus na Bride bithe,
Is tu creud na Moire mine,
Is tu gniomh na mnatha Greuig,
Is tu sgeimh na h'Eimir aluinn,
Is tu mein na Dearshul agha,
Is tu meann na Meabha laidir,
Is tu taladh Binne-bheul.
Thine is the skill of the Fairy Woman,
And the virtue of St. Brigit,
And the faith of Mary the Mild,
And the gracious ways of the Greek woman,
And the beauty of lovely Emir,
And the tenderness of heart sweet Deirdre,
And the courage of Maeve the great Queen*,
And the charm of Mouth O' Music**."
        *Literally, "the strong"
        **Literally, "honey-mouthed"

WHEN TO SUMMON BRIGID

If you are casting candle or fire magic rituals and spells, for protection against evil, to remove emotional, mental, or physical pain, in healing rituals, to protect your beloved one during pregnancy and labor, or if you are undergoing a changing phase. For example: loss of a loved one, breaking bad habits or wishing to raise your self-awareness.

Although Imbolc is celebrated in February, Brigid can be revered at any time of the year. She is the guardian of the home and families, and she also gives prosperity and helps in the harvesting of planted seeds. This ritual should preferably be done during the Crescent Moon or Full Moon so that your requests do not wane.

NECESSARY ITEMS

1. Sage smudge stick
2. 3 white candles
3. Milk
4. Honey
5. Seeds
6. Metal container

Purify yourself with a sage smudging and arrange the items where you will perform the ritual. Light the candles and place them in the three corners of the altar, pour the milk and honey in the metal container and throw the seeds in it. Make your requests to the Goddess, thank her for her light that shines daily even when we do not realize it. Finally, recite the following verses:

Brigid, Golden Goddess.
Brigid, Lady of Fire.
Brigid, Sun of Mankind.
Guide me, Lady Divine.

Bury the seeds so that they grow and your requests bear fruit.

Brigid Card

Standard Description: Brigid was a goddess of the Tuatha Dé Danann. She was a daughter of the chief of the gods, The Dagda, and was known as a goddess of healers, poets, smiths, childbirth, and inspiration. Her name means "exalted one". Also known as the "High One" or "Bright One". She is described as 'of great, shining beauty'.

Meaning: She was a Triple Goddess: Brigit of hearth, fire, metallurgy, and smith craft; Brigit of poetry (which the Celts deemed an immaterial, sensual form of flame), inspiration and learning; Brigit of healing and medicine; She Who inspired the skills of whistling and keening.

Upright card: You are on the path of healing. Be inspired. Your ability to create in many mediums is at an all time high. Spiritual exaltation is present. This card is a good omen for women looking to be protected during childbirth.

Reversed card: You need spiritual medicine. The fire of creation is dark. A fall from grace is imminent. You will reap what you sow. You have strayed from the path of healing.

Objects: Oak; fire; brass-shoe; cauldron; the number nineteen; Brigid's Cross.

CAILLEACH

PRONUNCIATIONS:	Cailleach (Irish: [ˈkaʎəx, kəˈʎax], Scottish Gaelic: [ˈkʰɛʎəx])
MEANING OF NAME:	Hag, old woman, veiled one
SACRED DAY/MONTH:	Imbolc, February 1st
GENDER:	Female
SEASON:	Winter/Early Spring
RESPONSIBLE FOR:	The creation of mountains, landscapes, cliffs
COMMON ASSOCIATIONS:	Wise women, fortune tellers, mountains, landscapes
ANIMAL:	Horned beasts or cattle
COLOR:	Icey blue
PLANET/STAR:	Taurus
SUGGESTED OFFERINGS:	Paper snowflakes, dirt,
MOST NOTABLE FEATURE:	She has red teeth and matted hair 'white as an apron covered with hoarfrost.' Over it She wore a kerchief and over Her gray clothing, a faded plaid shawl.
HERBS/STONES/INCENSE:	Snowflake agate, quartz

In Gaelic mythology, primarily Irish, Scottish, and Manx, Cailleach is seen as the Goddess of Winter (Scottish), the Divine Creator (all three) and is described, as well as depicted as an old hag. She is also viewed as an ancestor deity with ties to our ancestral roots. The Cailleach appears mostly as a veiled old woman, sometimes with only one eye.

Her skin is a deathly pale or blue, while her teeth were red, and her clothes adorned with skulls. She could leap across mountains and ride storms. In the Manx tradition, the Cailleach was a shape shifter capable of transforming into a giant bird.

She is a creator deity that shaped much of the known landscape; whether she did so intentionally was never made clear. Her tools of creation and destruction included her hammer, with which she was able to control storms and thunder. In some legends, she also controlled a well that would occasionally overflow and flood the land.

Neither good nor evil; her intentions vary from tale to tale. From her association with storms and thunder, she was a natural and wild destructive force. Yet, she also cares deeply for animals both wild and domestic. In all three Gaelic-speaking regions, she was the patron of wolves emboldened by winter hunger; while in Scotland, she also served as a deer herder.

The Cailleach is both ageless and immortal. As winter gave way to spring, she would take a drought that returned her to youth. In Manx legend, she spent half the year as a young woman and the other half as an old crone. In Ireland, she had seven periods of youth [The 7 Maidenhoods], after which she remained old permanently. The seasonal division between summer and winter, where the Cailleach ruled winter and Brigid ruled summer highlights the association of the two goddesses. On Samhain [sow-in], or October 31st to November 1st, the Celtic year ends, and winter begins, which marks the return of the Cailleach.

In Scotland and the Isle of Man, the Cailleach transforms into Brigid during Beltane. The Cailleach was also a goddess of grain, a key resource in surviving winter. The last sheath of grain harvested was dedicated to her and used to begin the next planting season. Like many Irish goddesses, the Cailleach was linked to sovereignty and rulership. Before anyone could rule the land, they had to first garner her approval. This shows a direct link to The Morrigan, the sovereign goddess.

The Cailleach was unique among Celtic deities, only appearing in Gaelic-speaking regions—namely, Ireland, Scotland, and the Isle of Man. While Brythonic Celtic regions told stories involving similar hags, none of these characters could rival the consistency the Cailleach. Such hags included Black Annis, a blue-faced hag of Leicester with iron claws who supped on children.

These hags were often closer to the popular notion of a hag, rather than the more capricious Cailleach. Outside of the Celtic world, the Cailleach has numerous similarities based on her individual attributes. As a creator deity, she bore similarities to the Greco-Roman Gaia. The Cailleach was also remarkably like the Norse deity Skadi, the goddess of winter and darkness, as well as the Germanic Holle, wife of Wotan (Odin) and master of winter's cold.

Though her stormy hammer closely resembled Thor's hammer Mjolnir, the Cailleach's behavior and appearance were closer to that of Thor's foes, the frost giants. In Slavic mythology, Baba Yaga carried many of the attributes of the Cailleach. An impossibly old woman just as likely to help as hinder, Baba Yaga made many appearances in Slavic folklore. Her leaping chicken-legged hut moved in much the same way the Cailleach did when she traveled between mountains.

On Imbolc, or February 1st, of each year, the Cailleach runs out of firewood for the winter. In the Manx tradition, she transforms into a great bird and collects firewood in her beak. In Ireland and Scotland, meanwhile, she collects firewood as an old woman. If she wishes for winter to last longer, she makes the day sunny and bright for her search. If she accidentally oversleeps, the day is stormy and gray. Thus, tradition holds that if February 1st is gray and wintry, winter will be shorter that year; if the day is bright, winter will return due to her preparation.

In the United States, this tradition was transformed into Groundhog Day, removing the Cailleach while retaining the central ritual. The Cailleach, the Bodach, and their children appeared to the people of Glen Lyon and Glen Cailleach seeking shelter. Despite their fearsome reputations (or perhaps because of them), the family was granted shelter. During this period, the surrounding glens became incredibly fertile. Before departing the area, the Cailleach gave the people a parting gift: the area would be eternally fertile, if they put up stones for her family between May 1st and October 31st—from Beltane to Samhain. Each year, this ritual is repeated.

In Literature

The maidens rejoice
When May-day comes to them;
For me sorrow is meeter,
 I am wretched, I am an old hag.
   - "Lament of the Hag of Beara", trans. Lady Gregory

The Cailleach has appeared in literature throughout the ages. In the 8th century poem, "Lament of the Old Woman," she reflects on her faded youth and laments its loss. In Donald Alexander Mackenzie's 20th century retelling of Scottish folklore, the Cailleach became Beira, Queen of Winter.

The work retained much of the Cailleach's classic characterization and, along with Lady Gregory's translation of old Irish tales, served as one of the more prominent sources of Cailleach myths.

WHEN TO SUMMON CAILLEACH

When working with yourself and your inner being. For self-healing, changes, she is a goddess of transformation and change. She is represented by Winter, ending of the harvest season, Samhain is connected to her. Recognizing Cailleach can be a step towards recognizing our own potential. For this we must destroy our conception of ourselves so that we can renew ourselves.

NECESSARY ITEMS:
1. Stones
2. Red Fabric
3. Green apple
4. Mirror
5. Paper and pen
6. Food you enjoy

Collect a variety of stones to decorate your altar. A good way to do this is to go for a walk in a wood, beach, or a rural area. Feel the smells, listen to the noises, enjoy the nature around you as you walk. Do not take any stone you find, let this selection be a channel with which the Goddess talks to your inner self. Back to your altar, open a circle (calling the Airts) and place the stones in the arrangement you think is best.

Cut the green apple in half and place it on top of the red fabric. Face the mirror. Ask yourself: What qualities do you identify on the reflection? Intelligence? Curiosity? Serenity? Write them down on paper. Then begin to appreciate the person you are now and the one you will become in the future, enjoying the qualities you have written and fortifying them every day. Try to change the traits you do not like by persisting in this renewal and always looking forward to your happiness. Close the circle (dismissing the Airts) and call to Cailleach, thanking her for the strength she gave you. Celebrate after with foods you like, fruit juices, cheese, and the green apple you cut.

CAILLEACH CARD

Standard Description: The divine hag, a creator deity, a weather deity, and an ancestor deity. In modern Scottish folklore studies, she is also known as Beira, Queen of Winter. The word Cailleach means directly "old woman". Her other name is "Veiled One". The Cailleach appears primarily as a veiled old woman, sometimes with only one eye. Her skin was deathly pale or blue, while her teeth were red, and her clothes adorned with skulls. She could leap across mountains and ride storms. In the Manx tradition, the Cailleach was a shape shifter capable of transforming into a giant bird.

Meaning: Great creative Earth Mother; Goddess of fertility and the cereal harvest; Goddess of birth and death; Hag of autumn; Corn [meaning grain, perhaps especially wheat]. Mother; Queen of the harvest; She whose regenerative power lurks in the last standing grain; She who "sits in" the last sheaf of harvest; She who ensures the fertility of the following harvest: [Matron of reapers]. The she/he who cuts, or binds. She, who is two spirited.

Upright card: Fertility and creation. The harvest is bountiful, whether it be one of a physical harvest or spiritual. Regeneration and new beginnings are coming but first a need to learn to be patient and stand still and listen.

Reversed card: You are not listening; you will miss the message meant for you. You are bound and stuck in place. You have no patience, and it is showing in your daily life and spiritual life.

Objects: Grains, rye, wheat, barley, oats; poppy; fox; mouse; spiral

SÍLE NA GIĠ

Pronunciations:	Sheila, Síle and Síla
Meaning of name:	Síle na gcíoch, meaning "Julia of the breasts".
Sacred Day/Month:	None
Race:	Unknown
Gender:	"Female" figure
Responsible for:	Folk deity used as an amulet for childbirth, symbolizing both life and death
Common Associations:	Vagina, female breasts, female form, womb, ovaries, female organs
Most Notable Feature:	Enlarged female parts

There is no known information on Síle na Giġ for summoning. There are no rituals that are standard to Síle na Giġ and she is thought to be either the representation of an older form of The Morrígan or Cailleach - some say she is the representation of the female form and divine ability to produce life from her body. The following summoning is a personal creation.

I will acknowledge that Kathryn Price NicDhàna has a divine take on Síle na Giġ, below is an excerpt from her article located on her personal website. I applaud Miss Kathryn, her thoughts and take on this subject matter really resonated with me, and she did a fantastic job of researching and gathering the information that supports her theories quite well. I would say she would be a recommended read on the subject matter.

> Possible meanings to be explored for Sheela/Síle include: to shelter or shield; the seed which is planted and the ground in which it grows; offspring, race or descendants of; raining; an effeminate person; to think, to consider, to have respect for; and perhaps my favorite possibility: cause or origin.
> In Scotland, we find the word sheiling – a shelter, and sheal – to shelter. Both are derived from the Icelandic root word for shield. These words are a product of the Northern influence on Gaelic languages and cultures and meaning certainly fit with the protective function of the sheelas.

P.W. Joyce gives the root Shee as a corruption of the Irish Sidh – a fairy hill. While this is probably too fragmentary to be the sole answer, it is still an interesting and appropriate association, especially as the mounds can be seen as both the tombs of the dead and the belly from which new life emerges. While originally only a word for the mounds, in later usage sidh also came to be applied to any otherworldly spirit or creature who might be associated with these places.

The Old Irish root word síl, or siol (both pronounced "sheel"), seems to be the strongest possibility. It is from this root that we get the rest of the above-cited words that could be related to Sheela/Síle: "síl – seed, offspring, race, descendants. silad – act of disseminating, spreading, to make known. sílaid – either the seed, etc, which is sown or the earth, etc, which is sown with it; causes, brings about, produces; generates, multiplies, spreads."

It was while digging through the Early Irish quotations in tiny print under síl and sílaid that I found something that really made me sit up and take notice: sila has been used to mean cause or origin. And it is pronounced the same as "Sheela" and "Síle." I felt a chill of recognition. This resonated so strongly with the intuitive impressions I'd been receiving in my work with her.

Ever since that moment I've found myself thinking of her as Síla ("SHEE-luh"), First Woman, Eldest of the Ancestors. This idea of Síla as "the origin" aligns with my sense of her strong connection to the ancestors, and the tales of the Cailleach as the mother of many tribes of humans, whose husbands have all died of old age, one after another.

I have generally continued to use this variation in the name, both to distinguish her from the more common personal name, Síle, in reference to the manuscript where this spelling was found, and to commemorate that sense of "rightness" that hit me when I found it. However, many prefer to use the more common spelling, Síle, and I sometimes do as well. In many ways Síle (Hag) may be the more appropriate variation, depending on which meaning one is leaning towards.

-- Kathryn Price NicDhàna

WHEN TO SUMMON SÍLE NA GIG

You summon Síle na Gig when you want to empower the feminine side of your being and make connections to the "First Woman, Eldest of the Ancestors" in your ancestral line. If you are dual spirited and want to work with your femininity you call on Síle na Gig. She is called upon for protection of the divine female within, she is called when matriarchal leadership is needed. You call Síle na Gig for primarily female sexual healing and power.

ITEMS NEEDED:
- Irish Peat Moss [Irish logs] *
- White cloth
- Red Cloth
- Black Cloth
- A personal item to you
- White quartz or selenite
- Red ruby [or replication of one]
- Black quartz, obsidian, or onyx [either will do]

Leave the altar set up until protection is no longer needed or working with the divine female energy is done. Open a circle (calling the Airts). Prepare your altar lining it with the three cloths and place your stones at the three points. Your obsidian [or black quartz or onyx], your ruby and white quartz or selenite at the two bottom corners. Add your item that is personal to you and light the sage or preferably the Irish peat moss (Irish log) in a saining burner. Let the peat moss burn out and then dismiss the Airts as you call the Síle na Gig and thank her for the strength and protection she gives you.

Saining is the Celtic "version" of smudging. Instead of fanning the smoke of sage with a feather, saining allows the smoke to rise as the incense burns while ritual altar work is performed. The word come from the Old Irish word sén meaning "a protective charm."

Trickster Hag, laughing and howling;
    Then veiled in the mist, silent as stone.
    Gateway and gatekeeper,
    Guide and challenger,
    Liminal-dwelling paradoxical crone.
    Síla of the branches, Origin of the Tribes
    Síla of the nymphs, Origins of Womankind;
    Eldest of the Ancestors, gynandrous crone and fertile youth,
    Hag and Maiden and in between; seed and ground and
truth;
    Síla of the bloodlines, Síla of the trees,
    Síla na Géige
    Sheela na Gig
    -- Kathryn Price NicDhàna

* Irish peat moss is an extremely strong smell, if you wish to substitute the item you can use an incense that appeals to you with an earthy tone to it. I recommend making a substitute to this item if you are asthmatic or have health issues involving the lungs.

In modern times, many blanket bogs have been modified by human action.
    The cutting of peat (called 'turf' when cut) for fuel began in the 17th century and continued at an increasing rate until the mid 20th century.

Síle na Giġ Card

Standard Description: The figure is meant to represent a survival of pagan, usually Celtic beliefs which have been incorporated into the newcomer Christian church. Disobedient artists/sculptors paying lip service to the old gods. However, Síle na Giġ or Sheela-Na-Gig is thought to be a representation of fertility, the strength of matriarchal presence and femininity. It is a stone carving that represents the reproductive organs of the female body with an over exaggerated and oversized vulva.

Meaning: Thought to be a gargoyle in modern day times, older traditions theorize that she is the representation of the matriarchal head of household. It also represents fertility and the ability of the woman to bring forth life from her womb.

Upright card: Listen to your female ancestors, they are speaking to you of your feminine divinity and power. You are stronger in your womanhood than you believe to be. The divine goddess is telling you to embrace your sexuality and not be ashamed of it.

Reversed card: You feel shame of your sexuality when you should not. Your female ancestors speak but you are not hearing them. You feel repressed and oppressed. You must break free of this shame and embrace all your being instead of only parts of it.

Objects: Spiral; Triple knot; red-heifer; horse; raven; hooded-crow.

RHIANNON

Meaning of name:	Appears to derive from the reconstructed Brittonic form *Rīgantonā, a derivative of *rīgan- "queen"
Sacred Day/Month:	Monday
Race:	Otherworld
Gender:	Female
Season:	Early to Late Spring
Responsible for:	Moon, horses, horseshoe, songbirds, gates, the wind, and the number 7.
Common Associations:	Fertility, sex magic, dream work, divination skills, beauty, earth
Animal:	Horses
Color:	Dark green, maroon, gold, silver, rich brown, white, black, charcoal gray, and ruby red.
Planet/Star:	Moon/Waning
Most Notable Feature:	Beautiful woman arrayed in gold silk brocade, riding a shining white horse
Herbs/Stones/Incense:	Narcissus and daffodils, leeks, pansies, forsythia, cedar and pine trees [evergreens], bayberry, sage and rosemary,[jasmine, any white flower]. Gold, silver, cat's eye, moonstone, crystal, quartz, ruby, red garnet, bloodstone, turquoise, and amethyst.

In modern practice, Rhiannon is a lunar goddess of fertility and rebirth, transformation, wisdom, and magic. A goddess of ethereal beauty, she is well known for granting wishes to those who ask for what they want. People with a special connection to horses will naturally be drawn to Rhiannon, the horse goddess. Starting a relationship with a horse is the best way to approach and show devotion to Rhiannon.

She embodies the cleverness of women in patriarchal systems, such as when she helps Pwyll trick Gwawl by giving him a magical bag. She never breaks the rules in that episode, but she helps bend them to a degree that allow her to pursue her true love. Her magical presence, while more subtle than that of other Welsh women such as Arianrhod or Cerridwen, nevertheless mark her as a manifestation of the Divine Feminine. She is a being of sovereignty, and her association with horses implies a cultured freedom that was hard won. When to summon Rhiannon. When you need to rely on your wit in a situation. Need to draw on the Divine Feminine. She is a goddess of transformation and wisdom and truth. Making a wish, she is known to grant those wishes.

Items Needed:
1. 3 candles; green or white
2. Fresh, colorful flowers in red, white, orange, and yellow
3. Cup with red wine or water
4. Incense: sandalwood, jasmine or rose
5. Paper and pen
6. Lighter (or matches)

When the sun begins to set, start decorating your altar with flowers. The blessings of the Earth will come around if we call upon them.
Stand up and take 3 deep breaths. Say:
You are blessed, beautiful Earth,
You secure me and nourish me.
Thank you for the trees, the roots, and the Spring.
Thank you for the wisdom that I hear in the wind
I welcome your Goddess gifts and accept your authority

Light the 3 candles being careful not to burn the flowers.
Say:
Hail to you, Great Sun.
You coordinate the flow of Nature through your powerful will.
When you rise you give me life, when you hide you teach me hope.
I pray for your light to reach me.
Light the incense and relax. Breathe slowly through your nose.

Close your eyes and let your body and mind fill with inspiration. Beltane is a celebration of fertility and growth, so we will use this opportunity to focus on the things in life that we want more of.

Sit by your altar and write down any of your personal wishes on the piece of paper, or simply meditate on them.

Take your chalice with both hands and say:

Earth Goddess, Gentle Sun.

Fromm your renewed union, a host of fruitful beings will rise.

Ancient Gods, I celebrate with you.

I ask for your blessings and protection.

I ask for the protection of those around me.

I offer you my prayers, thoughts, words, and actions.

Take a sip of your chalice and place it back on the altar as an offering. Let the candles burn until you leave the room. Then simply blow them out. Leave the offerings and your request on your altar until the next day. Offerings to Rhiannon: Garlands of roses, feeding the birds, oatcakes, oatmeal cookies, rose-scented candles, perfumes, and incense. Images of songbirds, horses and mules, horseshoes.

An old folk custom from western Ireland says that if you light fires just before dawn at each corner of a perfectly oriented crossroad (one that runs directly east, west, and north, south), then sit down quietly at its side, you can see Epona ride by, flying west from the approaching sunrise.

RHIANNON CARD

Standard Depiction: She is a strong-minded Otherworld woman, who chooses Pwyll, prince of Dyfed (west Wales), as her consort, in preference to another man to whom she has already been betrothed. She is intelligent, politically strategic, beautiful, and famed for her wealth and generosity. She is often considered to be related to the Gaulish horse goddess Epona. She and her son are often depicted as mare and foal. Like Epona, she sometimes sits on her horse in a calm, stoic way.

Meaning: Goddess of the year; Mistress of the Underworld; Beautiful Queen of the night and its dreams [both pleasant and unpleasant]; Muse of inspiration; Source of truth; She who is adored by all true poets.

Upright card: Heed the saying "the truth shall set you free". Your muse is around the corner, look for her but don't chase either the truth or your muse or you will never catch either. Let it come to you naturally. Use your dreams to inspire you, good dreams are coming to you.

Reversed card: The truth is darkened and in hiding. Chasing it only brings frustrations and hardship. Look for the signs back to the path of truth or suffer the consequences of chasing the truth with no end in sight. Your dreams are more nightmares than pleasant ones. Your fears are in those nightmares, and they plague you.

Objects: White horse; three birds; Rhiannon's Wheel. Gates.

DANU, THE DIVINE GODDESS
(AND HER COUNTERPART DÔN)

MEANING OF NAME:	"Mother goddess", "To flow", "good"
RACE:	Tuatha dé Danann
GENDER:	Female
RESPONSIBLE FOR:	Nobility, unity, power, wind, earth, fairies/fairy mounds
COMMON ASSOCIATIONS:	Mounds, the river Danube, motherhood, fertility
ANIMAL:	Fish, seagulls, horses
COLOR:	Amber
MOST NOTABLE FEATURE:	Her triple goddess form, crowns, keys, gold

In Irish mythology, Danu ([ˈdanu]) is a mother goddess of the Tuatha Dé Danann (Old Irish: "The peoples of the goddess Danu"). Though primarily seen as an ancestral figure, some Victorian sources also associate her with the land. Danu has no surviving myths or legends associated with her in any of the medieval Irish texts. She has possible parallels with the Welsh literary figure Dôn, whom most modern scholars regard as a mythological mother goddess in the medieval tales of the Mabinogion. However, Dôn's sex is never specified in the tales and was regarded as a man by some medieval Welsh antiquarians.

The closest figure in Irish texts to a "Danu" would then be Danand, daughter of Delbáeth. In the Lebor Gabála Érenn: The Book of the Taking of Ireland, it is noted the Tuatha Dé Danann get their name from the three sons of Danand: Brian, Iuchar, and Iucharba. These three are known as the "Gods of Dannan." However, Cormac's Glossary, a text that predates the Lebor Gabala Erenn, names the goddess Anu as the mother of the gods. In this respect, Danu/ Dôn, in my opinion and practice, is a dual Goddess/God. Some refer to Danu's counterpart as the Green Man (Cernannos) to which is a more modern take on the Goddess and her male counterpart. Some would suggest that Danu/ Dôn is a "hermaphrodite" type goddess/god and is gender fluid, myself included. With that said, the following ritual is for the gender fluid nature of Danu/ Dôn.

WHEN TO SUMMON

When you are working with both feminine and masculine energies, calling on brute strength that requires a gentle wise hand. When you need to flow like water in a situation or be empty and full at the same time. Danu/ Dôn is like Bruce Lee's teachings of "be like water". Danu Means "the Flowing One". She/He is shrouded in mystery, She/He is very popular, but little is known of her/him.

We do know the original 'she' was considered the most ancient of all the Celtic deities. She/He is the great mother/father of the gods of Ireland and the divine creator/creatrix who birthed all things into being. She/He is also an earth and sky goddess/god. She/He is the Mother/Father of The Tuatha De Danann, the Irish Gods, which literally means the Children of Danu/ Dôn. All the Danann can trace their Lineage back to Her/Him.

ITEMS NEEDED:
1. A blue altar cloth (to represent her flowing waters)
2. A yellow altar cloth (to represent his warm light)
3. A glass bowl full of water
4. River stones enough to circle the bowl
5. Four white candles (place in cardinal points, N,E,S,W)

Call the Airts before beginning. Try to imagine a shinning Goddess, Tall and proud with ivory skin and blue green eyes. She wears a flowing robe of watery blue silk and sliver. She wears a silver of spirals on Her head and holds a great sliver Basin from which all waters of life flows. Beside Her is Him. A bright shining, ivory skinned man with matching eyes. As tall as She is, smiling with a gentleness in His eyes.

On his head is golden spirals and he holds a great gold trimmed mirror that reflects the light, it is the warming light of protection and inspiration. Give them a gift. Sit for a while a listen. What does the Goddess Danu have to tell you? What does Dôn tell you? Stay if you like with them. She sits with you and wants to hear your woes, and your questions. He sits with you and wants to protect and comfort you from your woes and offer advice for your questions. Listen for to both of their answers.

Chant or sing to her. Sway like you are being rocked by the sea. Let your heart and soul be cleansed by her healing waters:

The Children of Earth remember the Mother of All.

All-Birther, fountain of healing,

Loving Sustainer remember us as we remember you.

☙

Chant or sing to him. Turn your face upwards as if a warming light is shining down on you. Let your heart and soul be comforted by his healing light.

The Children of Earth remember the Father of All.

All-Kindler, flame of comfort.

Lighter of Ways remember us as we remember you.

☙

It is time to say goodbye to the Goddess/God. Thank her/him. Find yourself back in your sacred space. Ground yourself and dismiss the Airts. Go in peace knowing you can visit the great Mother and Father anytime you need her or him.

Though Danu was the mother goddess and namesake of the Tuatha Dé Danann tribe, much about her remains shrouded in mystery. Danu was the source of the tribe's common heritage, as well as its nobility, unity, and power. As a goddess of sovereignty and power, Danu would grant gifts to rulers and those of noble birth.

Though such gifts varied in value and substance, it is nevertheless clear that the kings, chiefs, and Ollam of the Tuatha Dé Danann all drew their power from her. The Tuatha Dé Danann were creative, crafty, and skilled; it has been theorized that Danu was the source of such talents.

As a mother goddess, Danu was believed to have suckled many of the gods and instilled in them a sense of wisdom. Given the migratory nature of the Tuatha Dé Danann, it has been speculated that she was a wind or earth goddess as well. All things in Ireland depended upon her blessings. Her connection to the earth also tied her to the fairies, fairy mounds, and the many standing stones and dolmens of Ireland.

DANU/ DÔN

Standard Description: This Celtic goddess and god combination is portrayed as a beautiful and mature woman and man, they are associated with nature and the spiritual essence of nature, while also representing the contrasting (yet cyclic) aspects of prosperity, wisdom, death, and regeneration. She represents the cleansing power of water and he the comforting power of light. He is depicted wearing the antlers of a great stag. He is the god of the wild hunt, of the game in the forest. She is depicted wearing a golden crown and a flowing dress of the same color.

Meaning: Goddess Danu is a strong symbol of female strength and power, while her counterpart, Dôn is masculine comforting strength and protection. She embodies such traits as fertility, growth, abundance, agricultural bounty, and a sense of nurturing the land. While he embodies the primal sense of nature, the bounty of the hunt. He is a warm presence with a loving but firm touch, a fatherly figure who is firm but fair. The advice giver.

Danu the All-Mother is lunar in spirit. Danu is a lover of all life and was thus portrayed quite frequently with animals. In particular, she is associated with horses, seagulls, and fish, all of which move in free-flowing ways. This goddess is also symbolized in the physical elements, such as flowing bodies of water, air, wind, and the earth. Dôn the All-Father is solar in spirit. A lover of the hunt, he is associated with deer, wild boar, dogs, and the adder. His physical elements are that of air, earth, and fire.

Upright card: Prosperity, wisdom, regeneration. A cleansing with water and a bringing of truth, your truth to the light of day. Strength and power are in your hands. If you are dual spirited, gender fluid, non-binary this is your sign to embrace all your duality instead of one or the other. Your male side is as important as your female side. Seek advice from trusted sources. Flow free and uninhibited.

Reversed card: You are inhibited in some way. You are at odd with your duality and two sides. Steer clear of those who would stray you from the path with bad advice. You will struggle with prosperity and bounty. The elements work against you as does someone, or a group of people.

Objects: Moon, horse, seagull, fish, water, divine flow (menstrual cycles, moon cycles). Deer, dogs, wild boar, sun, light, gold, and silver.

CERRIDWEN AND HER CAULDRON AWEN

THE STORY OF CERRIDWEN

PRONUNCIATIONS:	Ceridwen or Cerridwen Ke-RID-Wen
MEANING OF NAME:	Poetry or song and – wen, (a contraction of gwen) – meaning white, fair or holy
SACRED DAY/MONTH:	July 3rd
GENDER:	Female
SEASON:	Summer
RESPONSIBLE FOR:	Grain, life, death, rebirth, inspiration, transformation, the moon, wisdom, poetry.
COMMON ASSOCIATIONS:	Full moon, transformation, change, herbalism, harvest, poetry, creativity
ANIMAL:	A white sow
COLOR:	White or Green
PLANET/STAR:	Moon
SUGGESTED OFFERINGS:	Vervain, acorns
MOST NOTABLE FEATURE:	Her cauldron

Cerridwen is a Celtic Welsh Goddess. Her name comes from "ceryd" which is Welsh for chiding love and "gwen" which is Welsh for white and blessed. She is the Mother and a Crone aspect of the Triple Goddess and is often represented as an old hag or witch and called Hag of Creation and the Old One. Cerridwen is a shape shifting Goddess able to shape sift from an old hag to a beautiful girl and various animals.

She is a corn goddess and is symbolized often as a sow as well, an animal of abundance and fertility, as the Goddess of Sovereignty. This totem animal also represents the fecundity or the Underworld and the strength of the mother. Cerridwen is one of the faces of the dark Goddess and a goddess of dark prophetic powers. Cerridwen's cauldron is one of the many cauldrons of Celtic lore. The Cauldron in Celtic tradition was central to the religious mystery and represented the regeneration in the womb of the Goddess.

Her cauldron was called Amen and was the Cauldron of Divine Knowledge, Wisdom, Rebirth, and Inspiration. It's transforming magic happens through change, experience, and divine inspirations. Cerridwen lived in the middle of Bala Lake in North Wales underwater with her husband Tegid Foel and her two children. Her two children were born from the womb as twins, a daughter Creirwy and a son Afagddu. Creirwy was a very beautiful fair maiden and Afagddu was a very ugly dark boy. Together they represent the light and dark. Since her son was so ugly Cerridwen was concerned about him and wanted her son to be more accepted by his peers and society despite his ugliness so she planned to create a magic potion in her cauldron that would make him a brilliant, wise, inspiring man and a talented bard.

The magic potion was to be stirred and boiled a year and a day as common in Celtic magic and to be condensed down to three powerful drops containing the wisdom of the world and the rest would be poison. Helping tend the cauldron of Cerridwen's magical potion for her son was a young man named Gwion-Bach. He helped stir and keep watch over it. One day when Cerridwen went out to collect more herbs for the brew the potion bubbled up and splashed onto his hand by accident the three drops of wisdom and in pain and he instinctively put his fingers in his mouth.

He instantly gained the wisdom and knowledge of the world and could understand all the secrets of the world past and future. This may be inspired by a Celtic divinatory practice of thumb chewing in early Ireland called Imbas Forosnai to gain wisdom and perception. Furious Gwion had licked the magical drops meant for her son Afagddu, Cerridwen began to chase him in rage, shape shifting into different animals. Gwion became a rabbit, and she became a dog. He became a fish and jumped in the water, and she became an otter. He became a bird, and she became a big hawk. Finally, he became a grain of corn, and she became a hen and ate him.

The grain of corn impregnated Cerridwen and she was pregnant for 9 month and 9 moons. She was so angry she plotted to kill the baby once she gave birth, but the reborn Gwion was too beautiful at birth to kill. Instead, she sewed up the newborn in a seal skin bag and threw him into the ocean. The baby was rescued by Celtic Prince Elphin son of King Gwyddno Garanhir from the water. He was called Taliesin which means "behold radiant forehead". He became the legendary and greatest Welsh bard and satirist in the land, a counselor of kings, and was perceived as the genuine incarnation of Druidism.

The Welsh belief that for true inspiration to be brought to the world there must be death and rebirth is represented by this story. Cerridwen's womb like her cauldron has potential to birth all manifestation and is the beginning and end of life.

❧

Neud amug ynghadeir o beir Cerridwen!
Handid rydd fy nhafawd
Yn adddawd gwawd Ogyrwen.

Is not my chair protected by the cauldron of Cerridwen?
Therefore, let my tongue be free
In the sanctuary of the praise of the Goddess.
--The Bard Taliesin

❧

When to call on Cerridwen and her cauldron Awen: When you need the wisdom of Awen and sanctuary of Cerridwen. Want to free your inner most self and feel safe while realizing any desired changes for your life and spiritual or psychological transformations.

CERRIDWEN RITUAL

CHANGE AND TRANSFORMATION

ITEMS NEEDED:
- 1 small white candle for Goddess
- 4 small green candles for renewal
- Blessing oil of your choice for Goddess candle
- Sandalwood oil or pine/evergreen oil for green candles
- Incense of your choice
- Cauldron for incense
- Matches
- Bowl of water with sea salt
- Paper and Pen

Place Goddess candle in middle of altar and other green candles in each of the four directions. Call to the Airts as you place the four directional candles. Anoint candles with oil and light them. Light incense and purify space.

Invocation: "Goddess Cerridwen, be with me here, and guide me to create the change and transformation I am seeking to create in my life right now."

Meditate visualizing the changes and transformations you would like to create in your life right now. After this is clear write down those specific changes and transformations in an area of your life you would like to make now and place on your altar.

Say: "Goddess Cerridwen bless and guide me on this journey of change and transformation. Awen may you enlighten my path and show me the way."

Dismiss the Airts and let candles burn out. Keep the piece of paper on your personal altar until the change and transformation has taken place or Awen has given you the wisdom to see the path to enlightenment and transformation.

I give you life
I give you death
it is all one

You travel the
spiral path
the eternal path
that is existence
ever becoming
ever growing
ever changing

Nothing dies that
is not reborn
nothing is born
that does not die

When you come
to me
I welcome you
home
then I take you
into my womb

my cauldron of
transformation
where you are
stirred and sifted
blended and boiled
melted and
mashed
reconstituted then
recycled

You always come
back to me
you always go
forth renewed

Death and Rebirth
are but points of
transition
along the Eternal
Path.

-Patty Kennelly,
Blogspot

Ceridwen/Awen Card

Standard Description: Ceridwen is the shape shifting Celtic goddess of knowledge, transformation, and rebirth. The Awen, cauldron of poetic inspiration, is one of her main symbols. Ceridwen pursues Gwion through a cycle of seasons until, in the form of a hen, she swallows Gwion, disguised as an ear of corn then rebirths him into the poet Taliesin. Black screaming hag; greyhound; otter; hawk; red-crested black-hen. Red and black colors signify her aspect as Death-goddess in this shape. While white signifies intelligence, knowledge, and foresight.

Meaning: Goddess of the moon, grain, intelligence, knowledge, foresight, poetry, and letters; White Lady of death; She to Whom skulls are mast; Shape shifting Presider over the year and its seasons. As Black-hag She is described as big-mouthed, swarthy, swift, sooty, lame, with a cast in Her left eye.

Upright card: Your creativity is at a peak, the knowledge you seek will come to you easily enough. Keep looking in the direction you have been looking. The seasons are cycling.

Reversed card: You are struggling in the path to knowledge you have taken. Let go of this path, it means only death of self. Don't let it consume and devour you. Change directions or meet a swift "petite mort" [little death].

Objects: grain; bee; cat; wolf; sow; cauldron of inspiration and knowledge; leather-bag (into which She put Gwion before throwing him into the sea); the color white.

Devotion, Veneration, Ritual Space, Offerings

Devotional Practices

The purpose of creating a devotional practice with a deity is to honor and connect with them, typically through prayer, offerings, and acts of service, just to name a few. Through this practice, we seek their guidance, their blessings, and to offer them gratitude and praise. Altars are nice for this practice for several reasons: they provide a focal point for offerings and connection and also provide a secure area to keep things that are a representation of that deity. While not completely necessary, they can be a valuable part of the practice.

RESEARCH: This is an absolute must when building a devotional practice. An understanding of their lore, their associations, as well as the context in which these stories took place is incredibly important for your practice. Avoid falling too far into the current trend of 'fan fiction as fact' when it comes to these deities. While it can often be nice to have the lore spun in a more positive light, one can miss out on important aspects of these deities when viewed through rose colored glasses (the current 'Persephone and Hades were secret lovers' trend comes to mind here).

OFFERINGS: should be left on a regular basis, though what that schedule is will depend on several factors. Start with what you feel comfortable with and then watch for omens and signs from deity. These will clue you in on whether they want you to up the frequency or change the offerings.

DEVOTIONAL ACTS: such as the ones provided with the deity descriptions [throughout the book], are another unique way to give offerings, as long as one stays mindful while doing them and expresses that they are doing them in that deity's honor. These can be as simple as spoken poems, simple words of mindful prayer.

DEVOTIONAL PRACTICES: to deities are well attested to, not only in northern European lore, but in cultures all over the world. We have archaeological evidence of votive offerings being left in bogs, wells, and other waterways, in addition to being left in mounds, cairns, and in temple areas.

These finds indicate a variety of offerings for a variety of reasons; broken weapons [see Economics of Destruction] and armor of the defeated would be offered to show gratitude for a successful battle, cooking and gardening utensils would be offered to ask for a bountiful harvest, and we have evidence of both animal and human remains that were left as a sacrificial offering for a variety of reasons, up to an including burial goods.

We also have enough written and archaeological evidence on the existence of various deity cults to know that devotional practices weren't limited to the occasional broken sword in a bog. Religious rites were performed in the home, typically by the female of the household, and then there were more public religious rites, often led by a person of authority in the settlement.

ECONOMICS OF DESTRUCTION

Over the pandemic, the Museum of London Docklands offered a virtual lecture on The Hoard, a find of epic proportions was made in Havering. The hoard contained both finished and unfinished weapons as well as a most curious inclusion of 'fragmented' pieces of metalwork along with liquid metal, raw ore, raw iron, fragments of forging as well as deliberately broken weapons. In a book titled Economics of Destruction by David Fontijn which details the practice of selective destruction of objects and deliberate fracture of important items such as weapons, jewelry etc, he provides sound reasoning as to why you would destroy a beautiful and no doubt meaningful object.

In Chapter 6, Gifts to Familiar Gods? He documents that metalwork deposited in this way represents gifts as well as concepts that the gods were similar to humans; "Metalwork deposited in the ground, then, would be the tangible proof of such offerings. There must have been a social belief that it was generally beneficial to society" so there in turn, the idea is to offer or deposit or to destroy is part of the giving aspect. Turning something valuable over, especially if it was a laborious prospect to craft or obtain and then systematically destroying that object would be difficult.

It requires a belief that the god in question would love something similar to you, because they were once human, and therefore have human needs/desires. There is also an economic part of the offering, in that there is a cost, a value in the item. As the item gains this value it almost becomes supernatural, as deposits may have accompanied people, they are the 'gift wrap' that binds the object with 'powers' this allows the object to transform a circulation of sorts. It moves from creation to destruction and then burial, during which the object becomes 'powered by the dead' and therefore is now superior or supernatural, and then broken into fragments, recycled and retrieved to create a new object that is now powered with otherworldly gifts.

This could be transformed in our modern landscape by creating specific objects (or commissioning/procuring) items for deposit or destruction. You could intentionally bury this item for a specific god/ goddess or ancestor and then go and 'retrieve it' and re-purpose it for harrow use. You could specifically destroy the object and give the fragments to various places in honor of gods/goddess, ancestors, wights etc. The options are endless. The idea of giving is to make the gift an real valued exchange. It does not mean it has to be expensive, you can make these offerings within whatever budget you have and within whatever materials are available but there should be some basics included when you think about offerings and how to make them.

1. Make the offering something of meaning
2. Be actively involved in the creation of it or curating it
3. Pick materials that mean something to the gods/ancestors/ wights
4. Think about the offering and its disposal? How are you going to dispose of it?, Where? Do you want to have a special ceremony? Do you want to do it alone or with someone present? Is there a special place you wish to place the offering?

If you are doing it with a ceremony, it might be fun and interesting to create as part of the crafting process, perhaps even crafting in the spiritual space you created for the god/goddess, ancestor or wight. Crafting it in the space, perhaps even just thinking and talking to the entity or ancestor could lend itself to concepts of silent embodiment of importance in crafting. You could 'donate' as part of the energy that went into the crafting of the object itself.

It might also be an amazing and perhaps harder offering to make if you destroyed or buried the tool used to craft, perhaps even the idea of being willing to part with an expensive tool, would be seen as a particularly large donation. Whatever we give, the concepts of how we see offerings is as important as the offering itself. Never giving something that has no value but instead something that has value and is slightly difficult to part with is not out of the realm of consideration. I highly recommend devouring the book Economics of Destruction to get a clear insight into the meaning and purpose of sacrificial offerings.

Disposal of Offerings

Sarah

There are many differing views on how offerings should be disposed of. Archaeological digs have found bits of broken weaponry and armor buried deep in bogs that may have been sacrificial offerings as well as bits of pottery and human remains buried throughout the landscape. However, in modern practice, we must be wary of our carbon footprint and the effects, if any, that our offerings could have on the land and native flora, fauna, and wildlife that might come across it.

There are a variety of ways in which offerings can be disposed of depending on your location, the offering, and what means are readily available. Typically, perishable offerings such as food and drink can be left outside, usually under a tree or by a large boulder on the property, if there is one. This can, however, attract some dangerous wildlife such as bears, coyotes, and other critters that you may not want around your home. In that instance, it may be better to burn what you can and put the rest in the trash.

Liquids can typically be poured outside without issue. Material offerings are a bit more flexible. If you have access to a bog or swamp or other body of water, they are perfect places for offerings to deities associated with them. If not, offerings can be tied to tree branches, buried in a specific part of your property, left to decompose (mainly with offerings to death deities), or burned, just to name a few.

Larisa

The age-old question of how to dispose of offerings. As the saying goes all routes lead to the gods and so there are several ways we can dispose of offerings. Truth is in these simple words. Disposal of offerings can be simple. If you are using biodegradable offerings. Please do not just go dumping things in water ways. Just because you think it's fine, or that it will 'dilute' in water, this is not always true and can harm wildlife. As a resident of Hawaii there are strict rules about what goes in the ocean. Many coastal communities have similar rules, make sure you check what is and is not ok to place in waterways that lead to sensitive reefs or at-risk habitats.

The same is true for anyone living in protective environmental zones. Just because we are an animistic religion that has land offerings at the root of our practices, does not mean you can do this wherever you want. Practice should be balanced with what is legal and what is environmentally conscious.

Liquids: if you leave out beverages of any kind, you can safely dispose of them down a drain if you have no outdoor place to deposit. If you do have an outdoor space, ensure that it's not where there are drains to the ocean or waterways. You also want to make sure you are in the place that does not affect the water table in any way.

Foods: if your food is cooked and compost-able, leaving it in soil in a; pot, compose, garden is a great way to deal with it. If it is not compost-able food, disposing in a compost-able container outside. The local wildlife will find it if there is any. If you live in a place that has no outdoor location, you can deposit offerings in the garbage if you need to or in a composting drain.

Most vegetables can range from 5 days to 1 month, an apple core or a banana peel will take +1 month. While an orange peel will take +6 months. Pistachio shells are another one that takes a long time, while composting it could take 3+ years. Lettuce takes 25 years to decompose. Wood from trees, like stumps, branches, and limbs will take a very long time to decompose, upwards of 50-100 years.

CREATING RITUAL SPACE

SARAH

In most Heathen groups, there is a standard set of practices used for setting up ritual space, as well as a few rules for the participants. The designated area is cleansed, both literally and energetically. There are a variety of ways this is done, from smoke cleansing, carrying a lit torch around the perimeter of the ritual space, and sprinkling cleansing herbal brews around the perimeter, just to name a few. The exact steps will vary from person to person or group to group, but the purpose of cleansing the ritual area is to prepare it to become liminal space, a space to greet the gods, wights, ancestors, or to work magic. Some people like to include god poles in their ritual space while others prefer a simple altar.

LARISA

My best suggestion is to find objects that have meaning to myself and family. I usually find these items in thrift shops which are a great way to make a spiritual space on a thrift budget. I personally don't believe the gods require an intense amount of money to be spent on things. I find placing objects in loose arrangements around the house is the best practice. All of my surfaces are generally a mix of spiritual and non-spiritual items, I like to mix my gods into daily life so statues of Hel or Frigga typically sit on shelves next to family photos and remains of lost pets or relatives.

If you can have a space dedicated to the gods that's amazing and you should do whatever you feel you can do in terms of the space available. Sometimes having animals or small children around makes having open access a bit tricky but I don't think the gods mind if objects move. For me, respecting spiritual items is important but so is living, and so I balance this by having a heart that understands that my gods are not punitive and would forgive an odd push or shove or theft from any little finger or paw. When setting up a 'table' for them, it should be noted that the space does not have to be a physical permanent place but instead could be a shelf or removable area that could be put away if needed.

If you live near an IKEA they have a cute mini storage box called MOPPE that could be used to hide objects away and then fix the top with smaller items that could be placed on top when in use. They also have a larger set called PALLRA that could be used in a similar way by having space to place things away and take out when needed. Small floating shelves if holding light objects can be held up with 3M Velcro strips, although I have found these don't always work unless you have a flat wall, however even floating shelves would only require small amount of hardware can be patched quickly if you needed to move. If you don't have the option to hang or place anything anywhere, there are many alternatives.

Canvas Art: picking pieces that appeal to you and perhaps contain visual representations of gods is a great way to incorporate them. Etsy has some amazing artists that you can locate different looks to bring in the spiritual.

Metallic Hanging Art: Displate is an amazing source for hanging art that you can get to symbolize the spiritual. Displate comes with glue on magnets that will hold the art to any wall even ones that are not flat.

Wooden Art or Statuary: there are some amazing statuary makers out there that make everything from tabletop to full standing statues of all kinds of gods, goddess etc. These can be displayed everywhere with little effort and provide a quick way to showcase your dedication.

A 2010 OUTDOOR ALTAR AT THE SPRINGBLÓT AT GAMLA UPPSALA, UPPLAND, SWEDEN. [Public Domain]

WITH A PRICK OF YOUR FINGER
BLOOD AND THE GODDESS

SARAH

Blood magic is common across many different cultures and is used for a variety of reasons. One use that is very common is binding magic and oaths. Binding magic is a type of spell work that, well, binds you to another person or entity for a prolonged period of time or, in some traditions, for life. Another use of binding magic is that of binding a person against performing harmful activities and blood or other physical items, like hair and nail clippings, can be used. It is often combined with oath takings but doesn't always have to include them. Some practitioners also use their blood as a 'tag-lock' for spell work, meaning a personal item that creates a sympathetic link between the spell work and the intended target, or even as ink for petitions and runic magic.

Another common use for blood in spell work is that of menstrual blood, which can be used in attraction, love, and fertility work. It can also be used in work designed to 'flush' something out of your life. Historically, however, menstrual blood was typically seen as a bad thing; many ancient cultures believed that a menstruating woman was a danger to herself and those around her.

It was believed that a menstruating woman could blight crops, cause damage to her lover, and cause her enemies to perish. But, it could also turn away tempestuous weather and cause crop-damaging insects to abandon the fields, so there was at least some value in it's baneful properties. Today, with our modern understanding of how a woman's body works, we know that is all crap and menstrual bloods usage in magic and spirituality has taken a different turn. It's about attraction, empowerment, and developing a connection with our bodies.

LARISA

"Once upon a time in midwinter, when the snowflakes were falling from the sky like down, a queen was sitting and sewing at a window which had a frame of black ebony. And as she sewed at the window and glanced up at the snow, she pricked her finger with her needle and three drops of blood fell on to the snow. And because the red looked so beautiful on the white snow, she thought to herself: if only I had a child as white as snow, as red as blood, and as black as the wood in the window frame. Not long afterwards she had a little daughter who was as white as snow, as red as blood, and with hair as black as ebony, and because of that she was called Snow White. And as the child was born, the queen died."[Snow White, Brothers Grimm]

There are aspects in Dread Sisters that relate to the concept of what one calls or creates can come true. We know that there was a strong animistic culture in the region. This seems to have crossed over into what blood could be or was. In some cases, it was physical blood in the sacrificial liquid that is used when creating a sacred space, a hallowed event, or preparing for the visiting witch that is about to call. The idea being that blood contains within it the power of the person or animal that it belonged to. You could in bronze age mindset, transfer your power through blood, as seen in Sigurd's consumption of blood that let him hear the animals.

The idea that drinking or consuming blood would unlock some aspect of hidden magic is not that far-fetched, although likely it might be due to the other herbs that were inside of these drinks. We can only make good guesses as to what herbs would be used in transitory drinks, but there are several passages in which drink seems to be a doorway to other worlds. The same can be said for foods. In the paper Eaten Hearts by Dr. Andrea Maraschi, we find a passage in Eiríks saga that describes the priestess eating a "porridge of kid's milk and the hearts of all the animals found there were cooked for her."

There is also an element of theater involved. In most cases when the witch came to call, she came appropriately dressed, it was her body that represented a 'different' place. By her wearing specific key triggers we are woven a visual story through her appearance. Whenever the seer, witch, priestess would eat the special foods created for her, it was served on a special setting which included "a brass spoon and a knife with a whalebone handle, attached to the blade with two copper rings, with a broken end" [The Icelandic Völva and the Old Polish Witch. A Comparative Analysis, Katarzyna Korneluk-Marloewicz].

She had a special place to sit;

> "He made a suitable place for her, as was customary when a woman of this kind was welcomed. A high stool was prepared for her, on which a pillow stuffed with chicken feathers was placed"[The Icelandic Völva and the Old Polish Witch. Marloewicz].. She came dressed in specific clothing, "when she arrived in the evening (...) she was dressed like this: she wore a blue rug tied around her neck, sewn with stones to the brim, glass beads around her neck, a hood made of black lambskin, framed underneath with white cat fur. In her hand she was carrying a [staff] topped with a tumor; it was decorated with brass and stones were embedded around the tumor. She wore a belt made of tinder around her waist, and on it a large purse in which she kept the magical items necessary for divination and magic. On her feet she wore fur boots made of calfskin with long, strong laces ending with tin tumors, and on her hands gloves made of calfskin, white and hairy inside "

[The Icelandic Völva and the Old Polish Witch. Marloewicz]

Dressing the part brought with it an aspect of transmutation, you are 'leaving' one space and entering another. This is a common thread in cultures that practice ritual dress or dressing for specific events. This ties into our modern day in the concept that certain clothing does signify a common ritual that is about to take place. We dress to be wed, we dress our dead, we dress to graduate, we dress to attend institutions, we have certain rules of conformity upon which our clothing bears a signifier to that role, situation, event.

There is evidence that transformation or darning a set of clothing could represent defiance or to be a call to action. In the paper, "Weaponizing Ordinary Objects" by Steven Dunn, it mentions that women would wear bloodied shirts to incite vengeance from other men, this was to remind them of the loss and provoke them to act. He also alluded to normal objects conveying 'sentiment', as the theses goes shares the story of a woman who was asked to make a shirt for another man, the woman stipulated that doing so would reveal her feelings for him.

It's clear that manufacturing things conveyed the persons intimate feelings. [Weaponizing Ordinary Objects. Steven T. Dunn] This makes sense when you look at folk traditions around embroidery, doll making, shirt making, spinning, weaving and other textile work, as there are remaining traditions of leaving one unlinked loop in crochet to 'release the spirit of the maker'. The idea that parts of us remain inside our work is not that crazy to think, we often use this in modern context by the phrase, "baked or made with love"we put what we want into what we make and thus in a way, even though mundane making we are imbuing magic. The same can be said about when we create things for our gods. We are imparting a magic into these creations by the shear act of conjuring them into being. There are elements that run head on into using blood in acts of magic, however these could be metaphorical for any liquid.

"The image of witches was also associated with nature, which was reflected in their clothing, equipment and living in the wasteland. In addition, it has been proven that the ingredients from which magic items, potions, ointments etc. Were made they took on the features of nature from which they were taken. As a result, they induced magical effects in the spheres of: love, life, health, weather, farm and landscape."

[The Icelandic Völva and the Old Polish Witch."

"Blood is a curious liquid in Old Norse literature, and its consumption may affect quite ambivalent transformations in characters. The prevalence of its influence in part stems from the inherent ambiguity which blood as a bodily fluid possesses, as is suggested in Janet Carsten's catalogue of its contradictory significances as a cultural concept across the ages. She writes that 'blood may be associated with fungibility, or trans formability, as well as essence; with truth and transcendence and with lies and corruption; with contagion and violence but also with purity and harmony; and with vitality as well as death'. Whilst not all these associations necessarily apply to blood's presentation in Old Norse literature, Carsten's conjecture that it may be thought of as a 'vector of connection between bodies or persons' serves as a useful starting point when examining the effects of its consumption." [Inspiration and Inebriation. Thesis]

All our dread sisters are linked to magical or practical liquids such as marshes, potions, healing liquids/streams, mead etc. All of these are complex metaphors for blood or transformative material. "Blood" therefore could be a few things. You could use it metaphorically by 'mixing' tiny bits of blood (like a drop) into a 'mixture' that could be used to smear on objects, secure sacred spaces, placed onto objects to imbue the 'self' onto them.

If we look to implanted and imparted understanding from external cultures that directly contributed to the formation of views in the Nordic region, we see in Sámi culture the view of the world as; "inhabited by different actors with whom people could communicate: animals but also sacred stones, giants, hidden people, animals, etc... in ancient times they splattered these (sacred places) with reindeer blood, and to these stones they brought animals antlers and other gifts, while begging the God in the stone for luck, prosperity and good fortune (reindeer luck) on the summer trails." [Sjamanistisk Forbund]

Throughout the sagas, blood or offerings seems to have mythological connections to the very idea of Ymir, that his 'blood' became the waters of life, and thus by extension within us exists a piece of that giant's blood. "Blood's significance, however, transcends its nutritional benefits, and in the mythological context it is a fundamental, generative, and protean fluid, with the creation of the sea from the blood of the primordial giant Ymir attested in Vafrúnismál 21, Grímnismál 40 and Gylfaginning." [Inspiration and Inebriation. Thesis]

If the concept of connective tissue exists in our animistic view, so does the aspect of marking time. We are in effect paying homage to the life we live; we are creating a fusion between the mundane and spiritual and thus in a way are constructing a communal relationship. By the 'blood' of our works alone we symbolically offer our rites of passage as ones that could be celebrated alongside our gods/goddesses. There are aspects of our modern life that have removed the sense and purpose of rites. We don't see the world as one in which we can stop and understand its significance. We don't pause to celebrate the in between spaces that rituals of daily life could fulfill.

In the book Deeply into the Bone: Re-Inventing Rites of Passage by Ronald Grimes he states that; "Passages can be negotiated without the benefit of rites, but in their absence, there is a greater risk of speeding through the dangerous intersections of the human life course...people often regret their failure to contemplate a birth, celebrate a marriage, mark the arrival of maturity, or enter into the throes of death...the primary work of a rite of passage is to ensure that we attend to such events fully, which is to say, spiritually, psychologically, and socially...unattended passages become spiritual sinkholes around which hungry ghosts, those greedy personification of unfinished business, hover."[Deeply into the Bone: Re-Inventing Rites of Passage]

Could we then consider offerings in a different way? If not through real offerings of blood, animal, flesh, components of animals, could it be offering of the self? Offerings of works? Is it possible that we could in theory transmute and conjure any offering to be a 'piece' of the self? I think it's very probable that we could do that. There is enough evidence to show that by the mere calling of something into being we are creating it. In a way Deeply into the Bone, summed it up best, "Ritual, like art, is a child of imagination, but the ritual imagination requires an invention, a constantly renewed structure, on the basis of which a bodily and communal enactment is possible."

We create the ritual through an artistic blending of modern understandings and ancient held believes to convey and summon our gods to a place in which we can curate and link to the very nature of our own forms and soul. If you were interested in using tiny bits of blood or spit, do so carefully and with respect for what it means. It does not have to be a huge amount, and it can be used to claim ownership as smearing some aspect of our own bodies on an object does convey with it a connection to the physical person.

It could also be herbs that are like blood such as certain kinds of red incenses that could symbolize blood, it could be red wine, which is similar in color, it could be a special curated fluid that you made to be representative of blood. Taking small amounts of ocean water would be appropriate in lieu of blood. If our blood conveys a certain component of the self, giving blood may be a natural way to connect to gods. However, there must be safety in this practice as blood is also a transmission method for disease and can make you sick regardless of what kind of blood it is.

If you choose to use blood in a ritual, you should be aware of how to do so safely without harm to yourself, anyone who donates it or from remains that were used with consent. Remember that when we create drinks or potions, we are creating a; "transformative drink has a unique potential as an agent of change"[Inspiration and Inebriation, Transformative Drinks in Old Norse Literature] and that "Symbolic action allows ritual participants to become actively involved with healing power, channeling it and manipulating it in ways that create profound changes in the self."[Deeply Into The Bone]

"While the duties of a seidhr woman could work on an individual level with personal motivations, the sorceress also acted for the collective benefit with offensive and defensive war rituals on the battlefield"

- Blood & Magic, A Micro Study of Associations between Viking Age women and their weapons. Alicia Halvardsson, Thesis

We must carefully construct all things to reflect the nature that they hold within them and the draining that will cause to the creator, for there is always a give or take. Even words themselves can be "symbolic objects [which can] represent power". Speaking with conviction and intention can create a powerful magical connection to any rite we wish to perform. Preparing your space for all rites would include ensuring that what you are doing is with intention, with purpose and with planning, for what one utters, could potentially be woven in the grand loom, from which one cannot un-tether.

IN SUMMARY WITH PERSONAL REFLECTION

LARISA

I am a feminist, but I am a believer in equality of genders, so my form of feminism includes men and trans women and anyone else marginalized. I have always been a bit more practical in nature, to me rituals that take too much time or too much effort are not part of heathen worldview/practice. I believe that much of heathenry has been way too much injected with pagan concepts to the point that one can't even tell which are not parts of the original forms of practice and which are parts.

I used to think a lot differently about heathenry when I first came into it. I have to say much of my ignorance and beliefs were since we didn't exactly have anyone to talk to where I lived, so I had no guide. As I began my long road of research, I kept evolving with each step. Initially I had a quite complex number of steps to approach the gods, I believed that you had to have the right things/the right time etc., But as I grew, so did my practice. I find myself these days working on a few aspects of myself as I grow in my tradition.

This allows me to adapt my views of how I will take part in offerings, ceremonies, and practice and how I feel about my gods. I am semi a stickler for informing my practice into what did happen historically but often buttress this with the modern understandings of things so that I create a holistic approach to my religious philosophy. Today, I am much more of an animist who feels my environment is alive and so our my gods and that they likely are fine with less of ceremony and more of practical, daily, subtle offerings that allow for me to bring my faith more into my life than just specific times of the year to call on them.

This approach is more I guess you could say cottage heathenry in that it bridges living with the land, the gods, the life around you and embracing it as part of the daily comings and goings. This more natural approach means my home has subtle elements of gods in it, like paintings and figures, those are my harrows. I feel this approach works for me as it requires little expense to be issued in terms of 'things' and relies on finding objects that are unique. I hope this book reflects ways we can all access the gods despite any limitations that we have to do so.

I am not a gate-keeper and will not dictate to someone who they can call, what they do in terms of practice, but I will push back if they seem to have come to this decision without thought or what historically makes sense and what doesn't.

I am not eclectic myself so I am strictly working in the confines of the Norse pantheon, however as I bonded with my sisters in this book, I found I did pick up at least a familiar relationship with the Celtic gods and also external concepts that I could place into mine to increase my own spiritual pathway. I believe adaptation is the key to forming a working faith that can and will expand and change, the ancients did, and they managed to leave an indelible link in history.

What gets in my craw is people assuming things to be true without worthwhile research into why that 'is' the case, if heathenry is the religion of homework, then this should lead to constantly being involved in active academic work that pushes us to discover something new. I also think that constantly making things 'closed practice' is preventing dialogue to really analyze things. It's clear that some aspects are tribal and culturally specific, but this may not always hold true depending on the practice.

No part of human history was born in a vacuum, there are almost no practices that developed all by themselves (in most cases, there are a few very rare instances when a practice did evolve on its own without cultural crossover). It's important to take all things and critically look at them. Does this practice fit in the confines of these gods? Does this practice fit in terms of what was accessible to this region? By asking these questions and others, we can approach all practices with respect and ensure that we are honoring the gods in a way that is respectful and without constantly drawing on traditions that they won't recognize. It's like the adage, appeal to people where they are.

The same goes for the gods, appealing to where they came from. There is space to add in what we have access to in terms of environment, plant materials, etc, but appealing to them means adding things that they would naturally see as something from their particular region and therefore this allows us to create a space for them that is decorated in a way that would be most appealing. If you're going to invite such an honored guest, giving them a meal that is cooked just for them, adorning the house for them, creating a special chair for them is part of the process to embrace them as a welcomed visitor/resident.

BLOOD OATH SISTERS AND MO ANAM CARA

SHEAL

With respect to Dread Sisterhood, in Celtic traditions we see something called the "soul friend" set of rituals. This concept dates to the Druids, and the Bandorai. The Norse (Danes) have a similar concept of blood oaths where two men (even women) would cut the palm and clasp each others hand, declaring that they are now blood oath brothers (or sisters). Anam Cara is a phrase that refers to the Celtic concept of the "soul friend" in religion and spirituality.

The phrase is an Anglicization of the Irish word anamchara, anam meaning "soul" and cara meaning "friend". The term was popularized by Irish author John O'Donohue in his 1997 book Anam Cara: A Book of Celtic Wisdom about Celtic spirituality. In the Celtic tradition "soul friends" are considered an essential and integral part of spiritual development. The Martyrology of Óengus recounts an incident where Brigid of Kildare counseled a young cleric that "...anyone without a soul friend is like a body without a head."

The Anam Cara involves a friendship that psychotherapist William P. Ryan describes as "compassionate presence". According to O'Donohue, the word anamchara originates in Irish monasticism, where it was applied to a monk's teacher, companion, or spiritual guide. However, Edward C. Sellner traces its origin to the early Desert Fathers and Desert Mothers: "This capacity for friendship and ability to read other people's hearts became the basis of the desert elders' effectiveness as spiritual guides."

Their teachings were preserved and passed on by the Christian monk John Cassian, who explained that the soul friend could be clerical or lay, male or female. For Anamcara rituals, it is a similar concept to blood oath siblings. Anam Cara (man-am care-ah) means soul friend, soul mate, or other various incarnations of a ritualized soul connection between two people much like the concept of blood oathing or blood bonding in Nordic and Indigenous cultures.

It is a sort of "womb to tomb" oath between two people. The modern day Anamchara ritual is a take on a very ancient concept of "spit in the hand and shake on it". Sherri Lynn Herrmann's theorizes correctly that Druids were attached to the chieftains in their roles as advisors, healers, and confidants and even war strategists. The following is a modernized bonding ritual from Sherri Lynn Herrmann's site Tiger Eye Designs.

Your Anamchara Bonding Ritual

Ritual from Sherri Lynn Herman

Tools Needed

Three Candles & Holders ~ To represent both of you and your union. The colors should have a theme of unity, for example, if your individual candles are blue and red, violet is a good color to choose for the unity candle

1. Three Cups or Glasses ~ One large and two small.
2. A Gift ~ For your soul friend. This should remain a secret until it is presented
3. An Alter Cloth or Floor Covering ~ Optional, though it can add to the over-all ambiance
4. A Box of Tissues ~ This ritual can be very emotional
5. Draw A Magic Circle ~ Gather all your items and take them to the place you have chosen for your ritual. Place the items on the ground (using the floor covering if you wish) between you and your intended soul friend and fill the two small cups with a drink of your choice. Draw a magic circle around yourselves es, sharing the duty equally. Sit down near the middle of the circle, facing each other.
6. Unity Chalice ~ Each of you in turn should sip from a small cup and then pass to the other to sip. Pour the remaining contents into the larger cup and state your friendship intentions aloud:

> I am your friend
> I am your teacher
> I am your student
> I am your dependent
> I am your solace
> I am your shield
> I am your child, sister, and mother

Each of you then takes a drink from the filled unity chalice
7. Light Your Candles ~ Now take a match and each light the candle that represents you. The unlit candle that sits between you represents your unity and the potential of two spirits on the same journey, each supporting the other. Join the flames of your individual candles to light the wick of the center one.

8. Make a unison statement at this point, such as: By this ritual I am bound to you as your friend of the soul, your Anamchara. See our flames shine brightly, burning hotter and stronger together then they can separately.

9. All my wisdom and all my secrets I share with you for as long as this life endures. Until we meet in the next life, so mote it be.

10. Trust that at this moment your emotions will be running very high, which is why you have that box of tissues nearby!

11. Exchange Gifts ~ Present to each other the gift or token you have brought to seal the ritual. A piece of Celtic Jewelry would be appropriate, as are magical crystals.

When you have exchanged gifts, set all your other materials aside, leaving only the unity candle burning between you and your soul friend. When both of you feel ready, extinguish (please use a snuffer or your fingers as blowing a flame out is disrespectful to the fire gods) the unity candle and close the circle. Lastly, take the liquid from your unity chalice outside and, together, pour it onto the ground as an offering to the Gaia, the Earth Mother. As you do this, visualize your joined spirits becoming a part of the Great Mother from whom you came.

DEATH WORK, BLOOD MAGIC & SHADOW WORK

SHEAL

Magic. Some people scoff at the sound of that word stating that it is purely fiction and pretend Hollywood glamours. From The Craft, The Witches and Practical Magic we have seen Hollywood twist and conform magic to their own purposes for the almighty dollar. We see their half truths and full out lies that Hollywood portrays magic to be. Movies like The Craft and Blair Witch Project taking the old "witches are evil" adage to create an attitude toward witches much like Salem Witch Trials or massacres like the Island of Angelsey.

Hollywood has a penchant for taking the darker happenings of human history and making a buck from it. They also have a penchant, and more in particularly, Disney, for taking it to the other extreme. Glamorizing the idea of magic to unrealistic extremes and creating an environment for vulnerable people to think that magic is the cure all to every ill, bad situation and whim.

It is because of mainstream media and in particular, Hollywood we had the 80s "Satanic Ritual Killings" that never existed and extremely psychologically disturbed people using the idea of magic as a catch all for their behaviors even today. I, myself, am guilty of such things in The Bone Jar and The Bone Jar: The Asylum Case for using historical legends and Pagan beliefs in the story lines.

We even have groups like MATOS pushing these disturbing ideals on-line with statements that perpetuate this idealism to the extreme. They state that "Some Initiates have stumbled upon evidence of a "Murder Society," a well-organized network of serial killers, complete with safe houses and an "underground railroad." This Murder Society is said to have contacts within many political institutions, law enforcement agencies, and even the CIA and FBI." This is an absolute absurdity that continues to degrade, infantilize, and minimize magic while perpetuating the occult belief that magic is of satanic, evil sources that should be stomped down and eradicated.

Magic is none of those things. Magic is intent placed in ritualistic physical interpretations of psychopomps to bring about help during personal resolutions to situations or desires while working with the deities that one walks with. It is another psychological and spiritual connection and tools of connection to either (for some) our ancestral lines, our gods, and goddesses, or both. True magic is neither evil, nor good or anything in between. The person using it may use it for nefarious reasons or may not.

They may use it for themselves or for others. It is a psychological and metaphysical transaction much like money is a physical transaction for services or goods. Magic is the living intention of change. It is putting intent into our actions, by 'spell casting' which is the act of verbally stating out what we wish to be true.

Then by subsequent acts of requesting assistance from the gods and goddesses one walks with while putting in the practical physical work to make these things happen. An example of this would be wanting prosperity to come to you, then asking the gods and goddesses for help through ritual magic, and then going out and finding gainful employment when you were not employed previously.

It is not that the gods and goddesses give you what you want just because you spilled three drops of blood but that they put their might behind your intent to help you move forward and work toward the wanted goal. It is not that our protection ward is the all-purpose protection to keep that terrible neighbor we fight with off our front lawn but that our intent is physically in front of us to remind us to remove ourselves from the situation and to not actively seek out discord with our neighbor. It is intent, with work, that can come to fruition. They are reminders of our own personal power in everyday life.

DEATH WORK

WHEN DEATH TALKS

SHEAL

Death work comes in many forms. It isn't always necessarily magic per say but rather working with death as a "living" force. An oxymoron that statement but that is what it truly is. Sometimes this force comes in the form of an ancestral link, a god or goddess that is associated with the dead or encountering the dead in various ways either to help or to be helped. Death is part of the life cycle; it is not the end of it but rather a transformation of life into another existence or being.

For the Celts and Druids, death was not an end but rather it was sloughing off the previous life to begin a new one. Druids believed in reincarnation, they also believed in other plains of existence as well. Places of great wealth and peace, where no one was sick, and death no longer existed. Places where our ancestors stood waiting for us to come through the change that was death into the new life of peace and comfort.

Places of gold and silver and merriment, no sadness, no illness, no pain. If you were not ready for such an existence you would be reborn into the world you came from to attempt learning what lessons you needed to. Some death work is of a healing nature. To kill what was broken or slough it away from yourself to replace it with something that isn't broken and to change what you were into what you were meant to be. It is facing what you are, knowing what needs to change and doing the work to change it.

Much like shadow work, and I would say that death work and shadow work go hand in hand even. Death isn't an end but a new beginning. Most pagan views of death are different than the ones seen in other more mainstream communities. Many believe that death is part of a sacred circle that is never ended. Death is also considered to be part of a sacred evolution. The soul goes through many changes and experiences before it reaches its possible final destination. Death magic is working with and honoring spirits of the dead (ancestors) as well as the power of death itself (endings, resurrections, new beginnings).

Those that work with death magic reflect upon the concept of death, come to terms with their own death, and work through spiritual "deaths" in their lives. Some may communicate with the dead regularly. Many believe that working to heal and help the dead will bring about a return of help from the dead to aid in magical workings. Rather than fearing death, those that work with death embrace it as a pivotal point in the cycle of life.

The death gods associated with this kind of magic and workings are often themselves associated with the end of life, but also with new beginnings. They represent transition, change, and rebirth. There are many ways to honor death. Burning effigies of the dead person, leave food out for them, pulling ancestral energies into your intent workings. Some intent work may include offerings to the spirits of the dead. These offerings could include herbs, flowers, wine, bread, or any other item that would please the spirit.

Death work also involves working with death as a force, dead plants, healing the dead, and other aspects of the end of life. Common techniques of death work include tending to the dying, giving offerings to the dead, and traveling to the afterlife. However, ancestral veneration is a main core tenant of death work. There are those who work with the bones of animals and even humans in their death work as well. In Canada, the laws are lax on human bone sales and trading.

There are places that sell human wet specimens as well as animal specimens. Bone tapping is considered part of death work to heal both self and the dead. Animal bones should be ethically sourced, my sources are roadkill stashes from various city works departments. I have access to these items due to living far north in the bush. Bones can be decorated with deity and practice symbols, used as decorations or tools of your altar. For Canadians, my recommendation is https://www.skullstore.ca/.

SHADOW WORK

YOU AND YOUR SHADOWS

Shadow work is much like death work. Except it isn't working with death as a living force but rather the suppressed parts of ourselves. Some would call this our shadow selves, our dark parts. It is work that is deeply rooted in healing the inner traumas we have experiences throughout our childhood and our adulthood. The ability to work through these traumas to better ourselves is a fundamental part of our spiritual practice.

UNCOVERING THE "TRIGGERS"

We learn to suppress certain parts of ourselves to please our parents, society, fit in with friends, or do well in school, we usually have no idea that we're suppressing anything. We just think we're being functional human beings. Then something triggers us. It's an external factor that catches you off-guard. In the spiritual community, the term "trigger" is often used to describe an experience that causes an unusually strong, sometimes overwhelming surge of emotions from you. When you're "triggered" it's typically viewed as an overreaction by other people.

They don't understand why you're so upset, and they might think you're being dramatic. You might get triggered when you arrange to meet up with someone cute from your dating app and you get stood up. Perhaps this experience makes you burst into tears at the restaurant and vow to never use a dating app again. Your friends might tell you to get over it but you just can't get over your hurt from the situation. This is probably something you can heal through shadow work.

Honor Your Feelings

One of the most important parts of shadow work is to honor your feelings. Your feelings are what alert you to any resistance, false self thoughts, or emotional wounds that are hidden in your subconscious. It's important to acknowledge these feelings because your subconscious issues could stop you from moving forward.

Discover the Hidden Story

There are many ways to figure out the story behind your strong emotions, but journaling or "Grimoires" are the quickest, simplest way to do this. The story behind your current pain is most likely from something that happened to you before. Start by jotting down possible reasons why you're upset.

If you become emotional when you do this, that's fine. Shadow work is not wallowing, it's healing. You'll know when you hit the right reason because you'll feel that strong emotion all over again. Next, think back to the first time you remember feeling unwanted. Journal about this memory. Dig deep to get all the painful details out on the paper. Don't hold back here. Write out anything that comes to mind even if it seems insignificant.

Heal Your Emotional Wound

Now that you've discovered the root of your pain, you can heal it. To heal your wound, change your inner story. For example, instead of, "I got picked last for gym class because nobody wanted me.", You can say, "I probably got picked last because the captains picked all their friends first." Remember, controlling your feelings is not the objective. Your feelings are your subconscious communicating with you and these signals are valuable information.

You can, however, control your reactions by simply changing your inner story to something more constructive. Most of all, we are all responsible for our own feelings and how we react to others around us. We may not be able to control others, but we can control ourselves. A Note About Deep Trauma: Shadow work can be intense, particularly if your trauma is deep. If you begin shadow work and feel overwhelmed with painful emotions, consider performing this work with a therapist, or a medical professional.

BLOOD MAGIC

It is in us, in our blood, in our ancestral line. Blood is essential for our mortal existence because it keeps us alive. Looking at blood in a mystical way, blood contains our life energy and the essence of our spirit. If we use blood for a spell or ritual, we literally put ourselves and our life force into our practice. Blood is associated with both life and death. The slain warriors on the field, the victim of violence, the hunter's prey all lay bloody in their final state. It's part of the cycle of fertility that perpetuates life.

A woman bleeds during her menstrual cycle, and there's blood at childbirth. If we lost too much blood, we would grow weak and die. If our blood is tainted, we will wither away. Blood is associated with pain and passion. We see it when we are injured either in a fall, or a fight. When we love doing something, when we are good at it, it's 'in our blood'. Someone we love, particularly family members, are our 'blood-kin'. Blood connects us to things and others. Even if we don't know someone, we can empathize with them, our 'heart bleeds for them'. Blood is a passionate connection in raw emotion.

FROM OUR ANCESTORS

Blood is in our own living bodies. It courses through our body delivering oxygen and nutrients to every part of us. When your heart pounds and your pulse races as your blood flows faster you hear the lifeline that is your blood in your ears. Our blood holds our DNA and contains the very essence for all that we are. Our blood contains the blueprint not just for us, but our complete ancestral line (bloodlines). Some people believe that the sins of their forefathers continue to exist in their veins, making them partially responsible for their actions.

This is a nonsense concept and is based on the ideology of "original sin" and does not have a place in natural spiritual beliefs such as Druidry. No one has ever been able to influence the acts of their ancestors; people who lived and died long before that person was born. Why should anyone take the blame for their wrongdoings? The only thing one should do, is take responsibility for their own actions in the past and present. The blood in my veins connects me to my ancestors in a way that it creates a spiritual bond with all my ancestors. My blood is a tool when I contact my ancestors for magical assistance.

One or two drops of blood is used to connect to their spirits, or to make an offering to or for them. This can hold the same for the gods and goddesses that I walk with in my spiritual practice. My blood is also a tool to connect to them on a spiritual level through the essence of my being. An offering to them for what I am about to ask for as magic is a give and take practice. You must give to take. Blood magic is not magic that involves killing people or animals in ritual sacrifice.

Blood magic is the use of a few drops of blood during a spell or ritual, usually your own blood. The negative connotations stem back to the fear of blood. Fear of our own mortality, fear of power, or fear of blood-borne diseases in our modern world are some of the many issues that are the driving factors behind a fear of blood. Blood: like any object or component you would use in magic, is simply a tool. It's a very powerful tool, but a tool, nonetheless. It's neither benevolent nor malevolent. You could use it for any number of purposes, though like any other tool it's not advised to use it for unethical purposes.

Blood and Menstrual Magic

Blood Magic

Intentions are powerful things but when adding blood to a spell or intention work it is what amounts to a "piece of yourself" and subsequently your ancestral line. This adds the extra power you may need for your protection spells. It is like backing the whole of your spell with your ancestral line behind it. Overall, there are safe practices that everyone can agree on when it comes to blood work within spells and blood magic.

Menstrual Magic

Although I do not practice menstrual blood rituals myself, menstrual blood is a very natural and powerful substance that holds your life energy not to mention your ability to give life as a divine female. Menstruation blood is typically connected to fertility rituals, literally as well as figuratively. Since I don't practice this method of blood magic, I will forgo any other comments on the practice and leave the teachings in more worthy hands than mine.

SAFE PRACTICES OF BLOOD MAGIC

- Please don't do these things
- Don't ever take more than a few drops.
- Don't ever take blood from an unwilling participant (this includes animals because they cannot give consent).
- Don't smear your blood on people, let people smear blood on you, or try to exchange blood in any way; remember that many diseases can be transferred through blood.
- Don't consume blood, either directly or by putting it into a drink; aside from the fact that you can catch diseases, blood itself is toxic to human beings. More than a couple of teaspoons can cause vomiting, potentially do some serious organ damage, or cause disease.
- Don't let others drink your blood, either directly raw or by putting it into food or drinks; this is essentially giving your power over to that person, and not in a good way.
- Safe Practices of Blood Magic
- Sanitize the area of skin with an alcohol pad or sanitizing gel.
- Sanitize a small poking implement, such as a pin or diabetic pick pen (I recommend the pick pen).
- Poke only enough to break the skin. Using a diabetic pick pen is helpful to keep the wound small and the bleeding at minimum.
- Squeeze out your few drops to collect for your use.
- Clean the wound immediately and put some antibiotic ointment on it. If it's still bleeding, put a bandage on it.
- Handle and dispose of anything that has been touched with blood with extreme caution until the end of your ritual or spell.
- Disinfect surfaces (of your skin and your workspace), implements and any other tools after performing blood magic.
- Keep the wound clean as it heals.

Water: Blood runs through our veins in liquid form.
Fire: Blood is connected to vitality, love, and passion.
Air: Blood transports oxygen through our bodies.
Earth: Blood cells represent the element earth.

Types of Rituals That Blood Magic Can Be Used In

Evocations and Invocations One way to protect an individual, location, or object is to assign an entity to the job. Saints Medals and spirit talismans may be utilized to bring an entity into service, one may appeal a god or goddess. Even a practitioner may create a servitor.

Protection Spells

Protection spells are used to protect home and hearth, family, or yourself. Most protection spells can be augmented with a few drops of blood. My usual go to for adding to a protection spell or ward protections is 3 drops of my own blood into the mixture or container.

Witches Jars

A Witches Jar is a container spell that acts as a protective decoy. Items are placed in the jar to represent the person to be protected along with items that represent that protection, especially things like nails, pins, and other sharp objects. The idea is that if a witch casts a spell against the subject of the spell, the spell will go into the jar instead of into the person.

Wards

Protective wards may be physical or energetic objects. A ward may be placed around boundaries or at entrances. They may be physical objects of a particular material (see Protective Materials and Objects above), normal objects inscribed with protective symbols or energetic wards, created by the caster and invisible to onlookers.

Mirror Spells

A mirror spell is a spell designed to reflect harmful energy sent toward you away and back to the sender. Generally, a small mirror is used for this spell. It is charged toward its purpose and placed near the subject's sleeping area with the reflective surface pointing out and away from the house. It is a good idea to make sure the sun does not directly hit this mirror to avoid the possibility of fire.

Maledictions, Bindings and Unbinding

Malediction comes from the Latin verb maledicere, meaning "to speak evil of" or "to curse." "Maledicere," in turn, was formed by combining the Latin words male, meaning "badly," and "dicere," "to speak" or "to say." You may recognize both of those component parts, as each has made a significant contribution to the English language. "Male" is the ancestor of such words as "malady," "malevolent," and "malign"; "dicere" gives us "contradict," "dictate," "diction," "edict" and "prediction".

Maledictions can sometimes combine bindings or unbinding, or just straight up cursing someone else. This usually involves a container of sorts, sometimes nauseous substances, and items that either are associated with the person, or the type of curse. A good example of a curse is a maledictions box where the name of the person is placed on a piece of paper, bound by twine while placing items in the box that would bring them displeasure, nightmares, or strife (or all the above) in both their dream states and waking lives.

Binding spells usually involve symbolic action of binding, wrapping, tying, or otherwise containing a representative object, particularly that of putrefied objects or fermented objects such as egg, soured milk and so on. In hand fasting rituals, the hands of the two individuals to be bound are usually literally tied together with a cord or ribbon. Other spells involve nailing or pinning a representative image or Ziploc bag to a surface, sealing it inside a container or wrapping it around with cords. Spirits are usually bound to a container that is symbolically sealed with wax or wrapped around with a cord. Unbinding often involves a physical reversal of the action of the binding spell, untying or cutting the cords, removing the symbolic object from the container it was placed in, etc.

DREAD SISTERHOOD

LARISA

Dread: greatly feared; dreadful.
Sisterhood: an association, society, or community of women linked by a common interest, religion, or trade.

Diving into this topic was partly a selfish pursuit to answer the question that kept swirling around my mind. Is it possible to see becoming closer to the gods (and perhaps walking with dread gods/ goddess) a literal and physical metamorphosis of sorts? Is it possible that as we become more aligned with our gods, aspects of our lives become radically changed? These questions are ones that I ponder as I noticed myself transforming in more than just physical ways, but ways that were unexpected.

I was tired of defending my lack of ancestor worship to some heathen groups that seemed to push the ancestors over the gods and the suppression of exploring outside topics that are not listed as standard. When you enter heathenry as a practice, the list of sources is limited to sources that came from authors who mostly came from neo-pagan backgrounds. This brought a few things to the practice that may have altered much of the original intentions. There were times in heathenry that practices directed to the gods were often scoffed at and instead large pushes toward only ancestors began.

This remained pretty much the standard to some degree or other. In heathenry, we can't really speak to the 'whole' of the path as each group had their own practices, but heathenry did have issues with certain practices entering the mainstream and that limitation did push many of us to create alternatives. My path was pushed both politically and spiritually. I began to explore animism, trolldom, hagdom and abolitionist feminism. Things in me began to transform in a way that created both an awakening to new ways of thinking and a righteous rage that wanted to unleash itself upon an unjust world. This mental shift hit me at the most unexpected time. I was listening to my normal podcast, The Majority Report with Sam Seider. The host Emma Vigeland interviewed one of the authors of a book called "Abolition. Feminism. Now", named Angela Y. Davis.

The podcast involved discussing the concept of what feminism was meant to be. How its intentions were to create this intersection of people. That true feminism is humanism. The desire to create a world for all humans to live out their true potential. I purchased her book and found this amongst its pages these concepts that aligned with how I feel about my own pathway. Her book expressed that true feminism is abolition. Abolition of systems of oppression, abolition of norms, etc. Even though this seemed separate from my spiritual life, her words struck me as indicative of how I have been walking my spiritual life, I have been abolishing the 'standard's and forging a path of my own.

Walking with darker gods or gods that have associations in the areas of death, dying, transformation requires a person to accept some amount of deconstruction to occur. This deconstruction can cause extreme changes in the person which may shift more than spiritual philosophies. It may cause a person to shift personal views across the board that can potentially touch radical concepts, possibly transforming the person on a fundamental level. The dread sisters seem to require some norms to be abolished. The dread sisterhood involves working with goddess that are holding marginal spaces.

They work in the places that others may not want to be working in as these are places of loss, mourning, pain, trauma, suffering, and the constant injustice for those who are undesirable in the world. The represent the things that are often discarded, and this gives them a unique position in the pantheon, because they are a symbol of what you can't ignore. It is the voices of the women living in the dark wood, the 'witches' if you will, who often speak for those who are powerless.

Working within the dread sisterhood can become a catalyst for a deep paradigm shift. You begin to see your life as not only belonging to you but also as an extension; of belonging to a [spiritual] collective. You could define this as an 'order' of sorts. As with most orders, giving a portion of the self away to the gods (or community) may be required depending on the gods you work with or path you choose. It is not always required upon the individual if they are not planning on joining the sisterhood, but if you are or are planning on doing work that requires a collective aspect, the needs of the individual may be put aside. If you choose to walk down a path that includes multiple gods or ends up that way, you will find in some cases the pathway a complex one. For it may mean you are at odds with other gods/beings or in concert with agendas that are not always exactly known to you.

Sometimes this pathway is thrust upon the person, as the road they are walking involves movement through worlds that may cross and intersect with gods/wights/trolls/other to which can teach/impart valuable lessons/skills. Being part of a 'sisterhood' in this case means you might find yourself at tea with a sea of goddess all of whom may require your service. It might increase a physical and emotional cost on you. There may be things you don't want to do, or aspects of this path that is uncomfortable.

Boundaries can be arranged in advance of most spiritual relationships, for the most part. If the need arises in which one must severe relationships with certain aspects, there are ways to exit the pathway respectfully. Often by giving the gods an offering that equals the gravity of the role may be required. Once inside the dread sisterhood, a transition occurs, we exit the pathway of the seeker and move to become the sacrifice. You transform, giving yourself over to the worlds held by the Dread Sisters and surrendering to a different path. The path that they offer is one that will force you to face aspects of yourself.

It forces you to face your issues head on. You may face past/present traumas that you have endured or caused, you may face parts of your personality which could be positive or negative to the relationships you have had in life within family/peer groups. They face you in front of a mirror and show you the imperfections you have (of which all of us have, as no one is perfect) and show you your true nature. They help you to abolish your norms and to embrace a true feminism of equality, safety, transformation, and targeted rage. The path they offer asks you to give a life in service to others, a life in service to the Gods, and a life that is not just for the 'self' but also for the communities within which we reside.

When you invite the Sisters in, you begin living with the spirit of the collective soul of the Goddess (the aspects of each of them, of who you have invited and summoned) and the mirrors that she places that show you what you need to see. For me, formation of my own personal views has been a very long road. I did not start out thinking that I would completely shift my own self-understanding.

Riding The Bones pushed me to do that. It forced me to confront what I knew within myself, and yet denied. I knew I was moving towards walking the line between woman and hag and that this pathway would be a integral stage of my transition. When I wandered down this way, a few thoughts began to form in my mind. I began to think about how our history was formed and thus a clarity of views began to align between my feminist brain and my spiritual brain.

I had an epiphany. What if we could use the concepts of abolitionist feminism in our spiritual life, embracing the political movements that many of us wander into and applying the same principals to our practices. When we form new pathways or new philosophies, we should be asking the following.

1. Is this practice truly reflecting the nature of our gods?
2. Is the practice equalizing gender?
3. Are the practices breaking norms?

Throughout Riding The Bones, we showed that people who formed our religious foundations were not static in view. When you slide into dread sisterhood you begin to critically view our current understandings, asking ourselves questions like these below;

1. Why is it that we have become so?
2. Why is it we don't offer counter narratives?
3. Why is it we see 'experts' that live in a 'certain' place as more important than a wider range of views?
4. Why do we not look outside academia to folklore and regional practices for answers?

These are things I ask myself a lot, and when I ask myself these questions, I feel myself aligning my view of the gods with greater clarity, allowing me to see the road ahead with greater resolve. It allowed me to have less fear of walking down it, that I could, face the pathway head on with little regret. I see the road wandering with my dread sisters flanking my steps as one that is constantly shifting. It allows me to develop closer relationships with gods that I may have avoided due to fearing what that could mean for me (emotionally, physically, mentally).

I believe that walking this path with; a willingness to be adaptive, a heart that is open to transformation, an acceptance that life is not linear but eternal (in many respects), that one should not go into this path without full awareness of its costs, is all part of the concept of dread sisterhood. The concept that we become 'other' on our own path but that this 'othering' is a badge of honor instead of one to be afraid of.

When we embrace that being part of this order means working outside the normal pathways, that this path may mean getting your hands dirty, that it may mean giving up aspects that you hold dear (this can be physical aspects ranging from fertility to sexual ability/ desires to material aspects like financial support). Perhaps an analogy would help, hopefully some of the readers would know of this aspect, but if not, this episode does still exist on a number of networks.

I refer to the example of Joan Clayton, more commonly known as the Cut-Wife, in episode 3, "The Nightcomers" from the show Penny Dreadful. This character is assigned the role of terminating unwanted pregnancies like a lot of midwives did back in the day. Although, this show is entirely a work of fiction, the concept that walking with darker goddess requires one to not always preform work that is glorious.

It often involves doing acts like this (although let me be clear, I am not advocating you take part in gruesome acts, but there are modern equivalents) you might have to be responsible for taking someone to an abortion clinic let's say, to serve the interest of the women in need, who are mostly cared for by the dread sisterhood. The dread sisterhood cares for those that society has removed as part of itself. They are that which stands for the girl in need of an abortion, or the sanctuary cradling our lgtbqia+ community hiding from those who would seek them harm, or the women who barricaded themselves in front of police during Black Lives Matter protests.

These women are the righteous angry women who link hands with the disenfranchised because we know in our core, the only true freedom is liberation of all humans. That task is in her hands (that of the dread sisterhood and its goddess) when you read the folktales surrounding them, you see women that not just sit in the edge of life and death, but are in the place of the doorways to which you must cross, they can shut it to those who seek ill to the others they hide within, or open it with an acceptance of a loving mother who wants only to comfort you.

Walking with them means you may also need to walk in the darkness carrying your other sisters (human/non-human) along the way. I believe in my core that Riding The Bones is more than just a pathway to dark hag like gods/goddesses/beings. Riding The Bones goes beyond this and becomes a key to transforming our own nature. I have traveled my own path sometimes in fear of how open I am in the way that I visualize the gods, but to me they were all consuming.

They consumed my thoughts, consumed my soul, helped build me up and tear me down. There was always something in these hag type goddesses that I could not quite put my finger on. They seemed to be drawing me to a place where I could finally own my true hagdom and there was power in that. What I am expressing may seem disjointed from the subject matter, but to me Riding The Bones is not just about dying/death but about transforming yourself in the light of darkness as well as the light of day.

It is RIDING yourself in and through the flames, embracing your inner self, your inner power, and above all being unapologetic in your path, your views and your voice. I don't use these 'inner' words from an esoteric or selfish view, but more that we must take care to push our inner desires to our outer desires and use our privilege (whatever we have or may have) to make change happen.

RELATIONSHIPS WITH THE DREAD SISTERHOOD

The concept that the gods are not always 'active' but also 'passive' and may be acting in ways that could be perceived as either 'too much' or 'too little', is often difficult to measure or judge. Not everyone will have the same relationship with the gods. There is a subtle tone in heathenry that would attempt to dissuade you from direct contact with gods, (although this view is fading). Instead, we are encouraged to focus on the ancestors as if we might bypass the effort required to cultivate relationships with the divine. The ancestors may be presented as the only thing to honor/worship because according to some, the gods don't care about you.

I believe much of the resistance to how we construct our faith is to prevent even the slightest dip into some monotheistic view. I do agree that we don't want to tip the scale and develop some heathen Christian hybrid, but instead develop spiritual relationships in a more realistic and natural view. I also believe that much of the resistance to forming spiritual bonds is that some feel it means you think you're 'better' than others or that you see yourself as 'special' or 'chosen'. I don't think I am either of those things. I believe that if I'd have choose a path for myself, it would have been a lot simpler to take a straighter path with only ancestor worship.

I wish I could have taken that path. For me, the ancestors were not an option. I did not feel at all linked to my roots, nor did I want to be. For me family ties carry with them a terrible amount of trauma that I cannot shake. I could not resolve these things even though I attempted to go as far back as possible and examined even the concept of 'generic' ancestor. For me that just didn't work or fit. I have never been that great at accepting spiritual abstracts, which for those reading my work may find confusing as I often deal in nuance and abstract. My practice however is different from my writing, I do live in a complex brain that holds multiple concepts at once. I don't however see this as abstract.

I deal in grounded views that balance what I can do with what I can practice and what I can do within the parameters of my life. To me direct god/goddess connection is not only possible but something achievable. For me solace and peace were found in the gods, but not through normal channels such as mediation or ritual practice. The development of my faith the gods was one fraught with pain, self-realization, and a push in me to reclaim the angry witch/hag within. My spiritual path met my political one head on and the collision caused my eyes to be open to a desire to reclaim my own power. I wanted to fight with those I kept reading about that were out there trying to make our world better for workers, for marginalized groups, for all of us.

I began to feel more confident with my voice being heard and would make it so by engaging in discourse with community members in hopes of showing alternatives to some of the views expressed within heathenry without much evidence. I started realizing that if I wanted to make things better or different, I would have to do it myself. Rolling up my sleeves, I began forming a plan to not just write better books on heathen practice but to practice dread sisterhood by moving myself to an active participant in movements. I came to the realization that the only true freedom comes when you apply your practices to every part of your life, when you choose to live in the true light of the goddesses and what they stand for, when you no longer choose to sit in silence, but speak with conviction, power, and passion. Finding that voice and using it gave me a sense of inner peace.

REFLECTING ON THE GODDESSES

There is a strong association and tie between the primordial dark goddess that held sway over the pits/bogs/grave and the primordial mother goddess who held sway over the home/crops/children/mothers as well as the hag/grandmother who resided in the 'wild' spaces. When we reflect on the powers of the goddess and the gigantic swath of things, they had powers of domination over it stands to reason why we call them 'dread'.

They are not just divine archetypes of primordial power, they are that which transports us between stages of life, therefore society brands them as "other". If there are aspects in the historical writings on most of the gods may seem very gendered but this is not how the ancient heathens intended the information to be relayed. Most of them are gender fluid, they may appear to be presented as male or female, but they can transform themselves into any form they wish.

They are gods after all, and don't really follow any specific rules such as gender, time, space, size, species, or other confines. There is concepts however, woven into the history of the dread sisters that does use wording like womb and usages of 'blood' that may or may not come from menstruation or some form of it. On occasion if you look at works from scholars like Maria Kvilhaug mead is a metaphor for 'blood' and this can be any blood from any place but the connotations of 'blood flowing' from a physical being in terms of a process of shedding (menstruation) is often linked primarily to dread goddess like Frigga, Freyja, Baba and Hel.

Interestingly not so much to Sif, Ran as these two border between two states of 'womanhood', Sif, Ran and Frigga are more linked to the concept of 'fertility' or at least 'abundant progeny' in that most of their 'powers' come from the creation of children through marriages. Although Sif has a strong tie to fertility in terms of creative fertility or fertility that has more to do with 'growing' things than it does specifically children the fact is that these two goddess/giants do border another state of womanhood, that of the 'mother' figure.

Frigga also borders this role and is the most linked to the concept of womanhood, however she has aspects in her that are related to deeper, darker magic. There are references that point to her silence not being a form of oppression but one that holds with it a magic of restraint. What she says, she weaves into existence. This concept is woven a lot in fairy tales as words hold weight in terms of what magical things can be birthed into being or used to stave off bad outcomes. [For example, Snow White has a passage of the mother 'pricking her finger' and wishing her child have lips as red as blood and Rumpelstiltskin being summoned away by the mere use of his name]

Freyja and Baba are opposite in terms of how they function. Freyja holds multiple functions. She is a death goddess in terms of her possession of half of the dead. She is also linked to witchcraft/magic and sexual freedom. Baba is more the end-of-life function in terms of how she is viewed through the lens of womanhood. Although she is an ogre and does also appear in both male/female forms, for the most part she is linked to 'grandmother' or the role of the wise woman who will impart knowledge willingly or unwillingly. Each of the goddesses/giants/ogres represent phases of life that we go through or actively must transition through to get to the other side.

They represent the nature of transformation itself, that we change over time, and that these changes create fundamental shifts [or should] in our opinions. We should be willing to allow these stages to be met with some self-awareness and self-kindness as none are easy to go through. Circling back to the original thoughts in the first section, how do we intersect views from the previous section into our current spiritual pathway we have another series of questions we might want to ponder. How can we see the gods/spirits/giants/etc through the lenses of radical abolitionist feminism?

We can take the concepts and apply them to how we see the dread sisters acknowledging them as more than just female archetypes. We see them as woven in the fabric of how landscapes and homes were created. We see them transforming the view of the 'womb' into something else. Transforming the womb into a metaphor more than a concrete word only symbolizing a place to hold children, it is now a well from which all things can 'spring forth' and the transformation of traditional roles onto a wide range of tasks that remove barriers. Here is where we start building our case that abolishing our views of what we are told about our dread sisters and what is true comes into play.

It is also where you start feeling a true feminism existing, in that feminism was woven into structures that existed. If feminism is inter-sectional and humanist, that view has long been threaded through the practices of the past and into the practices of the future. We should refrain from reducing the dread sisters into singular forms. The dread sisters remind us that we should embrace transitions on all levels. When we refuse to do that and refuse to acknowledge that transformation is a foundational stone to practicing heathenry. To be a dread sister means you embrace what you are, who you are and live free from the constraints that often keep us from achieving close links to our gods and the freedom to practice our faith the way we wish to.

Expressing through each Goddess and Being

Each goddess shatters norms. Freyja for example shatters the norm of what is sexually allowed for women. She breaks these rules by sleeping with dwarves and then is othered for her sexual liberal views and becomes a goddess of war.

"When Freyja woke up the following morning she instantly noticed the absence of her necklace and blushed in anger. She saw that her doors had been open by force and immediately knew that Loki was responsible for such a burglary. But she also knew that Loki would never risked getting caught by her unless Odin had told him to. What she did not understand, though, was how her secret was discovered.

She then hurried to Odin's hall and demanded what he did with the necklace for he was caught if he had anything to do with it. Odin grew angry with her and shot back that she could not talk about a sense of morality when she went sold her body to four greedy dwarves just for a necklace. Freyja repeated her question of where her necklace was and started weeping tears of gold. Odin told her she would never see the necklace again until she had met one condition to satisfy him.

The Allfather told her to find two Midgardian kings and start a war between them, and ensure that they only meet on the battlefield, each supported by twenty vassal kings. And when each soldier is slain she must raise them from the dead and have them fight again. The Allfather stated that those were his conditions: for her to set men to kill each other. Freyja inclined her head and simply told him to then give her the necklace."

Freyja's role changes as she becomes more war-like. This "othering" of her from this magical goddess to a goddess of death abolishes the norms of what women could do and relates to some changes and interpretations of how we see figures of Freyja depicted in amulets and figurines. We see examples of gender as per-formative and so Freyja is preforming both roles, thus breaking the boundaries of what women could do and what they could express both sexually and in terms of the roles they held.

Frigga: "Frigga is presented as a Queen but also as a representation of the land itself." Because of her marriage to Odin, she brings with her the power of land/sky this is an important union metaphorically and happens a lot. There are many scholars that focus on the importance of matches between great sky gods and great land goddess that explain why. Frigga transforms the idea of what a goddess is and does and what she can do.

Her promiscuity to is another aspect of her that like Freyja can alter the perceptions of what is permitted for women. She also is described as silent, but this silence is not to mute her, more that her words hold sacred and important meaning, and so speaking to them allowed, conjured them into being. [Friga, Frea, Frigga, Phol, U]

Sif: holds with her potency that is transferred and held on behalf of her husband. This power that she holds allows her to hold the greatest number of regenerative powers as well as pro-generate powers. "Sif was also worshiped as a goddess of the Earth and the land. Her marriage to Thor, god of thunder, the sky and agriculture, may be symbolic of the connection between the sky and the earth, linked by rain and fertility."

This is a common link with a few of the goddesses, they hold sway between the sky/earth. "Inflicting damage on Siv's hair was both a crime and an offence. Based on the frequently encountered cultural idea that access to someone's hair equates with access to the body as a whole, Margaret Clunies Ross (1994, 59-61) suggests that with this disgrace - humiliating Thor by severing this part of his wife's body" She holds power and sway over the very power of Thor.

Ran: holds the power over the waters itself. Her power comes from the very source where life begins, she is the 'well' the force in which all creation ebbs and flows, through her we abolish the concepts of what water means and allow ourselves to transform the word 'womb' to well because all wells spring forth a 'type' of life.

This is not always 'material' life but the life force that both nurtures the world through rain, creative regeneration, and a liquid matter that we both can enter or exit corporeally and non-corporeally. Ran in a way removes the archetypal feminine as she is the mother of waves, but these children do not come through natural means, she 'created' them more than 'birthed' them.

Angrobda: abolishes norms of 'beauty' she is both a giant/goddess and hag. She transforms the concept of what power a woman can have in that she holds great power over magic, over the ability to conjure fear and balance, as through her comes children that will destroy the gods. She is both an object of fear and yet has such deep profound sadness in her. In a fictional novel called The Witches Heart, the author Genevieve Gornichec she expresses this on Angrobda: "They say an old witch lived in the east, in Ironwood, and there she bore the wolves who chase the sun and moon.

They say she went to Asgard and was burned three times upon a pyre, and three times was she reborn before she fled. They say she loved a man with scarred lips and a sharp tongue, a man who gave her back her heart and more. They say she loved a woman too, a sword-wielding bride of the gods as bold as any man and fiercer still.

They say she wandered, giving aid to those who needed it most, healing them with potions and spells. They say she stood her ground against the fires of Ragnarök until the very end, until she was burned a final time, all but her heart reduced to ashes once more. But others say she lives yet". This passage indicates to us that regardless of how much we are destroyed through trials and tribulations we live, reborn each time.

Baba Yaga: Is the mother/father complex. In that we hold sway over both. She is also the most allusive when it comes to embracing the feminist within. She is the feminist that not only wears a pussy hat, but fights for rights of all who come to her. She is the equalizer that teaches us to be truly between both things, you must accept an inter-sectional view. One that is grounded in accepting queer and trans folk into our midst.

FINDING DREAD SISTERS IN METAPHORS

Each of the goddess has a dwelling. What this has to do with feminism and the idea of abolition is mostly centered around the fact that once a patriarchal view took hold, the home/dwellings/houses of the dead are moved from being feminist to being constricted. The concepts of the house moved from an a closer communal one in that the house was also the place in which one would be born/live/die and marry/divorce etc. It was more than a place to live, it was the 'hub' of activity depending on what role you held in society. Even the longhouse was the 'hub' of all functions.

SUMMONING THE BONES

Once however a stricter view on gender norms began sweeping through, the house moved from a central hub of activity and was replaced with other structures that would serve to be 'houses' of worship, funerals, marriage rights etc. The role of women in terms of the aspects of birth would be segregated to rooms in which would be less communal and more seclude as would rites of burial etc. As life changed and new religious views took hold, much of the history about the house was eventually replaced with a new version that was less linked to landscapes of living/death.

By removing the meaning of objects, doorways, cooking surfaces, 'rooms' of the house, we lost connection with how these were also viewed as 'places' which existed in both the landscape of the living and dead and would be viewed as part of the transitions between stages of development. We may not long really understand or have relationships with physical space in the same way our ancestors did, because we no longer have the same understanding of what these spaces meant. By removing the importance of the fluid nature of objects and creating permanence, we reduce the power held by feminists. In terms of abolition, we seek to return the concepts of the house as being a conduit of change.

Most of the dread sisters have a 'house' or place that they dwell in. We will examine how that makes them [The Dread Sisters] something to fear as they are linked to 'landscapes' as closely as they are to esoteric things like runes or divination tools. The natural and unnatural bridge they walk down makes them dread sisters. Associating the place that most of the goddesses live with the concept of the womb itself is not that hard to connect if we view the womb as a 'creative' place instead of linking it to childbearing. When we seek to understand where the concept of dread sisters come from, we look to figures in history that represent seats of female power.

No greater symbol of that is the vagina. The Sheela-Na-Gig [Image] The image of the vagina or parts of it such as the vulva appear in carvings all the way back to the stone age. "Paleolithic cave art is grounded in the imaginative idea of a universal creative womb as the generatrix of all life. Indeed, the very structure of the caves with their entrances, passages, and caverns, mirrors the primordial vulva, vagina, and womb of the Goddess." [Icon of the Vulva, A Basis of Civilization, Star Goode. 2021] It is difficult to articulate this point without using gender specific biology, I think that it is going to take a few decades to figure out some better formations of what the 'vagina' could be.

There are some changes in terms of actually seeing the 'vagina' as more like a metaphorical one, a magical 'symbol' of sorts. "Old Norse poetry is purely metaphoric: The Eddas concern themselves with telling the tale of individual learning, and gender is used, like any other attribute, to symbolize something in order to bring about the message. The male and female forces of the Old Norse cosmos do not represent men versus women: They represent the different, gendered aspects within a whole human being regardless of sex or gender. We are all Odin, we are all Thor, Loki and Freya in all her shapes – all at the same time." [Burning the Witch!–The Initiation of the Goddess and the War of the Aesir and the Vanir, Maria Kvilhaug.]

The real connection to the ideas of life and death being in the hands of women is likely due to the natural cycles that women held sway over [historically]. These three stages, that of maid/mother/grandmother literally marked out not just the stage at what the woman could do/be/ produce but also has significant ties to concepts of blood and magic that go well beyond historical sources. The idea of the primordial female power source is something that cannot be dismissed in this regard. When I wrote The One Time We Ate Grandma, concepts of how the 'body' became part the landscape is clear.

The links between the dwellings and the very power center that the goddess dwell in make this clear. Connecting the aspects of primordial dark/light means to accept and embrace aspects of ourselves. I am aware that this is a selfish pursuit to embrace what I am, fully fledged and burned into the abolitionist feminist that wants to change the systems of oppression around me, but to indelibly alter the consciousness of practitioners who have forgotten the roots to which we are grounded. These roots are in the soil of Baba Yaga, in the deep wet cave of the Sheela-Na-Gig, and in the bony fingers of Hel.

These forms build for us a gateway to feminine power, waiting for us to claim it. The concept of the womb is triggering to many people who either were not born with one or may not have the desire or possibility of procreating. In recent years, the womb being referred to as the 'well' is much more accurate. The 'well' is life if you live in a place where water is hard to find. When we look at neolithic life and how they noted landscapes we see that; "The connection between moisture, life, and the life-giving goddess contained deep cosmological significance. Human life began in the watery realm of a woman's womb. So, by analogy, the goddess was the source of all humans, plant, and animal life. She ruled all water sources: lakes, rivers, springs, wells, and rain clouds." [The Living Goddess, M Gibutas.]

We see this connection in certain goddesses that have places that exist within a 'marsh' - the concept of dwellings inside wetlands having dual meaning. But again, note, that it's not just human life, she is that which holds animal and plant life. The fact that the dwelling itself where the goddess/witch/hag dwells is a metaphor for the place of female power dwelling inside the well or spring evokes with it both the concepts of life in that this water can create and the concept of death in that it is that which holds the 'sacrifice' or 'body'.

The hero/heroine finds themselves in this space between birth/death where the most power would culminate. Goddesses like Frigga for example are most notable for having a dwelling that is within the marsh lands, her house sits on an inlet inside a 'fen' [A fen is a type of peat-accumulating wetland fed by mineral-rich ground or surface water. It is one of the main types of wetlands along with marshes, swamps, and bogs.] Water being linked to healing, birth, and the bog where bodies could be left/buried/sacrificed offers a small glimpse into how these goddesses can be labeled as dread sisters.

They are the material to which we travel corporeally and non-corporally, they are the boundary that you cannot control without extreme amounts of effort/sacrifice. It is possible to displace a bog, but the bog still exists low within the earth, they have a mysterious element to them in our supernatural brain. The bog is creepy at certain times of the year and likely was avoided during certain times (for example the bog would not be ideal to cross during low light or twilight conditions and or during environmental events like flooding as the bog would become severely treacherous. Bogs can draw you down, engulf you and disappear you for all time. The fact that the bog itself was seen as an extension of the goddess is not hard to understand.

HOUSES

Frigga, Baba Yaga, Freyja, Ran, Angrobda and Sif all have houses. Some of them dwell in watery regions [Frigga, Ran] some in wilder untamed places [Angrobda, Baba Yaga] and some in appointed constructed dwellings or halls [Sif, Freyja]. The houses they 'live' in have significance as they are connected to concepts that weave in aspects of the mortuary landscape as well as the landscape of the 'traditional' home. The well of the goddess was seen in the power that she held in the base of the house.

The hearth itself. Although seen as the 'heart' this could also be where the spark of divine creation resides. IF our goddess represents a metaphorical womb, and that womb represents the beginning of all life then the dread sisterhood holds with it the aspect of this creative process. Thus, when we walk into their 'dwellings' we enter the first stage of transformation. We allow ourselves to be consumed. We are consumed in that the home represents a healing, emotionally comforting place (for the most part) but also a deeply frightening concept because from the outside you cannot 'peer' inside.

They are in effect holding dual positions, that which wraps the 'babe' in warm cloth and that which binds the body in shrouds. In the paper, Lift me over Door-Hinges and Lintels, Eriksen suggests that the house itself reflects the entire process of death itself because it is a representation to the entrance exit principal. The very names for gable, window and roof having meaning into concepts that are part of the 'skull', the 'eyes' the 'legs' all aspects that you can see woven into the folklore about our dread sisters.

The house is a metaphor again for the 'coffin'. The house itself becomes this shifting thing that is not just a dwelling but a living, breathing entity that holds inside of it a great and powerful force. Traditionally this force is a witch, but she is not always a she and she is not always a goddess in the sense that we define it. It is more that the house holds with it some magical and mystical link to that primordial equal force of divinity that we are supposed to face and come out transformed. In a way the house is a metaphor for the genetrix of change. The idea that doorways, homes, houses are also linked to 'the otherworld' is clearly linked to the concepts of Baba Yaga. The position of her house is often described as forcing the person to face the 'crossroads between the living and the dead. "

Baba Yaga challenges us to go beyond that immature stage of development, moving from an undifferentiated world of early matriarchy, nor the overly differentiated world of patriarchy allows for a conscious world that can contain opposites. If we see the opposites in ourselves, we are less likely to judge and blame others. If we have identified too closely with the light, have too idealized an image of ourselves, then our shadow will surely come up and hit us on the backside. The same is true if we have identified with our negative side: we could be struck from behind by our goodness. Either position is a denial of our wholeness." [Dancing In the Flames. Marion Woodman and Elinor Dickson 1996]

This is the challenge that the goddess put to us, it is seeing our 'whole' selves the good and bad. They force us to accept what we are and to transcend our mortal coils to embrace a true form of feminism. For me this form is one of inter-sectional equality that spans all genders. It does not simply apply to women, but feminisms wrap itself in abolition. I believe goddesses like Baba specifically give us the ability to abolish things. I think all of them to some degrees are about transitioning our very consciousness. The goddess is all from the same route, the thing we must face; "to those who see her from a transcendent consciousness, she is fierce because she demands truth, sacrifice, and transformation."

This is true of them across the board as they all hold sway over both worlds: "The fact is the Goddess who gives life is the Goddess who takes life away. That fact allows for no sentimentality. In feminine thinking, we hold the paradox beyond the contradictions. She is the flux of life in which creation gives place" [Dancing In the Flames. Marion Woodman and Elinor Dickson 1996] Even if the women we discussed in our book are not traditional goddesses, like Baba Yaga who sits closer to the concept of ogre/troll and is more androgynous, we stand in and with women who seek to equalize the view of life and death to be more one with the self. Through this concept we become more in harmony with what we are. To be with these women, to call to them, to invite them, is to be with the great women who struggled to be free.

They are the others, the oppressed, the things that are discarded because they represent that which we fear. In several of the stories around the dread sisters, they represent the change of the young fertile man/woman being consumed by the tempter/temptress and thus becoming a man/woman through imparting both skills/wisdom as well as endowing them with certain aspects [for the most part this is the ability to conceive/create/gain power/gain strength] but also the transitioning to becoming part of the order.

You are going through them to come out the other end changed. Throughout most of the lore around our dread sisters we see this constant theme of being 'swallowed' or entering their dwelling through 'dying'. This shedding of that which was and transforming to that which will be is a way of taking part in a ritual of change. Initiation rituals of all sorts are abundant in our pathway. You can find historical and modern representations of these. Dread sisterhood requires an initiation like every other transition of life. This initiation imparts with it a sense of willingness to travel through it as a active participant. This initiation requires one to come out still 'living' and yet seems to have elements of resurrection/restoration [implication that you have died in some way and are now not you but a new you].

In the book Baba Yaga, Interpreting Baba, the author notes that historical precedent dictates that the original meaning of these stories is lost, but if you look at the hidden meaning, a bigger picture appears. "Baba Yaga is the guardian who lives at the gateway to the land of the dead. Her hut faces the land of the dead, and therefore, you cannot go around this hut or avoid it, but instead must walk through in.... the hut originally represented an 'animal' [so we see an overlay here of 'sacrifice or swallowing']" Those who enter her house enter in the same way a sacrifice enters. You are not there as an equal you are there to transform.

Consumed, you become something else. In Baba's example the story relays that the hero demands food and that this (according to the same book - Interpreting Baba) represents the idea of feeding the dead, "which allowed for passage onward into the spiritual world".

Eating and consuming special drinks/meals is often related to the idea of transfixing oneself between worlds. You are basically communing with and becoming part of the sacrifice. You are giving yourself. The giving of a sacrificial food or feeding the dead, allows you to consummate an almost romantic relationship with the dead, you are now seen as a 'caretaker' and thus welcome to be wandering about the place without bodyguards.

You are seen as 'trusted' by those on the other side, and this is important in working with dread sisters because the dead/dying will become actively part of the practice you will engage in. Even further in her story, Baba appears "stretched out and occupies the entire space of the hut" just like a dead body does. There are some aspects of 'shifting' shape in dread sisterhood that often overlaps with natural shapes of how bodies appear in physical and metaphysical space. There are likely some overlaps in why physical space can be bent that is lost to us, but we know that many of the dread sisters do shift space to suit them.

As her body appears to be like a corpse, she represents both the living body in the coffin and the coffin itself. She is living/dead, the representation of the things you fear, and the escape from those things does not come from a shining dragon or kissing a sleeping princess, it's facing the goddess herself. You see her for what she is and come out the other side changed. These deaths are not literal (for the most part) but metaphors for what becoming a part of the order of dread sisters means. You become a conduit for the dead and dying. You become that which lives outside the hut, inside the hut, and beyond the hut.

You can find similar analysis in all the stories of the goddesses and discover a tone of hidden initiations that one must wander through diligently. You become part of the transitory process. You abolish the norms that life has pushed onto women, you begin seeing a different potentiality. To be a dread sister means to be and see potential. To connect the dread sisterhood to powerful movements where you can invite the prospect of transformation within your own self, altering your home to be the conduit of change - these are the things that you must face, must walk through, to come out transformed.

In conclusion

Accepting that dread sisterhood means walking a pathway that will uncover deep and unrelenting critic of systems, including shaking the very foundation of who and what you are is no doubt alarming. To me, it's part of human nature and the reason for writing Riding The Bones. It is to face what we are afraid of, to wander through these fears and explore them. It is to adapt to our world, to hold our grief and honor it. The dread sisters teach us that ugliness is not something to run from and that it's not even ugly at all. It is the badges of time that we wear proudly.

The gray hairs that adorn us in radiant glow. The dry skin and removal of our fertile fields do not make us less than or other than. They make us strong! Defying what we have been told applies to the word woman is the first step. To see the goddess, hold no issue with gender constructs but instead to tell you I don't care what you are, come to me, as you are, humble and ready, for in this hut you will change much. Welcoming Dread Sisters into your house gives you a sense of what it is like to live in two thoughts, to maybe decide the pathway you want for yourself, for your community, for your family.

It allows you to own yourself and with that comes the opportunity, nay the responsibility to change things for the better. Stand now, with your dread sisters, hear their call, for they are loud, and wish to be known by you. As you go from this book to wander the fields of the marshes and look for them, carry not fear nor hesitation, but instead carry with you the desires to be and belong in the world of hagdom. We other hags are waiting for you with tea and cakes to welcome you into the house of those who live in the bog at the edge of the wood!

Follow these dread sisters with care, wearing iron shoes, for the pathway they build is not one to be wandered into lightly. If you find yourself face to face with any of the powerful hags in a place where they are not ready to face these dread sisters, my advice is to give them a big slice of cake and wish them all the best. They do not expect all of us to wander in the places they set for us, but if you do decide that this place is one that you feel called to. Well sisters, I bid you welcome, and will ensure the hut is ready for when you knock at the door.

On Dread Sisterhood–The Female Celtic Ties

SHEAL

"Everything that ends has a beginning – sun rises, sun sets; the first page of a book leads inevitably to the last; the opening sequence of a film to the credits; the opening and closing of a circle. Those endings – deaths – are the universal constant, the one experience everything that lives shares. Humanity has ever been fascinated with the ending of things, and where it leads – how the living conceives of the dead, and how the dead relate to them. To that end we have tried, over our millennia, to reconcile ourselves with the unknown that is death by storytelling about what comes after, and what it means to those still living."
--Meredith Catherine Moore Dread Sisterhood: Conceptions of the Feminine in Norse Depictions of Death

Miss Moore refers to women or the feminine role of women in death as a two-fold representation along with calling them "death-women". The Battle Women and the Bloody Dream Women are two concepts that are prevalent in Celtic lore and traditions as much as it is in Nordic lore and traditions, and I tend to agree with her distinction of the dominant role of women in death work and in my assertion that death work was as important in life work roles that women had such as midwives, and healers.

That women were the beginning and end of all lives through their ability to bear life and the role in the inner workings of the passings of their community members as death workers. As suck, if we take for example the bean chaointe (Keener), the Bandorai (Women Druids) and myths such as bean sidhe (Banshee) and Women Washers also known as bean nighe (known as prophetesses of doom) we see a recurring feature of women in death roles both culturally, spiritually, and in Irish legends.

She [Miss Moore] goes on to say that Gísli Sigurðsson mentions that rather than Celts influencing Nordic people, it is the other way around and that cross pollination of religious motifs reinforces the concept of death-women. She goes on to say that Valkyrie, or the concept of Valkyrie has strong ties to death-Goddesses in Irish culture and mythos (example: The Mórrigan and her Mórrigna).

She even quotes Donahue from "War-Goddesses" to support this ideology.

"Gísli Sigurðsson's 'Gelic Influence in Iceland' seems to support a literary connection with Gaelic roots, regarding saga literature and stories related to the mythology, though he maintains that the mythological framework in both Prose and Poetic Eddas are "no doubt Scandinavian". This literary contact does not preclude the idea of Valkyries in some manner being related to the idea of Irish war-goddesses as Donahue has mentioned them.

However on the other hand, Donahue finds that perhaps some of the Irish goddesses had Norse influence, given the high level of contact in Ireland with the Norse system of beliefs.36 The possible (though not universally accepted) cross-pollination of religious motifs complicates the issue from the standpoint of one trying to suss out the origin of these death-women, but for our purposes, the idea that this cross-pollination rendered two sets of feminine beings presiding over slaughter rather lends more credence to the idea that death and women could go together. [Meredith Catherine Moore Dread Sisterhood: Conceptions of the Feminine in Norse Depictions of Death Gísli, Gaelic Influence, 119. Donahue, "War-Goddesses", 5]

Miss Moore goes on, again, to mention that the Mórrigan is one such Goddess that is associated with death and death-women along with being related to battle women and death battle; going so far as to make the connection that Donahue does about ravens (sic birds associated with death) being a similar theme in both Nordic and Celtic cultures. She also says that the proposed ideology that an earlier manifestation of the Mórrigan, Allecto (Táin Bó Cúalnge) is one such example and I would say that the Mórrigan herself is such an example as well. She says by Donahue's words, in the Táin Bó Cúalnge she (Allecto/ Mórrigan) takes the form of a bird (sic Raven) and makes an "obscure prophecy relating to death and war".

This relates back to Valkyries and even Freyja and does cross back over into Nordic sagas. It also relates back to bean nighe, which relates to the Mórrigan's other form bean sidhe or her banshee form, making her both a battle woman and a bloody dream woman.

"With those goddesses, one finds the feminine related to battle and battle-death, and there is that strong association with birds, yet again. Donahue proposes that the goddess Allecto, in an early passage from Irish Tain Bo Cualnge, is a gloss for Mórrigan. In this passage, she comes in the form of a bird, and makes what Donahue describes as a rather obscure prophecy, though certainly relating to war and death.

He reports that ravens are mentioned at least twice, and then mentioned again in another Mórrigan prophecy before a different battle. This preoccupation with birds and the dead we know can relate back to Valkyries and Freyja, and we see it cross over into the sagas again, for example, in another of Gísli's dreams." - Meredith Catherine Moore Táin Bó Cúalnge Rescention I, ed. Cecile O'Rahilly. University College Cork: CELT, 2011, 30. "Céin bátár didiu in t-slóig oc tochin Maige Breg, forrumai Allechtu colléic, noch is í in Mórrígan són i n-deilb eúin co m-boí forsin chorthi h-i Temair Cúalngi & asbert frisin tarb..."; Táin Bó Cúalnge Rescention I, ed. Cecile O'Rahilly, trans. Cecile O'Rahilly. University College Cork: CELT, 2011, 152. "While the army was going over Mag mBreg Allecto came for a while, that is, the Mórrígan, in the form of a bird which perched on the pillar-stone in Temair Cúailnge and said to the bull..."; Donahue, "War-Goddesses", 5-6.

So, what does this mean and what does "Dread Sisterhood" have to do with it? Dread Sisterhood is the concept that it is a woman's role to deal in all things death (and life) and that this creates a sisterhood where women, through their divine feminine, are revered, and subsequently feared. It is a society within a society that teaches each other the ways of their sisterhood whether that be a Norse Seidhr or a Celtic Bondorai (or other female groups such as keeners). That it is spiritually and primarily a woman's work, that the divine feminine can give life, and/or take it and even predict it. That women are the connection between creation, as seen through the various goddess archetypes, and procreation. That she is both the giver and the taker of life, and if not the taker, the messenger preceding the taker.

"... The inescapable female connection between creation and procreation... And the sorceress - the witch, the wise woman, destroyer, and preserver of culture - is she not the midwife, the intermediary between life and death, the go-between whose occult yet necessary labors deliver souls and bodies across frightening boundaries?" Justyna Szachowicz-Sempruch, The Witch Figure in Nineteenth and Twentieth-Century Literature. Pages 376, 377

It is considered primarily a woman's work, not because they are women, especially not in Celtic cultures due to the simple fact Celtic women were equal to their men and if not, above them as it was a predominantly matriarchal society. Prime examples of this are the goddesses and their powerful positions of sovereignty over the lands not to mention women like Queen Boudicca, Queen Maeve and so forth. The husband's lands came from them as part of the marriage though remained with the women in titles. The Cattle Raid of Cooley is a prime example of Queen Maeve's lands remaining with her and not her husband or later her consort (Conchobar Mac Nessa and Allil). Not to say that men can't work shadow or death work, there is certainly titles that indicate that this is something that is entirely accepted by the Celts as well. The role of the Borekeen, the male master of ceremonies is a good example of this, especially in relation to the games played at wakes, as well as some other male roles that are both prime examples of male involvement in death and shadow work.

"It was only usual in most cases for wake games to be found at wakes of someone who had passed of natural cause or in old age. Young or tragic deaths were more sombre affairs and would not have seen this behavior to the extent the others would have. As mentioned at the beginning these games and revelry were presided over by a male master of ceremonies, the Borekeen. When death caused disruption in the community, the female was the agent ushering the soul into the otherworld, i.e. presiding over death and the male was the agent presiding over life, whose job it is to "reassert the continuing of vitality and the potential for renewal in the community" (Lysaght, 1997:65).

As a result, they were cosmologically opposed, (Ó Crualaoich,1990:147) in essence a balance or compliment to each other. As well as having a male figure presiding over the games, many of these games and pass times were male-centered. That is not to say that they were all just involving men, as there were many matchmaking type games played that involved both sexes, but most of the recorded games seem to involve just male participants. These were often in the form of feats of strength to show physical prowess and gain acclaim (O Suilleabháin,1969:38).

Story telling was also a favorite at wakes, even the more solemn ones, and we are told how these stories were often told by an elderly man (O Suilleabháin,1969:14), most likely a member of the community with some renown in telling stories. Like keening this sort of behavior at wakes came up against opposition by the clergy who at the synod of Cashel and Emly (1720) thought "the purpose [of the wake] is being defeated when immodest games are carried on which suppress the memory of death in the minds of those present" (O Suilleabháin,1969:149)

Going beyond that, gender fluidity was viewed much less of a problematic issue in ancient cultures as it wasn't viewed as a "sinful" state like it was post-Christianity influences, we have examples of this from both Odin himself learning the female magic of Seidhr, along with Freyja and Freyr, Castor and Pollux, Gwydion and Gilfaethwy all being possible examples of "dual spirited" gods and goddesses, and quite possibly a reference to a Celtic priest in female clothing from Tacitus. This possible reference found regarding trans people in Celtic culture comes from Tacitus in his book, Germania. As far as Romans were concerned, "Germany" was displaced east from our modern idea of the country. The people he was talking about were a tribe called the Nahanarvali, who were part of a larger confederation of tribes called the Lugii. Their home territory was in modern Poland, between the Oder and Vistula rivers.

Tacitus wrote: "Among these last is shown a grove of immemorial sanctity. A priest in female attire has the charge of it. But the deities are described in Roman language as Castor and Pollux. Such, indeed, are the attributes of the divinity, the name being Alcis."

The Mabinogion may have some surviving Welsh legend that may also support the concept of transgendered or dual spirited people within the Celtic communities. In the Fourth Branch of The Mabinogion, as a precursor to the tale of Blodeuwedd, there is a story about two sons of Dôn, Gwydion and Gilfaethwy. Gwydion goes on to have many other adventures, but Gilfaethwy is known only for his obsession with a young girl called Goewin. She's not interested, and she's a special virgin servant of King Math of Gwynedd making her untouchable. Gwydion and Gilfaethwy therefore kick off a small war by stealing some pigs from a rival king, Pryderi of Dyfed. While Math is away dealing with the inevitable retaliation, Gilfaethwy can rape poor Goewin.

When Math gets home, he finds out what the boys have done and is furious. He turns them first into deer, then into boar, and then into wolves. In each case one of the boys becomes a male of the species, and the other becomes a female, and they have children, whom Math adopts. What we have is a tale of divine brothers who go through species and gender changes and produce offspring, which is reminiscent of Loki and his shape shifting abilities that produce offspring as well, specifically Sleipnir while Loki is in female horse form. Are transgendered/dual spirited people present in the ancient societies of the Celts? Perhaps, but we don't have enough archaeological evidence to say whether there were or not. In a cautionary statement, I would say that every story and piece of history that can't be corroborated fully or at all may still have a seed of truth within it that we have yet to find.

They very much exist now, among many genders, that are accepted into today's society. Why not the ancient people of the Celts (and Norse). Did trans women in the Celtic ancient society, if they did exist, participate in the divine female death work roles? It is very possible they did indeed participate. We, unfortunately, do not have enough evidence. Yet, to say that they did or didn't exist and participate in death-women work or roles as battle-women or bloody dream women; I tend to lean toward that they did exist and did participate, considering that in Irish Celtic societies the women were as equal as the men were, if not above them and so described by the Romans many times.

The fact that woman are primarily death workers, in many ways, is quite true even today, considering that death doulas are primarily women (I, myself, was a death doula; personal support worker), and most healthcare workers at the nursing level, as well as nurse practitioners, personal support workers, and early education workers are all female dominant roles or rather traditionally so and again this is not to say there are not male counterparts, there are plenty. That held true for ancient Celts as well, such as bean chaointe; (physical battle women), living women keeners who would lament at funerals much like bean sidhe (the banshee), and bean nighr; (mythological bloody dream women) women washers who would wash the shrouds of the dead, both of which were built in the basis of the bean sidhe (banshee) a concept borne of the Mórrigan goddess archetype.

The woman washer was a banshee class of Tuatha (aka 'fairy') that would wail and lament for the unfortunate souls whose shrouds they were washing; this is much like the Mórrigan washing the bloody armor of a fallen warrior at the river side – both appearing to a person would be considered a bad omen or a prediction of their death. They were never the direct cause of their deaths but rather the foretellers of doom and messengers of death's arrival. The banshee was described in a similar manner, though they would scream and wail while pacing rather than cleaning the shrouds of the dead and are considered a demonic version of the previous named Mórrigna. Being so named due to the Mórrigan's domain over the dead (sic named after her). This concept also establishes the "Bloody Dream Woman" concept that Miss Moore speaks of in her thesis.

It is said that the bean nighe is likely the 'hag' (sic crone) version of the Mórrigan, a goddess of death and rebirth that is much like Freyja and Hel, to which she has been linked to both, including in our previous book Riding the Bones and was known as the triple goddess (The Maiden, The Queen, The Crone or The Young Woman, The Maiden, The Hag) while she has a secondary set of stories that depicts her as three warrior goddess sisters, Neiman, Anand and Badb. Unfortunately, there is very little literature for Anand; however, Neiman and Badb are also known as "Violence and Madness". Which relates both sisters to a battle-woman (Violence) and a bloody dream woman (Madness). They are considered part of the original three Mórrigna, to which a banshee would be considered one as well.

This means that Neiman and Badb represent both a battle-woman and a bloody dream woman; otherwise called violence; a physical act, the battle woman, and madness; a psychological act, the bloody dream woman. This supports Miss Moore's ideology that woman come together as death-women or death workers in a "dread sisterhood". It also supports her stance that our storytelling, and our cultural history storytellers from the past were using forms such as myths, legends, and sagas to attempt (and them) trying to reconcile what is beyond the veil, what is beyond death while trying to form an ideal of what our own mortality is and how we relate to those around us in that mortality as well as their mortality as compared to ourselves. As such, life is fleeting as it were, death is absolutely the only true constant and forming a sisterhood through death in all its forms, as death is not always a physical thing, is an attempt to connect with each other on the divine feminine level through the assumed roles based on a woman's feminine power that is inherently shared between them and dictated to them as per their societal roles.

WIGHTS OF THE DEAD

VALKYRIES

Famous for being beautiful maidens who serve mead in Valhalla and choose the worthy slain from the battlefield, these beings are actually a lot more complex. Their name means "choosers of the slain", indicating that not only did they take fallen warriors to Valhalla or Folkvang, but they may have also been the ones who determined who survived the battle and who did not. Many scholars have theorized the true nature of the Valkyries and believe that their nature was much more akin to that of priestesses who presided over death rites for the fallen or even agents of death itself, stirring up war and devouring the fallen, given their strong association with Odin.

DRAUGR

The zombies of Norse lore, these undead creatures are said to have incredible strength, the ability to move through stone, and the ability to change their shape and size. They are believed to reek of decay and appear mostly as rotted humans. They are notorious for guarding the treasures of their tombs and making any would-be grave robber pay with their lives. Draugr are also thought to have lore similar to that of vampires, but instead of sucking blood, they spread the contagion of vampirism, essentially turning their victims into draugr as well. In Eyrbyggja saga, it is said that Thorgunna's death was caused by an "epidemic"of revenants and Thorolf Lame-Foot's death was from a contagion brought on by the transmittable nature of the draugr's attacks.

FOSSEGRIM

As with most water spirits, the Fossegrim, also referred to a Näcken, Nixie, or Nøkken, is both beautiful and deadly and their gifts do not come without a price. It is said that the Fossegrim appear as beautiful, scantily clad men who play enchanting and haunting music on their violins by the waterside. For the price of a well-fed goat, the Fossegrim will teach a human to play the violin like a pro, but their beautiful and haunting melodies are also notorious for luring women and children into the water to drown.

While lore varies from region to region, some beliefs state that one could stop a malicious nøkken from stealing someone away by shouting the nøkken's name, which was believed to be lethal. Another belief was that the nøkken were omens of where a drowning would or had occurred; if one saw them screaming at a certain point on the water, that was where the drowning would occur. They were also able to shape-shift and would often appear as water horses, or bäckahäst, and appear on the shore on foggy mornings. Once a rider mounted the bäckahäst, they were unable to dismount and would be dragged into the water.

KRAKEN

The famous sea monster of Norse lore, the Kraken is depicted as a large squid or octopus who lurks in the deepest parts of the oceans and attacks boats, dragging them down to the depths.

FYLGIA

Stories about the fylgia are often ambiguous. On the one hand, a person's fylgia could be viewed as their guardian spirit who either watches over the family or who appears in dreams to pass on omens of things to come. In other lore, seeing your fylgia, whether awake or in dreams, is an omen of death.

GARMR

The blood-soaked wolf or dog that guards the gates of Helheim

ANIMISM

Largely due to such ethno-linguistic and cultural discrepancies, opinions differ on whether animism refers to an ancestral mode of experience or to a full-fledged religion. The currently accepted definition of animism was only developed in the late 19th century (1871) by Sir Edward Tylor. It is "one of anthropology's earliest concepts, if not the first".

SARAH

The home was very much a living, active part of lore and superstition. I'm sure we have all heard of house wights, or house spirits, but ancient people also believed that certain areas and elements of their home held special meanings and attributes, as well as special magical properties. Obviously, the hearth would be the center of the home, the heart, if you will, and certain elements of the hearth fire pertain to how the dead were viewed. It was believed that the dead who had remaining ties with the household would warm themselves by the fire every Saturday night.

Ancient people were very particular about how the dead were removed from the house as well, to protect the house and those who dwelt inside from an unwelcome visit from the recently deceased. The dead were to be taken out by a special door that was then bolted shut, or a special window, all in an effort to make the deceased forget where the front door was. In other traditions, the dead were buried under the threshold, except for suicides, who were taken out of the home through a hole dug under the threshold.

LARISA

There is metaphors throughout the lore, folklore and external sources that seem to indicate the home was part of an 'in-between' space and much of this lore has been woven into fairytales throughout the ages. The idea that the house itself is a transformative place, can be seen in an amazing paper called Lift me over Door-Hinges and Lintels by Marianne Hem Eriksen, in which the author details the concepts of the home as a transitory object to which bore striking similarities to the grave. I detailed much of these comparisons in the section Dread Sisterhood.

SHEAL

Objects, places, and creatures all possess a distinct spiritual essence. Animism [Latin: anima, 'breath, spirit, life'] is the belief that objects, places, and creatures all possess a distinct spiritual essence. Potentially, animism perceives all things; animals, plants, rocks, rivers, weather systems, human handiwork, and perhaps even words; as animated and alive. Animism focuses on the metaphysical universe, with specific focus on the concept of the immaterial soul.

Animism encompasses the beliefs that all material phenomena have agency, that there exists no categorical distinction between the spiritual and physical (or material) world, and that soul, spirit, or sentience exists not only in humans, but also in other animals, plants, rocks, geographic features such as mountains or rivers, or other entities of the natural environment: water sprites, vegetation deities, tree spirits, etc. Animism may further attribute a life force to abstract concepts such as words, true names, or metaphors in mythology.

Animism in Celtic Beliefs Systems

The Celts of the ancient world believed that many spirits and divine beings inhabited the world around them, and that humans could establish a rapport with these beings. The archaeological and the literary record indicate that ritual practice in Celtic societies lacked a clear distinction between the sacred and profane; rituals, offerings, and correct behavior maintained a balance between gods, spirits and humans and harnessed supernatural forces for the benefit of the community.

The Celtic religion perceived the presence of the supernatural as integral to, and interwoven with, the material world. Every mountain, river, spring, marsh, tree, and rocky outcrop was inspirited.

While the polytheistic cultures of ancient Greece and Rome revolved around urban life, ancient Celtic society was predominantly rural. The close link with the natural world is reflected in what we know of the religious systems of Celtic Europe during the late 1st millennium B.C.E and early 1st millennium CE. As in many polytheistic systems, the local spirits honored were those of both the wild and cultivated landscapes and their inhabitants. As Anne Ross observed:

"... God-types, as opposed to individual universal Gaulish deities, are to be looked for as an important feature of the religion of the Gauls ... and the evidence of epigraphy strongly supports this conclusion."

The ancient Celts venerated the spirits who inhabited local mountains, forests, and springs. Certain animals were seen as messengers of the spirits or gods. In tribal territories, the ground and waters which received the dead were imbued with sanctity and revered by their living relatives.

Sanctuaries were sacred spaces separated from the ordinary world, often in natural locations such as springs, sacred groves, or lakes. Many topographical features were honored as the abodes of powerful spirits or deities, with geographical features named for tutelary deities. Offerings of jewelery, weapons or foodstuffs were placed in offering pits and bodies of water dedicated to these beings. These offerings linked the donor to the place and spirits in a concrete way.

THE SACRED TREES

The Celts believed that trees had spirits and revered certain trees. The most sacred trees of Ireland were the bíle trees - old, sacred trees that stood in a central area and were often the social and ceremonial meeting place for a tribe or village. According to the Dindsenchas (lore of Irish places), the five sacred bíles of Ireland were the Ash of Tortu, the Bole of Ross (a yew tree), the Oak of Mugna, and the Ash of Dathi.

These trees were associated with the five Irish provinces then in existence. Among both the Continental and Insular Celts, the behavior of certain animals and birds were observed for omens, and certain spirits were closely associated with certain animals. The names of Artio, the ursine goddess, and Epona, the equine goddess, are based on Celtic words for bear and horse.

In Ireland, the Morrígan is associated with crows, wolves, and horses, among other creatures, and in Scotland Brigid's animals include snakes and cattle. Certain creatures were observed to have physical and mental qualities and characteristics, and distinctive patterns of behavior. An animal like a stag or horse could be admired for its beauty, speed, or virility.

Dogs were seen to be keen-scented, good at hunting, guarding, and healing. Deer (who shed antlers) suggests cycles of growth; in Ireland they are sacred to the goddess Flidais, while in Scotland they are guarded by the Cailleach. Snakes were seen to be emblematic of long (possibly eternal) life, being able to shed their skin and renew themselves. Beavers were seen to be skillful workers in wood. Thus, admiration and acknowledgment for a beast's essential nature led easily to reverence of those qualities and abilities which humans did not possess at all or possessed only partially.

IN THE HEATHEN BELIEF SYSTEM

LARISA

There is no distinction between living and non living objects it seems, at least if you look at the corpus of materials on the bronze, iron and Viking age. There are tons of examples in which non corporal objects come to live, give gifts, even in some cases impregnating people.

This again connects to the fact that the lines between the seen and unseen were blurry and non existent. The land is pivotal to life and so by seeing it as a living creature more stewardship is given to protecting sacred landscapes. Mountains were seen as enclosures and portals to realms unknown and are living parts of the landscape, the water that surround the land are vital for travel and for providing important drinking and irrigation systems.

If all parts of your world are alive, then so are the gods and heathenry is no exception from this concept. For those that do ancestral worship, the concept of animism is pivotal for it is what continually animates our dead to be with us. The definition of animism is that there is a soul linked to inanimate objects and by believing this we can see that this extends to that which we cannot see. The most comprehensive work on this subject is by Nordic Animism from Rune Hjarnø Rasmussen who is working on reconnecting this practice to modern heathens.

You can incorporate animistic views into your life by seeing the world around you as inseparable from yourself. I myself am very fortunate to live in Hawaii. The world here is deeply rooted to the land, they believe that the island must be maintained, it is sacred space from mountains to the ocean. The volcano's are seen as extensions of Pele. Living here has shown me a real life example of animism and I can see how this would and did exist for the Nordic people as the concepts are not dissimilar.

Seeing that all living things are deserving of our care, love and intention is not just reserved for environmentalists it is vital that we care for the world around us, we only have this one place to live and it requires us to be careful when doing things. Its important to remember in rites and practice as a heathen to respect the world around you, live knowing that you take with intention and give with intention.

I see this as a way to try within my means to live local, focus on foods that I can eat here, connect to the land around me by growing plants that are non invasive, by taking care of the land I own, offering to the gods of this place as well as my own, and understanding that I am not and will never truly own my land, it belongs to the island, I just get to live on it and take care of it.

"The Polynesian Hawaiians worshipped nature. They saw its forces manifested in a multiplicity of forms to which they ascribed godlike powers, and they based daily life on this animistic philosophy. Handpicked and specially trained storytellers chanted the exploits of the gods. These ancient tales, kept alive in a special oral tradition called mo'olelo, were recited only by day. Entranced listeners encircled the chanter; in respect for the gods and in fear of their wrath, they were forbidden to move once the tale was begun.

Any object, animate or inanimate, could be a god. All could be infused with mana, especially a dead body or a respected ancestor. 'Ohana had personal family gods called 'aumakua on whom they called in times of danger or strife. There were children of gods called kupua who were thought to live among humans and were distinguished either for their beauty and strength or for their ugliness and terror.

It was told that processions of dead ali'i, called "Marchers of the Night," wandered through the land of the living, and unless you were properly protected, it could mean death if they looked upon you. There were simple ghosts known as akua lapu who merely frightened people. Forests, waterfalls, trees, springs, and a thousand forms of nature were the manifestations of akua li'i, "little spirits" who could be invoked at any time for help or protection. It made no difference who or what you were in old Hawaii; the gods were ever present, and they took a direct and active role in your life."-Kevin Whitton, author of Moon Hawaii

On Being Called

An Excerpt from Riding the Bones by Sheal Mullin-Berube

When we started talking about this book, I jumped at the opportunity to not only write again with one of my womb-to-tomb sisters but both. I also jumped at the chance to talk about death because that is something that society says we aren't supposed to talk about, and I've always been the "bucker of societal norms" so to speak. Death has followed me everywhere since I could remember. From my earliest memories of death at 3 years old to the lingering smell of lilacs when grandmother was around from beyond the veil as a teenager. It plays a prominent role in my life, so much so that I studied and worked in a field that was surrounded by death in all its forms.

Working with Alzheimer's patients, where they call it the "million little deaths" to cancer patients as a palliative end of life personal support worker, death was my companion while I was my patients and their family's companion. I was the buffer between death and them. The interpreter if you will, to ease the message of passing from this plain of living to the devices of dying and beyond into the plain of the dead. I've always been drawn to death.

From my tastes in music like Hozier's Take me to Church talking about giggling at funerals and my artistic style while drawing being dark and gruesome, even my written fiction is death, mayhem and destruction, the call of death work and dark works is strong. Then, the call of The Morrígan came. When you are called by Morrígan you don't tend to ignore that call she doesn't really give you much of a choice to be honest.

Being a living haunted is a strange path which I will certainly touch on throughout this book. Most Druids and Celtic Shamans [more Druids] don't normally get called to dark workings or death work. I happen to be one of those few Druid-Celtic Shamans who has been. I was drawn early to Druidry and Celtic Shamanism but only answered the call later in life. It was my first encounter with the phantom smells of lilacs as a young child that first drew me to the dead and death work. I couldn't understand why I was smelling lilacs in my most stressed out moments as a child and young adult.

When I put the question to mom, she froze and stared oddly at me for a moment. Her next words were quite chilling, 'that was your grandmother's favorite flower, you were too young to remember that.' To this day, if I am upset or stressed, the phantom smell of lilacs crops up around me, even in the dead of winter where no lilacs bloom. It's like grandmother is popping in to say, hey it's okay, I'm here my child. Then came my first Shamanic act, without having the words for the work I was doing, as a young, barely teenager.

It came in the form of a letter, written to my grandmother Joan, my mother's mother, on an anniversary of her passing. I had given it to my mother at my grandmother's grave site in Montreal for her to read. While it drew from my mother tears of great grief and sorrow, it also drew from my mother the most endearing and genuine of smiles through those tears. To this day, she keeps that letter as a reminder of the release of her grief over her mother's passing.

Using this book and the Tarot we developed to build a tool for others to understand, not only the Nordic goddess Hel and the Celtic goddess The Morrígan but also their roles both culturally and historically was an opportunity I wasn't about to pass on. This book and Tarot aren't just about a guide to grief and death, divination tool, culture, history or personal anecdote either. It's about giving others a tool to take in their grief, their loss and not only understand it and process it but heal from it.

That is the ultimate duty of a Celtic Shaman, to come to the aid of others. To give them what they need to heal and be whole again. In this book you will find not only a Tarot deck but history of the goddesses, the cultures they come from and how those cultures deal with death very differently from the mainstream societal dealings with death. You'll find death rituals from both Norse and Celtic origins in this book as well. Take what you need, leave what you don't from this book and may you find your way with the light in the dark.

'LISTEN TO THE BLACK RAVEN SING, HAIL TO THE MORRÍGAN!'
ON INSTINCTUAL PRACTICE

SHEAL

WHAT IS INSTINCTUAL PRACTICE?

Instinctual practice is taking the history, culture and knowledge that you have accumulated and using that to follow your instincts on what rituals you perform and how those rituals are performed. For example, this past [I am Canadian, it lands just a bit before Samhain] Thanksgiving my second youngest as well as myself performed a thanking to the gods and goddesses by burying the turkey heart from out meal with apple cider beer, honey and milk in our front yard.

We buried this in the dirt, calling on the gods and goddesses and thanking them for the strength and protection they had provided us throughout the year. Those various gods and goddesses were Cailleach, The Morrígan, Síle na Giġ, Cernunnos and Hel [A Nordic Goddess that "adopted" me through my blood oath Völva sister, Larisa]. Instead of following a strict ritual we both followed our instincts instead. Feeling for what was asked of us by the gods and goddesses instead of "knowing".

I find this style of ritual and practice more relaxed and leaves me not worrying about whether I performed the ritual correctly or not. This can be especially helpful to newcomers to Druidry, Shamanism, Asatru, Heathenry, Wicca or any other beliefs that you may ascribe to or are just starting out with. Relying on instinctual practicing of rituals and beliefs allows you to focus on what you bring to the table instead of worrying what you perceive that the gods and goddesses think about what you are doing or who you are. They truly care more about intent rather than what or how.

ON GATE KEEPING

SHEAL

Why avoid gate keeping?
First, what is gate keeping?
Gate·keep·ing: noun: "The activity of controlling, and usually limiting, general access to something."

Gate keeping doesn't help anyone. It doesn't teach others about the history, the culture and beliefs of any of the communities we may be a part of. When we gate keep information and knowledge it only serves to take away from our beliefs and practices, as well as each other and ourselves. Some believe that gate keeping may dissuade others from appropriating the culture behind the beliefs that the community practices.

Appreciation is not appropriation. If the practitioner acknowledges and honors where the practice came from, who it came from and appreciates the culture of where the practice came from then this is appreciation. In that light, take from this what you need and leave the rest. You can add to it or take away from it. It is now your knowledge as well as mine. I share it with you as part of my culture as an Irish Celt.

I truly believe that my Celt cultural and practicing knowledge isn't just mine to hang onto but rather share with others in the hope that we find some sort of common ground and come to know each other as people in a meaningful and productive way.

I TAKE YOU AS YOU COME AND ACCEPT YOU AS YOU ARE.

CELTIC CULTURE & HISTORY

SHEAL

ON CELTIC CULTURES, HISTORY AND FAIRIES

The earliest evidence of Celtic culture is from the site of Hallstatt, Austria. The site has over 1000 burials with Celtic features, dated to approximately 1200 BC. There are a few practices of what the Greeks called the Keltoi (Kel-twah) that were especially interesting. Their hair, body painting, the way they fought and a more gruesome practice, head hunting was a few of the cultural practices among most Celts, including the Pict, the Gaulish, Irish, Scottish, and even the Welsh to name a few.

ON HAIR, HEAD HUNTING, AND ITS SIGNIFICANCE

Hair was very important to both men and women among the Celts. Particularly warriors. The Celts, like the Danes (sic Vikings) were very particular on hygiene. Though they kept their hair long and cutting another Celts beard or hair was considered insulting. Celts, particularly Gauls would fashion their hair with a mixture of lime and fermented urine that would color their hair a brighter yellow.
They would spike, plait, or dread their hair to resemble a horse mane. Julius Caesar and Strabo each described the Gaulish people as painted with woad and spiked, colored hair.
"By far the most civilized [of the Britons] are those who dwell in Kent. Their entire country borders on the sea, and they do not differ much from the Gauls in customs. Very many who dwell farther inland do not sow grain but live on milk and flesh, clothing themselves in skins. All the Britons paint themselves with woad, which produces a dark blue color; and for this reason, they are much more frightful in appearance in battle. They permit their hair to grow long, shaving all parts of the body except the head and the upper lip." – Julius Caesar

"Their [the Britons'] hair is not only naturally blond, but they also use artificial means to increase this natural quality of color. For they continually wash their hair with lime wash and draw it back from the forehead to the crown and to the nape of their neck, with the result that their appearance resembles that of Satyrs or of Pans, for their hair is so thickened by this treatment that it differs in no way from a horse's mane. The men of Britain are taller than the Celti, and not so yellow-haired, although their bodies are of looser build. The following is an indication of their size: I myself, in Rome, saw mere lads towering as much as half a foot above the tallest people in the city, although they were bandy-legged and presented no fair lines anywhere else in their figure." – Strabo

Hair was very significant to the Celts as it was believed that the head contained the soul, and the hair was a representation of the power of that soul. It was left long, even colored and treated in plaited or dreaded locks with lime and fermented urine to resemble the locks of a horse mane. In fact, the hair on their head, other than their beards for men, was the only hair that they left on the body. All other hair was shaved clean from their bodies ritualistically. Women also kept long hair, sometimes well past their knees. Queen Boudicca is described as having hair past her hips by the Roman Cassius Dio.

"In stature she was very tall, in appearance most terrifying, in the glance of her eye most fierce, and her voice was harsh; a great mass of the tawniest hair fell to her hips; around her neck was a large golden necklace; and she wore a tunic of divers colors over which a thick mantle was fastened with a brooch. This was her invariable attire. She now grasped a spear to aid her in terrifying all beholders."- Cassius Dio

As you can see, both men and women, and in this case Queen Boudicca, a woman of great and significant stature, are equal among each other. The women were sometimes described as being more than equal to the men of the Celtic peoples (sic in strength).

Women could hold property and wealth as well; they were equally great warriors themselves on the battlefields as the matriarchal society of the Celts was the basis of this equal standing. Lands and wealth were procured through the maternal side of a family, the woman's father's wealth came with her within a marriage, particularly among the elite and noble families.

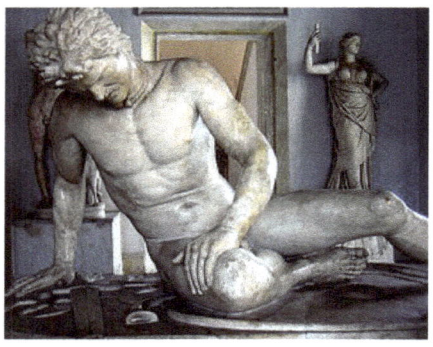

The Dying Gaul, or The Capitoline Gaul, a Roman marble copy of a Hellenistic work of the late 3rd century BCE Capitoline Museums, Rome

[CC BY 2.0 Anthony Majanlahti]

"Physically the Gauls are terrifying in appearance, with deep sounding and very harsh voices. The Gallic women are not only equal to their husbands in stature but rival them in strength as well."– Diodorus Siculus Ammianus Marcellinus, a Byzantine writer, wrote of the Celts: "Nearly all the Gaels are of a lofty stature, fair and of ruddy complexion: terrible from the sternness of their eyes, and of great pride and insolence. A whole troop of foreigners would not be able to withstand a single Gaul if he called his wife to his assistance, which is usually very strong and with blue eyes."

The sculpture, The Dying Gaul, again depicts the importance of hair in detail. It was commissioned by Napoleon Bonaparte and was so sought after that it was replicated so often by other kings and rulers. The sculpture shows a Gaul, sitting on his shield, naked and wounded.

His hair, albeit depicted erroneously by Napoleon's sculptor as short, is limed and pulled back in the warrior's fashion that is described by Strabos, and others. Around his neck is a Celtic Torc. Along his right side is a fatal wound in his chest. That statue has a two-fold message, one of defeat, but also one of great respect for the Gaul sitting upon his shield, an homage if you will, to a formidable enemy worthy of dignified respect despite being defeated.

"The white marble statue, which may originally have been painted, depicts a wounded, slumped Gaul or Galatian Celt, shown with remarkable realism and pathos, particularly as regards the face. A bleeding sword puncture is visible in his lower right chest. The warrior is represented with characteristic Celtic hairstyle and mustache with a Celtic torc around his neck. He sits on his shield while his sword, belt and curved trumpet lie beside him. The sword hilt bears a lion's head. The present base is a 17th-century addition."

The statue serves both as a reminder of the Celts' defeat, thus demonstrating the might of the people who defeated them, and a memorial to their bravery as worthy adversaries. The statue may also provide evidence to corroborate ancient accounts of the fighting style. Diodorus Siculus reported that "Some of them have iron breastplates or chain mail while others fight naked".

Polybius wrote an evocative account of Galatian tactics against a Roman army at the Battle of Telamon of 225 BC: The Insubres and the Boii wore trousers and light cloaks, but the Gaesatae, in their love of glory and defiant spirit, had thrown off their garments and taken up their position in front of the whole army naked and wearing nothing but their arms... The appearance of these naked warriors was a terrifying spectacle, for they were all men of splendid physique and in the prime of life.-- Polybius, Histories II.28

The Roman historian Livy recorded that the Celts of Asia Minor fought naked, and their wounds were plain to see on the whiteness of their bodies. The Greek historian, Dionysius of Halicarnassus regarded this as a foolish tactic: Our enemies fight naked. What injury could their long hair, their fierce looks, their clashing arms do us? These are mere symbols of barbarian boastfulness.— Dionysius of Halicarnassus, History of Rome XIV.[3]

The depiction of this Galatian as naked may also have been intended to lend him the dignity of heroic nudity or pathetic nudity. It was not infrequent for Greek warriors to be likewise depicted as heroic nudes, as exemplified by the pedimental sculptures of the Temple of Aphaea at Aegina. The message conveyed by the sculpture, as H. W. Janson comments, is that "they knew how to die, barbarians that they were".

This description of Celts brings us to their peculiar behavior with their enemies, being that hair and head were so important to them, the head-hunting behaviors of the Celts was a rather gruesome ritual. Fighting your enemy naked was one thing, the reverence of taking the enemies head was another. It was thought that the power of a person was in their head, and subsequently their hair atop that head.

The Celts were avid head-hunters. Displaying the heads of the vanquished enemies around their doors of their homes even. Taking the enemy's power by taking their head, and the more you had the more respected a warrior you were. Even Queen Boudicca ritualistically took the heads of her enemies, even their horses, and placed them at the river's edge in masonic jars as a testament to her strength and prowess against the Roman enemies.

Having a large collection of enemy heads was a sign of prestige to the Celts, and they would even go so far as to decorate the doors to their houses with the heads of their enemies to show off how successful they were in battle.

At one site in France there is even a pillar with special niches carved out to display severed heads. Since the Celts considered the head to be the source of life and the location of a person's soul, warriors saw great value in beheading their defeated enemies.

"Amongst the Celts the human head was venerated above all else, since the head was to the Celt the soul, center of the emotions as well as of life itself, a symbol of divinity and of the powers of the other-world." —Paul Jacobsthal, Early Celtic Art.

The Celtic culture of the severing of heads is documented not only in the many sculptured representations of severed heads in La Tène carvings, but in the surviving Celtic mythology, which is full of stories of the severed heads of heroes and the saints who carry their decapitated heads, right down to Sir Gawain and the Green Knight, where the Green Knight picks up his own severed head after Gawain has struck it off, just as Saint Denis carried his head to the top of Montmartre.

Separated from the mundane body, although still alive, the animated head acquires the ability to see into the mythic realm. Diodorus Siculus, in his History V, 29, 4- 5; first century B.C.E. Had this to say about Celtic head-hunting:

> "They cut off the heads of enemies slain in battle and attach them to the necks of their horses. The blood-stained spoils they hand over to their attendants and carry off as booty, while striking up a paean and singing a song of victory; and they nail up these first fruits upon their houses, just as do those who lay low wild animals in certain kinds of hunting. They embalm in cedar oil the heads of the most distinguished enemies, and preserve them carefully in a chest, and display them with pride to strangers."

Strabo speaking on how Poseidonius describes head hunting practices of the Celts: I mean the fact that when they depart from the battle they hang the heads of their enemies from the necks of their horses, and, when they have brought them home, nail the spectacle to the entrances of their homes.

At any rate, Poseidonius says that he himself saw this spectacle in many places, and that, although at first he loathed it, afterwards, through his familiarity with it, he could bear it calmly. The heads of enemies of high repute, however, they used to embalm in cedar-oil and exhibit to strangers, and they would not deign to give them back even for a ransom of an equal weight of gold. The Celtic head-hunters venerated the image of the severed head as a continuing source of spiritual power. If the head is the seat of the soul, possessing the severed head of an enemy, honorably reaped in battle, added prestige to any warrior's reputation. According to tradition the buried head of a god or hero named Bran the Blessed protected Britain from invasion across the English Channel.

The symbology of the Druidic orders in the form of a possible tattoo.

How Others Saw the Druids

The Romans and the Druids

The Romans killed many Druids and destroyed many of their books. The Roman Catholic church believed that female Druids were sorcerers and witches in cooperation with the devil. They also saw the knowledge of the Celts as a huge danger for their domination. The well-known Saint Patrick burned more than a hundred Druid books, and destroyed many places connected with the old cult.

Julius Caesar describes the Druids as the following:

"The Druids usually hold aloof from war, and do not pay war-taxes with the rest; they are excused from military service and exempt from all liabilities. Tempted by these great rewards, many young men assemble of their own motion to receive their training; many are sent by parents and relatives. Report says that in the schools of the Druids. They learn by heart a great number of verses, and therefore some persons remain twenty years in training. And they do not think it proper to commit these utterances to writing, although in almost all other matters, and in their private and public accounts, they make use of Greek letters. I believe that they have adopted the practice for two reasons ± that they do not wish the rule to become common property, nor those who learn the rule to rely on writing and so neglect the cultivation of the memory; and, in fact, it does usually happen that the assistance of writing tends to relax the diligence of the student and the action of the memory. The cardinal doctrine which they seek to teach is that souls do not die, but after death pass from one to another; and this belief, as the fear of death is thereby cast aside, they hold to be the greatest incentive to valour." (Caesar, The Gallic War VI.13-14)

SAINT PATRICK VS THE DRUIDS

One such person is Saint Patrick. He was described as "driving the snakes off a cliff from Ireland". There are no snakes in Ireland, however, it is believed that a particular tattoo that Druids had of a snake on a "T" symbol was the reference point for "driving the snakes". Saint Patrick had a very discernible distaste for Druids and made that quite known according to some texts.

It was a tattoo that Druids were marked with to symbolize their beliefs and membership in either of the 3 Druidic orders. There have never been and will never be a native snake species in Ireland. This was a reference to the symbol of the serpent used by the druids who were eventually driven out of Ireland. This is what is being referenced when the legend of Saint Patrick driving the serpents into the ocean and out of Ireland is being told.

He was also a book burner (Druidic texts), stole and incorporated Irish pagan beliefs into Christianity to commit cultural and religious "genocide" with. He was not the saintly person that most people think he is. There's even debate on whether his legends were fake propaganda from the church and that Patrick never existed as he's portrayed.

"A certain magitian that was in high favor with the King, and whom the King honored as a god, opposed himself against S. Patricke, even in the same kind that Simon Magus resisted the apostle S. Peter the miserable wretch; being elevated in the ayre by the ministry of Devils, the King and the people looked after him as if he were to scale the heavens, but the glorious Saint, with the force of his fervent prayers, cast him down unto the ground, where dashing his head against a hard flint, he rêdred up his wicked soul as a pray to the infernal Fiendes."

The Vita tripartita Sancti Patricii (Tripartite Life of St. Patrick) relates:

"Lóegaire mac Néill possessed Druids and enchanters, who used to foretell through their Druidism and through their paganism what was in the future for them." Coming to a certain town, the Saint, according to history, "found Druids at that place who denied the Virginity of Mary. Patrick blessed the ground, and it swallowed up the Druids."

On Faries: The Tuatha De Danann

The Tuatha de Danann (Irish Faries) were the most significant and prevalent of the beings responsible for forming Irish culture and history; however, there were plenty of other supernatural races, including the Gaels, the Fomorians, Firbolg and the Milesians. The Tuatha de Danann were a magical race that possessed supernatural powers. Most of them were god-like creatures or divine beings that were worshiped. The Tuatha de Danann brought skills and wisdom to Ireland when they arrived.

They gained those skills from four wise men who resided in the four cities: Senias in Murias; Morias in Falias; Urias in Gorias; and Arias in Finias. The Tuatha de Danann also brought four treasures from the four cities; treasures that were said to be beneficial to Ireland. Those four treasures are Lugh's Spear, The Sword of Light, Stone of Lia Fáil and Cauldron of Dagda.

Regarding Tuatha de Danann's disappearance, there had been several claims; one of the theories states that the Tuatha de Danann did not fight the Milesians at all. That was because their foretelling skills suggested that they were going to lose the country to the Milesians. Instead, they built their own kingdoms under several hills around Ireland [mounds of Ireland]. The other theory claims that the two races entered a battle in which the Milesians won.

They took over Ireland and had most of the races around Ireland as their allies. What happened to the Tuatha de Danann after the defeat was divided into two different opinions. Some say that their Goddess Danu sent them to live in Tír na nÓg, the Land of the Young. On the other hand, others claim the Milesians came to terms with sharing the land with the Tuatha de Danann. However, the latter had taken the underground part as their own land.

People of the Sidhe

The Fairy Folk of the Mound

The Irish mythology mentions a race named the 'Sidhe', pronounced as 'shee'. Historians believe that the Sidhe is another reference to the Tuatha de Danann. They were regarded as gods of the earth. There was also a belief that they had the ability to control the crops ripening and cow's milk production (Cattle Raid of Cooley), and people in ancient Ireland worshiped them with sacrifices to have their blessings in return.

There are few "rules" if it were about fairies or, in this case, Tuatha that I grew up with or learned about. One major significant rule about Tuatha is the use of the word "Fae". Most old school Irish witches and practitioners will tell you (and even every day Irish folk) not to ever call the Tuatha "Fae". It is akin, and I speak about this briefly in Riding the Bones, to calling them "little fuckers".

The last thing one would ever want to do is to annoy or anger the fairies in any significant way. It can bring strife, hardship, and malevolent mischief into your household. The other is that not all fairies are Goddesses or Gods and not all Goddesses and Gods are fairies, and some fairies are not benevolent or good.

Pollyanna Jones has a few general tips that speak to fairies and how to live side by side with them. However, I personally, do not agree with the term 'Good Folk' or the descriptor 'Good Folk' as it generalizes all fairies into the same definition, to which they certainly are not.

"Fairies have been both loved and feared throughout the ages. With supernatural powers, they are described in folklore and fairy tales as being able to both gift and curse, or at least cause mischief to humans. Items going missing, a spate of breakages of household items, sickness in animals, and periods of bad luck were suspected to follow an instance of upsetting the fairies. As a result, various superstitions and customs developed on establishing healthy relationships with the 'Good Folk' to avoid displeasing them."

Tip One: Fairies dislike discord within their host's homes. Bad language and arguments are bound to cause upset; seemingly these magical folk enjoy their peace and quiet. Offerings of milk and honey could be left to appease the fairies should they have been upset by their human companions.

[Author's Note: While I do agree with the offerings bit in this tip; I do not agree with the bad language and arguments causing upset. Some fairies thrive on that kind of negative discord.]

Tip Two: Circles of mushrooms known as fairy rings were described as left behind by fairy footfalls after a night of dancing under the moon. It is considered very bad luck to break a fairy ring, causing seven years of bad luck to fall upon anyone who damages them. Some people avoid walking inside them entirely, believing them to be portals to the fairy realm.

Tip Three: Anything shiny is supposed to attract the fairies, and you may find that these items go missing only to appear in the most unexpected places once the fairies are bored with their newly found toy. A more recent phenomena is that of placing "fairy nests" or fairy doors in the garden in the hopes that the fey will make such a place their home, helping a garden to thrive. This is a very recent idea, following on from the Victorian concept of flower fairies, and romanticism and taming of these folk.

Tip Four: The elder tree is believed to be associated with the fairies, and bad luck or seven years in fairyland awaits anyone who would pick flowers from this plant on Midsummer's eve.

Tip Five: Not all fairies are benevolent! Should you find yourself out walking alone at night and hear the nickering of a horse or see a strange light up ahead, do not follow, for you may find yourself waylaid and Puck led. Survivors of such experiences often awoke in a muddy ditch, fooled by fairy lights into straying off their path and into disaster.

[Author's Note: Most Irish will tell you it is the disembodied sounds of barking dogs rather than horses. Especially while crossing a large field.]

Tip Six: For those fearful of fairies dwelling in their homes, yellow flowering broom plants outside the house are thought to act as a deterrent. As are any items crafted from iron.

Tip Seven: Whilst invisible to most humans, there were ways in which one could obtain the enchanted eye. One would be to wash their eyelids with the dew collected on May Day's eve. Another is to gaze through a hole within a hag stone: a stone with a naturally formed hole within it.

Tip Eight: "There are ways to know when a fairy is present nearby, without the aid of a hag stone. The bobbing of a head of bog cotton, when the air is still, laughter heard without an apparent source, or a sudden swirl of leaves crossing the road marks the passing through of one of these magical beings.

It is courteous to nod your head or tip your hat to acknowledge them if you are to be known as a friend to the fey. Be warned though, once you are noticed, this can never be undone!"

--Pollyanna Jones

ATTRACTING THE FAIRIES

If you would like to attract fairies to your yard or home, it is wise to be cautious in what kind of fairy or Tuatha you attract. Silver Rain has a rather simple ritual for attracting fairies to the yard and it doesn't involve milkshakes; however, they do like sweets and have a decent sweet tooth. I do warn you, that you may not like the fairies you attract, and they are not all benevolent and welcomed. Please use this ritual with caution.

You will need the following items for this spell:

5. 1 Large Jar
6. Mixed Hard Candy
7. Cup of Sugar
8. Lavender Oil
9. Rose Petals
10. Your Voice

Casting Instructions : 'Celtic Fairy Caller Spell'

On a full moon go deep into the forest or woods, don't forget to take your ingredients along. Go to a spot where the moon shines the brightest.
To your jar add your mixed candy and say;
      "Sweets, sweets, that's what you are,"
      Then add your sugar and say,
      "Sugar, sugar, that's what you are,"
  Add your oil and rose petals and say,
      "With the moon light above, I call upon the Fairy Queen
    and King, bring forth your tides, I am here to harm none, only
    to greet and love."
Dig a hole big enough to fit your jar in, allowing the top to be open, but do not let any dirt get inside. Leave the jar for one week, do not go back until the week is up. Then sit close by the jar, do a little meditation, and you will start seeing the fairies-- Silver Rain

WORKING WITH OTHER BEINGS, IN HEATHENRY

LARISA

The giants are often so badly portrayed that many practitioners of Ásatrú actually have full out disclaimers on their site that do not allow the names of giants to be mentioned in rituals, and will not accept anyone who follows Loki, in fact have spoken against people who blot to Loki in conjunction with Odin, even though they are blood brothers according to the Edda, and apparently were historically blotted to together..

In modern practice, the giants are still very much feared in Ásatrú, as if they have nothing better to do than attack humans, which is speculation at best. The term Utgard appears regularly in writings on giants, as a word that is supposed to indicate that these things are 'outside' the realm of the gods, and therefore should be avoided. The world tree is often described as having a giant fortress or wall called Utgard that keeps the giants in or us out, no one knows which.

But, in many stories, the giants are freely walking all over the place, and in fact can leave the world of Jotunheim where they live and go pretty much anywhere. There are a variety of giant types, you have some living in Jotunheim, some in Muspelheim, then you have natural occurring giants made of a variety of elements, they seem to be created out of a variety of elements.

There are giants of the water, rocks, mountains, fire, and ice and more, each one is different and there seem to be a variety of family groups living in different places. It is hard to define what is or who is a giant. When you look at the creation story of the Northern Europeans, you find that all the gods and giants were born of one single god named Ymir. From this one being came all beings. Ymir was said to be a hermaphrodite that bore children from his legs, armpits and other parts. He seemed to be a creature that was a-sexual and created all the gods from his body.

Since, the giants were created from him, as the gods, dwarfs etc, and then the gods and giants are related. Odin's parents were part giant; as were Thor's and many of the gods have giant blood mixed into their own.

"The giants are unbelievably old, they carry wisdom from bygone times. It is the giants Mímir and Vafþrúðnir Odin seek out to gain this pro-cosmic knowledge. Many of the gods' spouses are giants. Njord is married to Skaði; Gerðr becomes the consort of Frey, Odin gains the love of Gunnlod, and even Thor, the great slayer of their kind, breeds with Járnsaxa, and mother of Magni. As such, they appear as minor gods themselves, which can also be said about the sea giant Ægir, far more connected to the gods than to the other giants occupying Jötunheim. None of these fear light, and in comfort their homes do not differ greatly from those of the gods."

"According to the Lore, Odin, Villi and Ve created Ask and Embla from some wood that was lying around. If this is so then Odin is a Jötunn, as are his brothers, because both of their parents are Jötunn's – Borr and Bestla. Based on this, wouldn't the creatures they created also be Jötunn's; meaning, Ask and Embla .. the `first humans'? If so, what makes us human or different from those that created us? Modern Heathens tend to look upon the Jötunn's as `dark', `chaotic', `disruptive', and the like; so that their followers are also considered `trouble makers'. Conversely, most Rokkr consider themselves as `balance keepers', keeping the `dark ones' `content' and `well inclined'. Both stances are wrong. Nowhere in the Lore, that I have ever been able to find, does it mention an all-out disdain, let alone war, on humanity – Jötunn's against men."

However, according to modern books...the historical texts might be way off. According to the book Asyniur by Sheena McGrath "many of the giants are primal forces that contribute to creation and the order of the universe", "Giantess often had magic powers, especially of foreknowledge and supernatural wisdom......Jarl Haakon, built a shrine in southern Iceland to the giantess Thorgerdr Holgabrudr and her sister Irpa who helped him in battle...

In Norway, there is evidence of worship to Goi a giantess, daughter of Thorri....a memorial stone found in Hynnestad, Sweden shows a single female figure riding a wolf and using snakes as a bridle. This probably represents Hyrrokiin the giantess who pushed out Baldur's funeral boat when no one else could. She may have been featured in funeral rites....The Swedes worshipped Skadhi as we know indirectly from place names but also from her words to Loki that could counsels would always come from her groves and shrines" (McGrath, 1977).

> Grave mounds were often found with bowls of milk for the dark elves, warriors were buried with their finest weapons to be taken back to the dwarves, the giants homes were left, rivers named after them, mountains in many countries still bear the name of old giants, even river ways were named for them.

Outside of the giants, there was also a historical worship of dark elves, which were said to transport the dead in burial mounds, now, today, again we find that many Ásatrú don't worship them directly, or give them any offerings, and there are often statements at blots to keep out negative wights and elves, but no offerings. This is likely because the lore is lost on these creatures. In most instances, the elves and dwarves don't seem to be interested in what humans do, and don't require any specific worship or offerings.

It somewhat surprised me to find out that only one modern writer has actually covered the topic of dwarf worship, but apparently they really require a lot of caution when dealing with them. There have been old folk tales of elves that kill humans and dwarfs that will swindle you out of precious items, and a great deal of information on how to avoid them. But, it still surprises me that anyone who forges is not somewhat calling the dwarfs close by. Outside of the dark elves and dwarfs, the only creatures that seem completely off limits to humans are the light elves. This could be because no one knows what they are, or that they are not visible to humans.

The Dwarves

There is little written about these beings, we know that they dwell in caves and are the chief forgers of the worlds, they create many of the important items that the gods use, but for some reason are perpetually avoided by humans. More than likely this is because they cannot be exposed to sunlight as they will turn to stone, and therefore don't get out much. They don't seem concerned at all with human matters, and in fact are considered by some to be incredibly treacherous. They seem to also hoard money, and are responsible for commerce in the nine worlds.

When humans wander into their realms, they generally disappear or will talk to them if they find them interesting, it is mostly that humans have to be careful with how to talk to them, as they have a short fuse. Here, Tolken's work is not far off in its understanding of dwarfs, they are fighters, and often quick to judge. They sometimes seem to be lacking intelligence, and then in other stories are full of it, so the idea of what they are is still unknown. Even their size is debatable. There are sources which mention them as the same size as humans, but others that say the look more like the dwarves in stories, short and stubby. Gender is questionable in the dwarf world, there seems to be no way to tell males from females.

THE DARK ELVES

The dark elves live in subterranean areas. There are two schools of thought, they either live in mounds or underneath the earth, and it is not clear on where they live. They appear like Halfling creatures similar to Golim in Tolkein's the Hobbit. They are known to steal children, kill or eat humans, and attack anyone who comes into their realm. Similar to the fairtale Rumplstilskin, dark elves are said to take human children and replace them with changelings that are half elf/half human. There are some folk legends of them living in dark, damp caves.

LIGHT ELVES

Not much is known about them, they seem to be similar to the fairtale version of elves, complete with pointy ears, although may be more like the Tolkein version, human like with elf features, perhaps living in natural dwellings. Great care is given to these things still, in Iceland they will build around suspected elf dwellings rather than disrupt them, as disturbing their natural dwellings can bring bad luck.

The best source to understand the dwarves and elves is a book titled: "Elves, Wights and Trolls" by Kveldulf Gundarsson

In which he gives some general rules when dealing with these other beings, he talks mostly in relation to elves, wights and trolls and states the following recommendation:

   •Do not refuse food or favours in general, even gifts that
   seem worthless may prove to be of great value

•Be very careful about accepting drink given by trolls, which is often too strong for human flesh to bear, and burns when it touches. The wine of wights can also be perilous, as it loosens the human mind or soul from its ties to the earth, an makes it too easy to go deeply into the otherworld. The same is true for joining alf-dancing, possibly because of the ecstatic/trance-inducing effect of the dance

• If asked to do them a favour, do it wholeheartedly, even if it seems inconvenient

•Be careful to give warning when you light fires outdoors, toss boiling water on the ground or relieve yourself outdoors

•Do not ever lie directly to or about the alfs

•Be very careful about actually visiting the alfs in their homes or joing them in their activitieves, particularly dancing: folk who do that generally do not come back the better for it if they came back at all. Depression and various degress of mental disorder and distraction or common results of spending too long amoung the alf

•Do not speak first when addressing them

•Do not boast about favours or gifts given by them

•Do not ever mess with their mounds, rocks or other dwellings without permission.

•Finally he mentions that we should be careful on how we ask them as they are easy to offend b being nosy, and to not ask for gifts.

He mentions a few other tidbits about dealing with them and how to address them, care for their dwellings and properly offer to them. Often gifts are left outside the home in some place which people feel are enchanted by them, or sense they are living, these places will often have a small hole or object set out in which offerings and gifts are left as hopeful offerings of good behaviour.

RULES FOR GIANTS

After speaking with my two giant followers, they provided a list of do's and don'ts for dealing with the giants. Although I cannot verify whether these are true or not, they seem to be common sense based rules that should apply to any dealings with anyone, but are very solid for giant workings.

•Always show respect

•Don't challenge them unless you want a fight you probably won't win - a lot of Iron Wood Jotuns have animal ways of interacting and take challenges seriously.

•Don't wander around uninvited and avoid any areas you're told to keep out of - you're considered unprotected if you wander wrong and may be fair game for anyone who wants to go after you.

•Pay attention to body language - there are times to be serious and times for fun and games - make sure you're doing the right one.

•Do what Angrboda tells you - she's in charge of the Iron Wood and usually has a good reason for what she does even if she doesn't tell you why (she doesn't tolerate fools)

•Don't show your fear (try not to anyway) but definitely don't be arrogant - the first might create a lack of respect for you while the latter will create hostility.

•Sharing good food and/or alcohol is generally appreciated.

•Be prepared to be tested - they'll push you to test your worthiness to be there.

•Don't assume all Jotans are the same - especially Jotunheim vs Iron Wood - both sides will be insulted and that's very bad for you.

•Eat what Angrboda serves you - it's rude not to, and may be a test as well as a custom.

•Don't badmouth Loki (he's a case of "we can because we're family and you're not"). Don't badmouth Angrboda's children - it will anger her and that's bad.

•Never try to be sneaky or lie. They'll know immediately

ADORNING THE BODY

HAIR

THE SIGNIFICANCE OF HAIRSTYLES & THEIR POWER IN CULTURES

SHEAL

WHAT IT MEANS TO ME AS AN IRISH WOMAN AND DRUID

The significance of hair for most cultures comes from similar premise. For the Sadhus of India, their holy men dread their hair to show their dedication to their culture and religion. The Rastafarians dreads are like the Sikh's turban to say, "I am approachable, and I will help you if you need me." While the secondary meaning of Rastafarian dreads is to symbolize the Lion of Juda.

Even the Polish plait with its cultural significance in societal standing within their communities shows how hair is important to many cultures. Dreads are a hot topic debate these days with debates on who is 'allowed' and 'not allowed' to wear dreads raging in both social media and mainstream media circles. As someone who wears plaits, dreads, and braids as a cultural connection to my Celt ancestors as well as a connection to my spiritual beliefs and gods/goddesses I am disturbed by some of the debates going on and the gate keeping nature of these debates.

In Senegal, the Baye Fall, followers of the Mouride movement, a Sufi movement of Islam founded in 1887 AD by Shaykh Aamadu Bàmba Mbàkke, are famous for growing dreadlocks and wearing multi-colored gowns. Cheikh Ibra Fall, founder of the Baye Fall school of the Mouride Brotherhood, popularized the style by adding a mystic touch to it. Warriors among the Fulani, Wolof and Serer in Mauritania, and Mandinka in Mali were known for centuries to have worn cornrows when young and dreadlocks when old.

Larry Wolff in his book Inventing Eastern Europe: The Map of Civilization on the Mind of Enlightenment mentions that in Poland, for about a thousand years, some people wore a knotted hairstyle like that of some Scythians. Zygmunt Gloger in his Encyclopedia staropolska mentions that the Polish plait (plica polonica) hairstyle was worn by some people in the Pinsk region and the Masovia region at the beginning of the 19th century.

Photo of Polish plait, 1734–1766

The Polish plait can vary between one large plait and multiple plaits that resemble dreadlocks. Some of the earliest depictions of dreadlocks date back as far as 1600–1500 BCE in the Minoan Civilization, which is one of Europe's earliest civilizations, centered in Crete (now part of Greece). While the Vedic scriptures of India date it back even further to 400-500 BCE. Frescoes discovered on the Aegean Island of Thera (modern Santorini, Greece) depict individuals with long braided hair or long dreadlocks.

We seem to forget that dreads did not originate solely in Africa and is not solely a black community practice or cultural hairstyle, instead the Egyptians cultivated the dread from the Indians of India. Particularly the Aghori Ascetics of India where the name for their dreads is Jaṭā (literal translation is dreadlock). In the Vedic scriptures, the god Shiva is described as having dreads and holding back the Ganges with his dreads to protect the land and people from her raging waters by allowing it to trickle to the land through said dreads rather than wash it and the people away.

An Aghori sadhu in a cave near badrinath.

--Photo by Archit Ratan Photography

"Bhagiratha continued his worship for furthermore years, only this time he was worshiping Lord Shiva. After a few more years, Lord Shiva was pleased and agreed to hold Ganga in his hair. When Brahma released Ganga, she came down with tremendous force from the heavens. Lord Shiva blocked her with his hair locks (sic dreads) not letting a single drop fall on Earth. Lord Shiva eventually captured Ganga fully in his hair till her force came down."

In ancient Egypt, examples of Egyptians wearing locked hairstyles and wigs have appeared on bas-reliefs, statuary, and other artifacts. Mummified remains of Egyptians with locked hair and wigs have also been recovered from archaeological sites. During the Bronze Age and Iron Age many peoples in the Near East, Anatolia, Caucasus, East Mediterranean, and North Africa such as the Sumerians, Elamites and Ancient Egyptians were depicted in art with braided or plaited hair and beards. In the Rastafari movement dreadlocks are symbolic of the Lion of Judah which is sometimes centered on the Ethiopian flag.

Rastafari hold that Haile Selassie is a direct descendant of King Solomon and the Queen of Sheba, through their son Menelik I. Their dreadlocks were inspired by the Nazarites of the Bible. Rastafarianism only became mainstream when Ethiopian immigrants brought it to the Caribbean and Jamaica, exposing celebrities such as Bob Marley to the movement where he brought it to that mainstream community through his music and Hollywood. Pre-Columbian Aztec priests were described in Aztec codices; including the Durán Codex, the Codex Tudela and the Codex Mendoza, as wearing their hair untouched, allowing it to grow long and curl around itself. Bernal Diaz del Castillo records:

"... Here were priests with long robes of black cloth ... The hair of these priests was very long and so knotted that it could not be separated or disentangled, and most of them had their ears scarified, and their hair was clotted with blood."

We see other instances of dreads in other cultural scriptures as well. Samson is described as having dreads in the bible while various Roman generals and kings describe the Celts as having "snakes upon their heads". Indigenous peoples of the Americas are depicted in 1920s and 1930s black and white photos with dreads as well. Anyone's hair will dread and lock if left to its own devices.

For myself, as a Celt with roots tied into the Irish and Gaulish peoples whom hair had a huge significance, even going so far as to chemically treat their hair to resemble a form of swept back 'dreadlocks' and spiking of the hair, my use of dreadlocks, plaits and braids are as much a cultural practice as any other culture that practices the same hairstyle. It is a practice that brings me closer to my ancestors as a way of venerating those ancestors while displaying an outward appearance of my spiritual connection with my gods and goddesses.

Cree chief Pitikwahanapiwiyin with dreadlocked hair, 1885

Public Domain Image from Prof. Buell, O.B. From Catalogue #3241485 Library of Canada

Being white does not negate that practice as it is not singularly contained to one sole community. The significance of this practice, as a white woman of Irish decent and a Bandorai (female Druid) is deeply rooted in my overall practice and self image as a Druid. It is the display of my spiritual prowess, connections, and strength as it was for my warrior Gaulish/Irish women ancestors in battle. It is the life force of my being in a physical form. These forms of hairstyles are not cultural appropriation nor something that anyone should gate keep. It does not belong to one community as can be seen from cultures originating in Poland, Ireland, Greece, Egypt, and India to name a few.

Hair & Dress Amoung Heathens

<u>Larisa</u>

As I mentioned in Riding The Bones, adorning the body was often a way to make connections between the present and the past or the 'ancestors', gods or others. There was concepts woven throughout the lore in which we see a clear connection between the body and its appearance while living and when exiting this life for the next one. Hair and ritual wear/clothing would have been an extension for that. In a few examples that we have of Nordic women practicing some kind of ritual magic, there was a 'particular' look that was present. In a few research papers there was consensus that women had a distinctive fashion that did change over time but mostly featured a simple chemise, tunic, apron, clasps, jewelry and broaches.

Although its very common to see many heathens dressing in traditional garments found commonly in the Viking age, such as the apron dress and tunics, its not required. There is however something that happens to a person when they 'wear a costume' or outfit that is for specific purpose. When connecting to our gods, garments could be a way of presenting ourselves for the moment. For example, for me, as a Hel practitioner, I wear a set of Nordic beads affixed with a Hagalaz similar to the construction of prayer beads, this is a choice I make to honor her and keep her close.

Each bead has a color representing a god/goddess or realm of the world tree so that I am always 'walking with the gods' as it were. You could construct a garment just for the purpose of ritual and adorn your hair with braids (similar to ones found on bronze age game pieces, broaches and the like) or wearing it down with simple styling.

You could offer your hair as a token to the gods, because as I said in Riding the Bones each part of us is connected to them. If we are spun by the gods then certainly our hair is part of the fibers that forms us. Your hair, body and other parts are therefore an aspect of the sacred. There is a good song by Karl Donaldson that has one line in it that says "as our bodies ward", I think this is very true of heathen rites and space.

It is by the placing of ourselves inside the mindset of ritual, crafting a space, decorating the body, adorning it with fine linens, hanging symbols of our gods from our necks, each item added, symbolizing our deep connection to them.

Intentional Clothing: We could safely say that there is a bit of 'magic' in creating things to wear. It's often said about crochet for example, that you leave one stitch 'open' to release the energy of the person who crafted it. The idea that we can 'imbue' things with energy is not that weird of a concept. Especially when animism is a prevalent theme within the culture of heathenry/paganism, its normal to think and feel that the things we touch with our hands have connection to us the 'maker'. If you choose to make a garment specifically for ritual use and no other purpose, it would be a good idea to decide how and what your going to make and how you feel this garment would be 'viewed' by the gods.

Metaphorically, I see dressing and preparing one self as being 'part' of the sacrificial landscape of ritual. You are the 'petitioner' entering the space in order to be with the gods and to commune with them. This does not have to be an elaborate event. You could do simple things, for example, lets say I wanted to have the gods with me at an important event or just to go with me grocery shopping, then I would take a second to ask the gods to walk with me, by slowly placing my symbolic objects on me. This imparts the meaning that I feel about these objects and makes me feel connected to them through simply donning a shirt that I have embroidered an animal sacred to Hel on, or wearing a color that represents a god/goddess.

Hair: Personally, I see hair as an extension of my animated body. It is fused into me and is part of me. I also see hair as a deeply connected item to the gods I follow and to my family. Hair to me is a symbol of my practice. I have only cut my hair twice, once as an offering and once just before I gave birth as I needed to get the weight off, other than that I have lived with long hair as part of my devotional work. In research papers such as Masking Moments and Analecta Archaeologica Ressoviensia, mention that hair was a social and religious item to the Nordic peoples. "The length of hair could also be connected to other issues. Within Norse medieval literature there are several examples where promises are made to not cut the hair until a deed has been accomplished or a revenge has been taken care of". [Masking Moments. Danilsson, I]

According to a study done on Gotlandic picture stones, Gorasson noted that hair may have represented "power and life" and cutting it would have been done with intention. In the article inside Analecta Archaeologica Ressoviensia titled Death, Hair and Memory by Howard Williams he makes an interesting observation that shows us how and why things like hair would be considered important' "Combing and managing the hair of siblings, children, masters and mistresses might be among the tasks shared and thus defining relationships between household and family members.

Certainly the intimate caring of cadavers might have been regarded as an extension of these quotidian tasks. Hence, hair management was no less social than dress in early medieval communities, but required actions that related to the body's surface that might have relied upon interactions with others. Moreover, grooming implements were uniquely associated with hair transformation and hence could have taken on specific roles in making apparent obligations and relationships between individuals and groups in life and death through the manipulation of the body's surface." I believe that this sums up what I am trying to say, we are the sum of our parts as it were. When we dress. When we prepare ourselves, we are taking part in a system that bestows and imparts a connection to the living and dead world.

In the section on "The One Time We Ate Grandma" in Riding The Bones, I explained in detail how these connections are important for several reasons but the biggest is that we are part and parcel of the creative sources that we came from. We are all connected to both this realm and the next and thus by dressing ourselves for an important event is the same as preparing oneself for the last crossing. All aspects of our life is connected to the idea that we are members of a heathen family.

Even though many of us don't communally care for our hair, when we brush our hair, care for our hair, we are connecting with ancestral memories, or our gods and thus these acts are the same that we do upon those leaving this world. For to intimately be involved in the care of the body is sacred. We are always and forever adorning our body for the sacred world to which we are constantly and forever entwined. However you feel expressing these connections, ensure that you do them with intention, choose items that have connection to you, that present your connection to the gods is a simple and easy way to practice a living and breathing daily devotion.

THE DRUID PRACTICE

Druidism has never fully disappeared. Nowadays, many people still try to follow the ancient tradition and many researchers continue to work to rediscover the ancient wisdom of the Druids. We can only surmise, as most of the worldly Druidic knowledge was passed from word of mouth and kept close to the chest that Druidism was both a science and a 'religion'. It was and is the study of the relationships between opposites.

Summer and winter, spring and fall, men and women, consciousness and unconsciousness, force, and flow. We do know that the Druids believed in metempsychosis, or reincarnation much like the community of the Celts did. It is considered a transmigration of the soul wherein that soul would pass from one living body that had died into a new living body. That body could be another human being or an animal or living thing (trees, butterflies, etc).

METEMPSYCHOSIS: mə-tĕm″sĭ-kō′sĭs, mĕt″əm-sī-
Noun

REINCARNATION. Transmigration of the soul; the passing of the soul of a person after death into another body, either that of a human being or that of an animal: a doctrine held by various ancient peoples and by Pythagoras and his followers, and still maintained by Brahmans and some others: also loosely used of such a transfer of the soul of a living person. The passage of the soul, as an immortal essence, at the death of the animal body it had inhabited, into another living body, whether of a brute or a human being, transmigration of souls.

We also know that the Druid was the consort of the kings and queens. An equivalent so to speak much like the Arthurian wizard or sorcerer. Much like Merlin, the Druids advised, consorted, and protected their kings and queens. They were sought out for rituals for battle, for harvest, advice when the situation warranted divine intervention and so forth.

Druids were the highest elite only second to the king [or queen] and even then, they were sometimes revered higher than a king [or queen]. In the case of some queens, it is thought that some of them themselves were Bondorai, or female Druids. Some of the most powerful queens, Maeve, Boudica, and consorts, Fedelm, Scáthach were thought to be such Bondorai.

FEMALE DRUIDS: BANDURI OR BANDORAI

The Forgotten 'Priestesses' of the Celts

In medieval Irish legends they were called Banduri or Bandorai. The Druids were the ancient religious leaders, scientists, and researchers of the Celtic society. For centuries, there was a common misconception that Druids were only male. However, numerous historical records attest to the fact that there were women among their ranks. The term "Druid" comes from the Indo-European word "deru", which means "the truth" or "true". This word has evolved into the Greek term "drus", meaning "oak". In modern Irish language the word is "drui".

According to the Irish traditions, there were two main names of the Druid women: baduri and the banfilid, meaning female poets. Most of the names of the female Druids are, to this day, forgotten. The name Fedelma was recorded in ancient texts, as a woman in the court of Queen Medb of Connacht, who was a 'banfilid". She lived in the 10th century AD in Ireland.

WHO WERE THEY?

The Druids were the intellectual elite. Being a Druid was a tribal function, but they were also poets, astronomers, magicians, and astrologers. It took them 19 years to gain the necessary knowledge and skills in alchemy, medicine, law, the sciences, and more. They organized intellectual life, judicial processes, had skills to heal people, and were involved in developing strategies for war. They were an oasis of wisdom and highly respected in their society. Julius Caesar was fascinated with the Druids.

He wrote that they were scientists, theologians, and philosophers, and acquired knowledge that was extraordinary. According to experts in Caesar's writings, the great Roman leader was aware of the female Druids. Unfortunately, most of the Roman writers ignored women in general, so it is not easy to find reference to them in historical texts. However, Strabo wrote about a group of religious women who lived on an island near the Loir River. In 'Historia', Augusta is a description of Diocletian, Alexander Severus, and Aurelian, who discussed their problems with the female Druids.

Strabo speaking of divine women:

"In the ocean, he says, there is a small island, not very far out to sea, situated off the outlet of the Liger River; and the island is inhabited by women of the Samnitae, and they are possessed by Dionysus and make this god propitious by appeasing him with mystic initiations as well as other sacred performances; and no man sets foot on the island, although the women themselves, sailing from it, have intercourse with the men and then return again. And, he says, it is a custom of theirs once a year to unroof the temple and roof it again on the same day before sunset, each woman bringing her load to add to the roof; but the woman whose load falls out of her arms is rent to pieces by the rest, and they carry the pieces round the temple with the cry of "Ev-ah,"133 and do not cease until their frenzy ceases; and it is always the case, he says, that some one jostles the woman who is to suffer this fate.

Tacitus mentioned female Druids, describing the slaughter of the Druids by Romans on the island of Mona in Wales. According to his description there were women known as Banduri (female Druids), who defended the island and cursed the black clad. Tacitus also observed that there was no distinction between the male and female rulers, and that the female Celts were very powerful."

According to Plutarch, female Celts were nothing like Roman or Greek women. They were active in negotiating treaties and wars, and they participated in assemblies and mediated quarrels. According to the 'Pomponius Mela', virgin priestesses who could predict the future lived on the island of Sena, in Brittany.

"There arose a very grievous and irreconcilable contention among the Celts, before they passed over the Alps to inhabit that tract of Italy which now, they inhabit, which proceeded to a civil war. The women placing themselves between the armies, took up the controversies, argued them so accurately, and determined them so impartially, [p. 348] that an admirable friendly correspondence and general amity ensued, both civil and domestic. Hence the Celts made it their practice to take women into consultation about peace or war, and to use them as mediators in any controversies that arose between them and their allies. In the league therefore made with Hannibal, the writing runs thus: If the Celts take occasion of quarreling with the Carthaginians, the governors and generals of the Carthaginians in Spain shall decide the controversy; but if the Carthaginians accuse the Celts, the Celtic women shall be judges." - Plutarch.

Plutarch's Morals. Translated from the Greek by several hands. Corrected and revised by. William W. Goodwin, PH. D. Boston. Little, Brown, and Company. Cambridge. Press Of John Wilson and son. 1874. 1.

Tacitus describes black clad women defending the Island of Mona:

"Tacitus gives us the vivid account of the slaughter of the Druids by Roman soldiers on the island of Mona (Angelsey) in Wales. He says there were cursing black clad women there defending the island. Since the island was the most sacred stronghold of the British Druids one can assume that these women were Ban-druid (female Druids) though since he does not say this outright, we can never be sure." Ellen Evert Hopman.

Ellen Evert Hopman goes on to describe Strabo's accounts of women from an island that he didn't call druids or Bandorai, however it is evident that it is likely that they were Bandorai or as Tacitus called them; Ban-druid. These women lived at the outh of Loir River, and Diocletian and Aurelian are described as seen to consult with these woman as did Alexander Severus.

"Strabo describes a group of religious women living on an island at the mouth of Loir River but he does not call them Druids. In the Historia Augusta (a late Roman collection of biographies, in Latin, of the Roman Emperors from 117 to 284 CE) we learn that Diocletian and Aurelian consulted with female Druids as did Alexander Severus."

Hopman goes on to describe another, more specific Bandorai, or rather a Banfilid (female poet) from the Ulster Cycle, she is the consort of Queen Maeve herself, Fedelm. Along with Col and Eraise, two Bandorai from the Cattle Raid of Cooley. Yet again, she refers to Eirge, Ean and Banbhuana, other female druids mentioned in the Siege of Knocklong among others.

"In Irish traditional accounts there are references to "bandruid" (female Druids) and "banfilid" (female poets). Fedelm is a female seer and Accuis, Col and Eraise are female Druids mentioned in the Tain (The Cattle Raid of Cooley). Eirge, Eang, and Banbhuana are Druidesses mentioned in the Siege of Knocklong, and Dub and Gaine are mentioned in the Dinsenchas."

To understand the female druid, we first must understand the woman's equality in Celtic society, and it is helpful to look at the status of women in Celtic society before the Roman and Christian incursions and after. The marriage laws are a good place to start.

The ancient Brehon Laws recognized nine types of marriage:

1. In the first degree (the most desirable) both partners came to the union with equal wealth and status.

2. In the second degree the husband came to the union with more wealth, so he was in charge.

3. In the third degree the wife came with more wealth, so she was in charge.

In all cases divorce was available to wives and in the first two degrees of marriage the husband had to pay a bride price to her father the first year and every year after that a large portion of the "coibche" went to the bride herself so that she could remain independent if the marriage failed. In the event of a divorce each spouse could claim any property they had brought to the union and the wife kept all the coibche she had accumulated as opposed to Christian women, who would not see this kind of fair treatment again until more modern times.

Brehon Laws also refer to how their society was set up, who was at the top of that hierarchy, who was beside that person, how the solidarity of the society was ruled in kinship as well as land and territory rights and obligations. Rent was never a thing in Celtic society like it was in other societies, land was never bought or rented, it was inherited and rules together as a clan or kinship.

"Analysis of the extant remains of the Brehon law manuscripts has revealed the character of ancient Irish life, society, and social institutions. The basis of that society was the clan. Kinship with the clan was an essential qualification for holding any office or property. The rules of kinship largely determined status with its correlative rights and obligations. The solidarity of the clan was its most important characteristic. The entire territory occupied by a clan was the common and absolute property of that clan, although in the course of time a large and increasing proportion of the good land became limited private property. Thus, the area of arable land available for the common use of the clansmen gradually diminished.

Land was seldom sold and not often rented in ancient Ireland. Nobles and other persons holding large areas would rent to clansmen not the land itself but the right to graze cattle, and they sometimes even rented out the cattle themselves. There were two distinct methods of letting and hiring: saer ("free") and daer ("unfree") The conditions of saer tenure were largely settled by the law; the clansman was left free within the limits of justice to end the relationship, and no liability was imposed on the clansman's joint family.

On the other hand, daer tenure, whether of cattle or of the right to graze cattle, was subject to a security. The members of the tenant's joint family were liable to make good out of their own property any default in payments. No contract affecting land was valid unless made with the consent of the joint family. Other contracts had to be made in the presence of the noble or magistrate. The parties to a contract had to be free citizens, of full age, free to contract, and under no legal disability. A witness was in all cases important—and, in some, essential—to the validity of a contract. The criminal laws uniformly discountenanced revenge, retaliation, the punishment of one crime by another, and capital punishment. Reparations were paid to the family of the victim."

We know that Celtic women wore trousers, in fact, the Celts invented trousers. Gallic females went to war with their husbands and Irish Celtic women fought alongside their men. In some Roman reports they said the women were even more fierce than the men. It took a series of laws issued over several centuries after the Christian missionaries arrived to wean Irish women away from weapons, indicating problems with compliance. So, what happened?

Why did an indigenous culture that featured educated and powerful women devolve into a culture where women were demoted to the status of chattel? By the first century Britain the Romans were deliberately suppressing the Druids who were the intellectual elite, the advisors to the nobility, and the glue that held the kingdoms together.

Roman propaganda campaigns claimed that the Druids were the perpetrators of "savage superstition" and of horrific human sacrifice. That Bandorai were described as seers who were working of their own accord and not the powerful royal advisors and clergy they were. A policy of deliberate extermination was carried out, including the terrifying slaughter of the Druids at Angelsey.

THE CONQUEST OF THE ANGLESEY DRUIDS
[As told on ancientorigins.net]

When the Roman legion under Suetonius Paulinius, a commander who had distinguished himself in Armenia, approached the Penmon Peninsula on the Isle of Mona in 59 BC, terror immediately struck their hearts as the denizens of the evil isle emerged from the dark forests onto the shores:

"...A circle of Druids, lifting their hands to heaven and showering imprecations, struck the troops with such an awe at the extraordinary spectacle that, as though their limbs were paralyzed, they exposed their bodies to wounds without an attempt at movement."

The soldiers were particularly overcome by the wildness of the women who seemed to them like representations of the most deranged of female Roman deities: "In the style of Furies, in robes of deathly black and with disheveled hair, they brandished their torches."

It was at this point that Paulinius had to calm his soldiers down, and rouse them to battle:

> "Then, reassured by their general, and inciting each other never to flinch before a band of females and fanatics, they charged behind the standards, cut down all who met them, and enveloped the enemy in his own flames."

What followed was an orgy of destruction as men, women, and children were struck down by the swords and spears of Rome and sacred groves and clearings were incinerated in a cataclysm of Roman fury, fired by the unholy demonstration on the beach.

Although inflicting a near-lethal blow to British Druidism, the Roman legions were unable to fully complete the job, as news of Queen Boudicca's rebellion diverted the armies back east to the imperiled settlements of Colchester and St. Albans. After their spiritual center had been leveled, most of the surviving Druids escaped, bringing with them their totem, the Bardic Mantle, and slipping back into the obscurity of unknown Ireland, leaving only a few scattered remnants behind.

In 79 AD, following the massacre of an auxiliary squadron by the Ordovices tribes of north Wales, Gnaeus Julius Agricola, a Roman commander who had been a junior officer in the 59 AD campaign under Paulinius, finished off his superior's work with a further invasion of Anglesey. Employing the help of native auxiliaries who were well acquainted with the geography of the region, Agricola launched a surprise attack by ordering his subordinates to swim across the straits that separated Anglesey from the mainland:

> "... He then launched them upon the enemy so suddenly that the astonished islanders, who looked for fleets of ships upon the sea, promptly came to the conclusion that nothing was hard and nothing invincible to men who fought in this fashion."

The Druidic inhabitants were so outmaneuvered that they quickly sued for peace, bringing to an end the last pagan vestige of Wales and the conquest of Anglesey, as no further mention of disturbances on the island were ever chronicled again. Secure in the knowledge that his flank was secure, Agricola's next task was to stamp out the defiant native tribes of the north of England. The Romans never conquered Ireland and the worship of the 'pagan gods' continued there officially until the death of king Diarmat in 565 CE.

As Christianity gained power in all areas; Roman ideals of matronly behavior and womanhood took over, though in the few centuries that it was allowed to flourish the Celtic Church continued to exalt powerful priestesses such as Brighid of Kildare and Beaferlic of Northumbria. As the Roman Christian church gained ascendancy female Druids were labeled "evil Witches" and "sorcerers" to smear their reputations and make people fear them.

Religious orders founded by women were systematically dissolved upon their founder's death, preventing continuity of female centered orders. The Druids were demoted in the laws to figures of ridicule – mere magicians, stripped of their sacral function and status. Women in Celtic areas were forbidden to bear arms and their status dropped in most areas of life and society. What the romans did to the Celts, and more specifically the Druids was akin to the Salem Witch Trials. Stomping down the rights, laws, and positions of women because they did not match their own. Even in some instances ridiculing and demeaning their societal positions beside their men.

Prestigious Historical & Legendry Bandorai

Cassius Dio mentioned a Druidess named Ganna. She went on an official trip to Rome and was received by Domitian, the son of Vespasian. According to the description of the Battle of Moytura, two Druidesses enchanted the rocks and the trees, to support the Celtic army. The most famous descendant of a Druid woman was Queen Boudicca, whose mother was a Banduri. Boudicca was a queen of the British Celtic Iceni tribe. She led an uprising against the Romans in the 1st century AD. The Bandorai worshiped goddesses and celebrated with feasts in different months and seasons. One of the deities they worshiped, the goddess Brighid, who was later adopted by Christian nuns as 'Saint Brigid'.

Archeologists have discovered several proofs for the existence of the female Druids. Many female burials have been discovered in Germany between the two rivers Rhine and Moselle. The women who were buried there were dated back to circa 4th century BC. Some of them were buried with a special torc on the chest. According to researchers, only a Druidess could have a high enough status to receive a burial like this. Two burials located in the Vix in Burgundy, France and Reinham in Germany were dated back to the 5th century BC, likely belonged to female Druids.

Moreover, on the Rue de Récollets, in Metz, France, there it was discovered an inscription dedicated to the female Druid in honor of the God Sylvanus. It is difficult to confirm which of the noble Celtic women were really Druids, but it is believed that most of the well-educated women whose graves contained luxury goods were the elite of their tribes and quite possibly Druids.

Scáthach, (Gaelic: "The Shadowy One"), in Celtic mythology, female warrior, especially noted as a teacher of warriors. Scáthach was the daughter of Árd-Greimne of Lethra. She lived on an island (thought to be the Isle of Skye) in an impregnable castle, the gate of which was guarded by her daughter Uathach.

At this fortress Scáthach trained numerous Celtic heroes in the arts of pole vaulting (useful in the assault of forts), underwater fighting, and combat with a barbed harpoon of her own invention, the gáe bolg.

Her best-known student was Cú Chulainn, who stayed with her for a year to learn the skills that helped him win many battles. Number of other heroes of Celtic mythology also owed their prowess to the training of the Amazon Scáthach. – Britannica https://www.britannica. com/topic/Scathach

In the first century CE Tacitus wrote that "the Celts make no distinction between male and female rulers" and powerful Celtic women appear in the tales. By tradition Macha Mongruad founded Emain Macha (Navan Fort) in Ulster. The two most famous warriors in Irish history; Finn MacCumhail and Cú Chulainn, were both trained by women.

Finn was raised by two females; a Druidess and a warrior woman who taught him the crafts of war and of hunting while Cú Chulainn learned the arts of war from Scáthach who had her own Martial Arts school.

Boudica was a Celtic queen who led the last British uprising against the Romans in 60 AD. She was a priestess of Andraste, Goddess of Victory. Saint Brighid of Kildare (Kil-Dara, Church of the Oak) had a different kind of power. She was the daughter of the Druid Dubhtach and according to the Rennes Dindsenchas was a "bandrui" (female Druid) before she converted to Christianity.

She had both men and women in her religious community and she and her nuns kept a Fire Altar which was tended continuously until 1220 when an archbishop ordered it quenched. This Fire Altar mirrored the perpetual fire of the Ard-Drui (Arch-Druid) that had burned at Uisneach for centuries (thankfully the fire has been re-lit in modern times and is now being tended once again by nuns and lay folk in Kildare and all over the world).

Archaeology gives us more evidence for female Druids. An inscription was found in Metz, France, that was set up by a Druid priestess to honor the God Sylvanus and the local Nymphs of the area. It was found on the Rue de Récollets; "Silvano sacr(um) et Nymphis loci Arete Druis antistita somnio monita d(edit)" (Année Epigraphique 1983, 0711)

Two famous burials, the Vix burial and the Reinham burial point to very powerful women of their time. The Princess of Vix (who may have been a priestess) dates from the late sixth to fifth centuries BCE in present day Burgundy, France. She was a woman of wealth and authority whose rich grave goods came from as far away as the Mediterranean Sea.

Her wood paneled chambered grave held a huge bronze "krater" (a large ornamental urn used to mix wine and water for banquets), elaborate jewelry of bronze, amber, diorite, and serpentine, and a golden torque (a neck ring), symbol of noble status. She had fibulae (brooches) inset with Italian coral.

Many other female burials have been discovered between the Rhine and the Moselle rivers, where the women are laid out on wagons with rich jewelry and more impressive grave goods than some of the warrior chieftains of the time. The Reinham burial dates to the fourth century BCE by the river Biles in Germany and was an oak lined chamber filled with precious objects and jewelry. The body was laid out on a chariot with food and drink provided for her Otherworld sojourn. She was also buried with a torque on her chest, symbolic of her noble status.

Boadicea, oil on panel. Charles Gogin 1844-1931

The 'Staff Carrying Woman'

LARISA

For the heathen side, I am not going to go that much into the history of the 'Vikings' because I am not a historian. There are a few great books on the subject that will give you a good overview. I do want to stipulate two things;

One: Although the Edda's are important to read it would be a great idea to go outside of that and grab some stuff from Academia.edu, books on the greater bronze age, books on the iron age, some good reference books like The Seed of Yggradsill and The Goddess Iðunn from Maria Kvilhaug as well as some basic primers in Nordic age rituals, rites and life in general. Why? Because the Edda does not have much in it that tells us 'how' to practice, its the basic myths and stories which may or may not be that helpful.

Two: Not everyone believes the same things or has the same views, in heathenry there are no rules, so anyone telling you what to do, should not be. Your practice is your own and you decide how to make it.

Instead of focusing on the corpus of history of the Nordic region, I want to focus some of the practices mentioned. There are a few sources such as the, Medieval Nordic leechbooks and grimoires (galdrabækr) which illustrate that magic was used in everyday life for a number of practical purposes: for instance, spells and unusual recipes were employed with the aim of predicting the gender of an unborn baby or to discover if a sick man was going to die, namely by dropping a woman´s milk in urine. Spámenn and spákonur are the magical terms used in the sagas for men and women who were able to look into the future.

There seems to be a few specific names given to certain types of magic practiced:

Galdur is more ceremonial ritual form of magic, mostly practiced by the priest or priestess; it involves an intense knowledge of runes, rune stances, rune sounds, poems and runic songs.

Seiðr is a more shamanic, intuitive practice, involving the practitioner going into an altered state and speaking prophesy from beyond.

Spá-craft the fairest of the soul-crafts of old, and the one which had most to do with the worship of our forebears, is spá-craft (Old Norse spá) - the skill of seeing that which is unseen to others and of telling what should come to pass.

A meaningful difference between spá-craft and Seiðr: the one was usually prophetic and usually weal-working, the other was usually a magical craft and often woe-working. However within these groups there are variants and crossovers. All sorts of magic can twist one's Wyrd or cause harm unmeant; but when practicing soul-craft, you are traveling out into a perilous, unknown world filled with Wight's who may well not be friendly.

Some of the hazards of this sort of travel include getting troll-shot (also: Alf-shot, witch-shot, dwarf-shot), which can cause physical symptoms ranging from mild muscle spasms to bone cancer and nervous degeneration; having a part of your soul-complex stolen (in which case an experienced shaman has to be engaged to retrieve it) or eaten; being latched on to by an unpleasant Wight which follows you about causing various sorts of trouble thereafter; and, worst of all, getting permanently lost, which, after some time, will cause your uninhabited body to rot and die - something which shows up quite often in, for instance, Finnish legends.

Spinning is intrinsically connected with fate and with magic in the Old Norse literature. The goddesses of spinning inspected the spindles and distaffs of women of the household at Midwinter, rewarding the families of industrious spinners with good luck, and lazy spinners with disaster for the coming year (Motz, 152, 154), so that the industry of the spinning women of a house directly influenced the luck of the family. Spinning may have been used to 'bind' fate. There is a great example of this in the wonderous tale of the groteque loom that was made of human body parts. " Laxdoela saga seems to have an example of this, when Guðrún is sitting at home spinning while Bolli is out killing Kjartan. When he comes home and tells her about it, Guðrún's reply compares her spinning with his killing...Guðrún manipulated Bolli in the deed, and her spinning has been compared with that of the norns, and also with the valkyries' weaving on the grotesque loom of men's body parts."

Spinning was connected to fate, and therefore when garments were spun or created, it was believed that this would plant fate into the wearer for good or ill. "Weaving magic could be used to help as well as harm. Often in riddles mail shirts are likened to magically woven protecting shirts. These shirts were called gørningstakkr or witch's shirts, and examples can be found in Eyrbyggja saga when Katla weaves a wound-proof shirt for her son Odd (ch. 18), in Vatnsdoela saga, where Ljót weaves one for her son Hrolleifr (ch. 19), as well as many other places in Norse literature. The motif is also well known in Finnish runos, where a mother weaves a magical shirt that is proof against the feared and deadly metal iron."

Seiðr: " Seiðr, or to 'sit out' (sitja úti) at night in order to raise and control the spirits of the dead. Fictive descriptions of seiðr are remarkably consistent. The seiðkona or võlva is an itinerant who is invited to visit a householder and prophesy for his household. She must be lavishly entertained and paid with gifts. She may arrive accompanied by a group of helpers, or the women of the household may help her to achieve a trance through singing and/or drumming. The magic is performed on a high platform or mound.... May also employ the use of rhythmic drumming to induce a trance"[Meeting The Other, Mckinnell. J]

Much about this practice is unknown and the books that exist on it are somewhat questionable. Some stipulate that you have to be given the title, but by who? We don't really have an official 'community' that one could go to and petition to be called a 'seiðkona or võlva' so there is no real way of proving that you are one or gaining the title. These practices were done by people of all classes so there is no real way to discern that only some or only by certain ancestral connections one would automatically be or not be a seiðkona or võlva.

It has been speculated that Seiðr was considered unmanly because it allowed a man to strike at enemies with magic or poison, or perhaps that the rituals attending Seiðr included some sexual rites in which the Seiðr-worker was the recipient of sexual attentions. It is more likely that the Seiðr-practitioner was at times undergoing spirit possession or even possession by the gods, as happens in voudoun. By allowing one's self to be "ridden," and to allow another spirit or entity control over one's body, one totally gave up control and became passive, the antithesis of the expected ethic for masculinity.

A great article on seiðr and one of the best resources i Spinning Seidr, by Eldar Heide. In this short 10 page thesis the author describes seiðr as a practice that was entwined with physical spinning as well. The article mentions that in these states, "the seiðr performer could send forth his mind, in animal shape or other shape, or could ride in the sky....it appears that the sorcerer's mind emissary could be regarded as something spun: a thread or rope." Most of the practices are woven through a few sources as well as embedded in stories.

"It has been noted that women's magic-religious activities are always associated with their socially accepted and defined roles. Sometimes women's magic and religion reflect their domestic duties, while at other times magic and religion are the antithesis of a woman's socially expected role, acting as an outlet for rage and frustration but abhorred by the men who define a woman's role in their society (Geertz, 126-141). This is likewise true for magic in the world of the Norse woman. The woman of the Viking Age found magic in her spindle and distaff, wove spells in the threads of her family's clothing, and revenged herself on the powerful using the skills of sorcery.

"It is the ethymology of the word seiðr itself that helps us find a key as to why spinning is traditionally associated with fate... a thread that is used to bind or catch spirits or other beings. The whole context of textile production takes place in female, domestic surroundings and that is where their real power lies. For the trained spinner the repetitive, monotonous movements of spinning come almost as a reflex. Spinning leaves the thoughts free to wander and work the mind into a trance like state. To a novice though it looks like magic, as if 'something' is made out of 'nothing', to transform an amorph lump of wool into a structured, coherent thread. Spinning can therefore be seen as a metaphor for creation and growth, for fertility and motherhood, and again it comes as no surprise that the implements used for spinning, spindle and distaff, have a phallic connotation."

A good example of how the practice works is mnentioned in the Eybrbyggja saga through a seer na,e Katala. er story involved transforming the staff into something supernatiural, accoring to Marianne Guckelsberger, "it is a certain frame of mind, a way of thinking that changes the function and property of things. As a talented seiðkona she was able to manipulate weaker minds and trouble the visual perception of the men, and this happened because she decided to do so, and not because of some inherent quality of the tools she used. The motiv of a woman using a distaff in a supernatural way has been a powerful and persistent visual image through the ages that has inspired folk lore and art. "Die Hexe", a copperplate by Albrecht Dürer, where a naked woman is riding on a goat, holding a distaff may serve as an example." [Spinning and weaving in Viking Times and its use in seiðr]

Võlva: "The aim of the võlva is to gain control over spirits... The trance involves a seizure in which the võlva opens her mouth wide and gasps for breath (Hrólfs saga kraka, Hauks þáttr hábrókar). She may deliver her prophecies within the trance, in which case it is sometimes said that 'a song came into her mouth' from elsewhere.24 This is always in fornyrðislag metre; in it, she may refer to herself either in the first person (Hrólfs saga kraka, Baldrs draumar) or in both first and third persons (Võluspá, Õrvar-Odds saga, Bósa saga). In other cases, the võlva prophesies in response to questions when she has returned to her normal state... Might raise the spirits of the dead by 'sitting out' at night at a crossroads, on a mound or in a cave." [Meeting The Other, Mckinnell. J]

There are concepts woven in the lore that some of these women may have carried a staff, and this staff may have been an extension of the woman, there is evidence to indicate there was an idea that inanimate objects were a live and could also die and be reborn, "some staffs may have been regarded as animated objects which had to be ritually 'killed'" which may explain why some were found in graves.

They did a variety of 'magical' things such as fortunetelling, blessing, hexing, manipulating weather/ fish/animals, healing, causing mild harm to people/animal/ property, communicating with the dead, communicating or meditating with the 'unseen' world, communicating with the 'gods'/fate/spirits of the land, war magic, death and pain relief, and likely midwifery.

Finding practices that work for you and that can be reconstructed are going to take a keen intellect as they will require some extensive research. Some good beginners guides will be provided in the bibliography area under Resources.

The importance of the distaff as a main attribute of the völvur (who may be regarded as chief among the seiðkonur) also becomes clear in the story of Þorbjörg lítilvölva in Eiríks saga rauða. During a time of famine she was invited to the farm of Þorkell in Herjólfsnes in Greenland. We hear that she was elaborately dressed in a blue or black cloak decorated with stones, that she wore a necklace of glass beads, a hood of black lambskin lined with white catskin, a belt from which a pouch with her charms hung, calfskin shoes and gloves with white catskin. But the main attribute that signalised her position as a seeress was the staff of sorcery in her hand: „Staf hafði hún í hendi og var á hnappur. Hann var búinn messingu og settur steinum ofan um hnappinn" (Eiríks saga rauða ch. 4). The description of her rich clothes, her amulets and her staff are verified in numerous graves that have been excavated in Scandinavia of what are interpreted as burials of powerful and revered seiðkonur, for example in Fyrkat and Oseberg (Price 2004, 117; Price 2008, 245).

Runes

It is mentioned in numerous papers, poems and books that 'runes' may have been used by the seiðkona or võlva or by others depending on how you read some of the stories. It's unclear if these were carved on stones or rocks, but there is mention of some seiðkona/võlva(s) 'casting lots' so what those looked like is up to speculation. If you want to use them, find a set that works for you and pick up a quick guidebook to give you an overview. Some heathens see runes as literal translations of the meanings, so if you lets say, toss runes and get Fehu, some readers would interpret this as wealth and some readers who focus on the more non literal translation may say it means you are to gain something (physical, emotional) because wealth may not mean literally money.

One important note. On facepainting. There is no evidence anyone in the Viking age painted thier faces for any reason, if you want to do it, thats fine but please be aware and sensative to not copying the same marks that belong to indigenos people, particularly chin marks. Ashing the face, marking it is normal for heathens to but its best practice to go for more abstract looks.

THE WILD HUNT

SHEAL

Hunting deities, whose role acknowledges the economic importance of animals and the ritual of the hunt, highlight a different relationship to nature. The animal elements in half-human, antlered deities suggest that the forest and its denizens possessed a numinous quality as well as an economic value. Hunter-gods were venerated among the Continental Celts, and they often seem to have had an ambivalent role as protector both hunter and the prey, not unlike the functions of Diana and Artemis in classical mythology.

From Gaul, the armed deer-hunter depicted on an image from the temple of Le Donon in the Vosges lays his hands in benediction on the antlers of his stag companion. The hunter-god from Le Touget in Gers carries a hare tenderly in his arms. Arawn of Welsh mythology may represent the remnants of a similar hunter-god of the forests of Dyfed. Additionally, in Welsh mythology the hunting of a sacred stag often leads the hunters into the otherworld.

As with many traditional societies, the hunt was probably hedged about with prohibitions and rituals. The Greek author Arrian, writing in the 2nd century CE, said that "the Celts never went hunting without the gods blessing and that they made payment of domestic animals to the supernatural powers in reparation for their theft of wild creatures from the landscape". Hunting itself may have been perceived as a symbolic, as well as practical, activity in which the spilling of blood led not only to the death of the beast but also to the earth's nourishment and replenishment.

The Story of the Wild Hunt

As Told by Sheal Mullin-Berube (excerpt from Facebook post)

The story begins back in ancient Ireland where the old Irish Gods, the Fomorians, were subdued by the Tuatha Dé Danann or the Shining Ones. The Fomorians are often described as misshapen or grotesque and represent powers of violence, destruction, and chaos. While the Tuatha Dé Danann banished them from the mainland of Ireland at the battle of Mag Tuired, they were never destroyed.

In fact, we may see some of their influence in the division and divisiveness of our time. The Wild Hunt is a ceremony that is traditionally performed in November; however, can be performed in December on Solstice, that has multiple elements, one of which is to balance the dark forces with light. This tradition is not confined to Ireland, with versions practiced in Europe from Nordic lands to Ireland with records of practice in Italy at the time of the inquisition. The ceremony is traditionally focused on beating back the powers of darkness and the hunger of Winter. It also focuses on four other main points:

- Dancing with the Fairy folk as they move from their summer to winter homes.
- Helping the Dead through the practice of shamanic psychopomp, moving lost souls from the middle world to the light.
- Balancing the World, a warriors' action; encountering forces of darkness, like the divisiveness rising in our society, and infusing it with light.
- Bringing Light to the world by extending Divine power into the world.

FAMILIARS

SHEAL

Were they familiars or were they really abandoned child adoption? Familiars; are they a pseudonym for adoption or fostering abandoned children?

" A. P. Elkin studied the belief in familiar spirits among the Australian Aborigines: A usual method, or explanation, is that the medicine man sends his familiar spirit (his assistant totem, spirit-dog, spirit-child or whatever the form may be) to gather the information. While this is occurring, the man himself is in a state of receptivity, in sleep or trance. In modern phraseology [spirit-ism], his familiar spirit would be the control [control spirit]."

1579 woodcut
A witch feeding her toad familiars

In European folklore of the medieval and early modern periods, familiars were believed to be supernatural entities that would assist witches and cunning folk in their practice of magic. According to records of the time, those alleging to have had contact with familiar spirits reported that they could manifest as numerous forms, usually as an animal, but sometimes as a human or humanoid figure, and were described as "clearly defined, three-dimensional forms, vivid with color and animated with movement and sound", as opposed to descriptions of ghosts with their "smoky, undefined form[s]".

When they served witches, they were often thought to be malevolent, but when working for cunning folk they were often considered benevolent. The former was often categorized as demons, while the latter were more commonly thought of and described as fairies. The main purpose of familiars was to serve the witch or young witch, providing protection for them as they came into their new powers.

The practice of familiars is thought to be a form of adoption and quite possibly a form of adoption involving indentured servitude. This brings me to my theory that familiars may not have been as animalistic in nature as the accounts of witch familiars are made out to be but rather that witches were adopting the abandoned children of their time as their possible human child familiars. When witches and cunning-folk described their familiar spirits, there were always commonly unifying features. The historian Emma Wilby noted how the accounts of such familiars were striking for their "ordinariness" and "naturalism", even though they were dealing with supernatural entities.

Familiar spirits were most commonly small animals, such as cats, rats, dogs, ferrets, birds, frogs, toads, and hares. There were also cases of wasps and butterflies, as well as pigs, sheep, and horses. Familiar spirits were usually kept in pots or baskets lined with sheep's wool and fed a variety of things including, milk, bread, meat, and blood. Familiar spirits usually had names and "were often given down-to-earth, and frequently affectionate, nicknames."

One example of this was Tom Reid, who was the familiar of the cunning-woman and accused witch Bessie Dunlop, while other examples included Grizell and Gridigut, who were the familiars of 17th-century Huntingdonshire witch Jane Wallis. The description of a witches familiar, that of a small creature such as a cat or dog that could take on a shape shifting human form of substance leads me to believe that the accounts of a witch's familiar could be an embellishment to explain away child adoption or child slavery in the form of indentured servitude. That it was the abandoned children of their societies that they were informally adopting rather than leaving them to their devices to succumb to the elements or to starve to death.

The fact that they even gave them affectionate nicknames is akin to behaving in a manner as if toward a child rather than an animal. To treat the animal as if it were their child even hints at the theory that familiars may have been adopted or fostered abandoned children rather than animals. It is even spoken about in the legend of Taliesin and how he became the legendary poet and bard, although he was transformed into a seed of grain rather than an animal and he was Cerridwen's adopted apprentice first before becoming her adopted baby Gwion. According to the Hanes Taliesin, he was originally known as Gwion Bach ap Gwreang.

He was a servant of Cerridwen and was made to stir the Cauldron of Inspiration for one year to allow for Cerridwen to complete her potion of inspiration. The potion was initially intended for her son, Morfran, who although was considered frightfully ugly, she loved nonetheless, and felt that if he would not grow in beauty then he should have the gift of the Awen to compensate. Upon completion of this potion, three drops sprang out and landed upon Gwion Bach's thumb. Gwion then placed his thumb in his mouth to soothe his burns resulting in Gwion's enlightenment.

Out of fear of what Cerridwen would do to him, Gwion fled and eventually transformed into a piece of grain before being consumed by Cerridwen. However, this resulted in Cerridwen becoming impregnated with the seed and upon giving birth, she could not bring herself to kill the baby Gwion. She instead cast him into the ocean in a large leather bag, where he was found by his adoptive father Elffin, who named him Taliesin [meaning 'Radiant Brow'].

According to the above story of Taliesin, he was twice adopted. One by the goddess Cerridwen in a form of divine pregnancy and the second by Elffin who found him cast in the ocean. The legend speaks to both adoption for succession and adoption as familiaris (sic a familiar to the king). It also speaks to the fact that Cerridwen's familiar, Gwion Back ap Gwreang, was her indentured servant who helped her practice the art of witchcraft.

Another more familiar story of a witch's familiars or seeking of an apprenticeship is Hansel and Gretel from the Grimm Brothers. In one passage you have the parents looking to abandon their children due to poverty and the inability to harbor and care for their two children. The wife tells the husband they will bring the children to the forest and leave them there.

> "I will tell you what, husband," answered the wife; "we will take the children early in the morning into the forest, where it is thickest; we will make them a fire, and we will give each of them a piece of bread, then we will go to our work and leave them alone; they will never find the way home again, and we shall be quit of them."

> "So, Hansel and Grethel sat by the fire, and at noon they each ate their pieces of bread. They thought their father was in the wood all the time, as they seemed to hear the strokes of the axe: but really it was only a dry branch hanging to a withered tree that the wind moved to and fro. So, when they had stayed there a long time their eyelids closed with weariness, and they fell fast asleep."

This is the key component of my theory that familiars may have been a metaphor for adoption or fostering of abandoned children. In another passage we see the witch takes the children in and feeds them.

"Then the door opened, and an aged woman came out, leaning upon a crutch. Hansel and Grethel felt very frightened and let fall what they had in their hands. The old woman, however, nodded her head, and said, "Ah, my dear children, how come you here? You must come indoors and stay with me, you will be no trouble." So, she took them each by the hand, and led them into her little house. And there they found a good meal laid out, of milk and pancakes, with sugar, apples, and nuts. After that she showed them two little white beds, and Hansel and Grethel laid themselves down on them, and thought they were in heaven."

In the next passage we see the woman, an old hag described as a wicked witch capture Hansel and trap him in a cage while forcing Gretel to become her indentured servant. This supports my theory that some fosters or adoptees would have been slaves or indentured servants rather than apprentices.

"Then she went back to Grethel and shook her, crying, "Get up, lazy bones; fetch water, and cook something nice for your brother; he is outside in the stable, and must be fattened up. And when he is fat enough, I will eat him." Grethel began to weep bitterly, but it was of no use, she had to do what the wicked witch bade her. And so, the best kind of victuals was cooked for poor Hansel, while Grethel got nothing but crab-shells.

... "Now then, Grethel," cried she to the little girl; "be quick and draw water; be Hansel fat or be he lean, tomorrow I must kill and cook him." Oh, what a grief for the poor little sister to have to fetch water..."

Then we see the old woman refer to Gretel as a "stupid goose" in the story when she tries to trick her into entering the baking oven to check the fires. This is where there might be reference to an animalistic representation of Gretel as the witch's animal familiar rather than the child that she is.

"But Grethel perceived her intention, and said, "I don't know how to do it: how shall I get in?"

"Stupid goose," said the old woman, "the opening is big enough, do you see? I could get in myself!"

By the end of the story, the witch is vanquished, and Gretel comes to rescue her brother. When she does this she is quoted as saying;

"Duck, duck, here we stand, Hansel and Grethel, on the land, Stepping-stones and bridge we lack, Carry us over on your nice white back."

This is very similar to a ritualistic summoning of an actual animal familiar, a duck, to come take them away from the awful place to escape to freedom. She likely learned this summoning from the witch as a forced adopted apprentice or indentured servant. If you notice, if was not Gretel that the witch imprisoned but made to serve her, the female of the two children. While the male of the two children was made to be a feed animal to fatten up and eat later.

This may be in reference to the fact that most witch covens are primarily female. It could also be theorized that witches eating children may be a metaphor for them adopting or fostering the children within their own households as makeshift apprentices or indentured servants. The eating of someone's being or soul could be likened to the transformation of the person into something else, or someone else.

Much like Taliesin was when he was eaten as a grain of rice and then transformed through Cerridwen becoming impregnated and changing him from one being into a perceived omnipotent god-like being of legends. We also have a few other sources that show that the practice of fostering, and adoption were not unknown to most communities including the Celtic ones, as well as practitioners of magic.

For example, in the paper called Blood of my Blood, Incest, Parricide and Family Strifes in Ynglinga [Saga Jules Piet 2016] it is said;

"There are six women a man has the right to kill for. One is a man's wife, two a man's daughter, three a man's mother, four is his sister, five is the foster daughter a man has brought up, six is the foster-mother who brought a man up..."

We see it in Icelandic history as well. In the book The Witch Figure, Folklore Essays it is stated that:

"...The old Icelandic foster mothers are conventional rather than realistic figures; the normal practice was to foster a child at the home of a neighbor or friend in an ordinary family setting. There is, moreover, a very close parallel between the stories of the supernatural foster mothers and the spiritual marriages of shamans in such Siberian tribes as the Goldi, the Buryat and the Yakut. These 'wives' may be represented as the daughters of a powerful male spirit, like some of the giantesses of Norse tradition; they help the shaman during his life, doing battle for him in animal form, and again like the giantesses and Valkyries they can change their aspect, varying from that of a beautiful girl to a hideous hag or threatening monster."

[The Witch Figure, Folklore Essays London, 2004]

So it is clear that fostering and to a lesser extent, adoption is a functional practice surrounded by both the idea of familiars, creating kinship and perhaps even a pliable in youth indentured servant who grows up in the house hold of the witch who is taught the inner workings of the house hold by the witch within. This, of course is only a working theory and there is very little to no literature to reference on my theory. I also theorize that this may be the true origin of the saying "taking in a stray" as well, considering that the familiar was described as small animals in the more known popular literature at hand.

ANIMAL FAMILIARS: THE CELTIC CAT SÍTH

In a more traditional description of the familiar we have the Irish cat sí which is a fairy creature from Celtic mythology, said to resemble a large black cat with a white spot on its chest. The cat-sìth is the Scottish version of the cat sí. Legend has it that the spectral cat haunts the Scottish Highlands. The legends surrounding this creature are more common in Scottish folklore, but a few occur in Irish. Some common folklore suggested that the cat-sìth was not a fairy, but a witch that could transform into a cat nine times.

The cat-sìth may have been inspired by the Scottish wildcat itself. It is possible that the legends of the cat-sìth were inspired by the Kellas cats, which are a distinctive hybrid between Scottish wildcats and domestic cats found only in Scotland. The Scottish wildcat is a population of the European wildcat, which is absent from elsewhere in the British Isles.

"The Kellas cat is a large black cat found in Scotland. It is an inter specific hybrid between the Scottish wildcat (Felis silvestris silvestris syn. Felis silvestris grampia) and the domestic cat (Felis catus). Once thought to be a mythological wild cat, with its few sightings dismissed as hoaxes, a specimen was killed in a snare by a gamekeeper in 1984 and found to be a hybrid between the Scottish wildcat and domestic cat.

It is not a formal cat breed, but a landrace of felid hybrids.

It is named after the village of Kellas, Moray, where it was first found.

Illustration of the Kellas Cat, Public Domain, Artist Unknow

The purported first live cat was caught by the Tomorrows World team and featured in the 1986 programme 'On the Trail of the Big Cat'. The historian Charles Thomas speculated that the Pictish stone at Golspie may depict a Kellas cat. The Golspie stone, now held at the Dunrobin Castle Museum, shows a cat-like creature standing on top of a salmon which may allude to the characteristics ascribed to a Kellas cat of catching fish while swimming in the river.

The Kellas cat is described as 24 to 36 inches (61 to 91 cm) long, with powerful and long hind legs and a tail that can grow to be around 12 inches (30 cm) long; its weight ranges from 5 to 15 pounds (2.3 to 6.8 kg. The animal snared in 1984 was 15 inches (38 cm) to shoulder height and 43 inches (110 cm) in length. A specimen is kept in a museum in Elgin.

The Zoology Museum of the University of Aberdeen also holds a mounted specimen that was found during 2002 in the Insch area of Aberdeenshire.- Wikipedia The demonic cat-sìth called Big Ears could be summoned (Gaelic name taghairm) to appear and grant any wish to those who took part in the ceremony. The ceremony required practitioners to burn the bodies of cats over the course of four days and nights.

Yet still, some believe that the cat-sìth was a witch that could transform voluntarily into its cat form and back nine times. If one of these witches chose to go back into their cat form for the ninth time, they would remain a cat for the rest of their lives. It is believed by some that this is how the idea of a cat having nine lives originated.

The cat-sìth is all black except for a white spot on its chest. It is described as large as a dog and chooses to display itself with its back arched and bristles erect.

Cat Sìth as the Soul Stealer

The people of the Scottish Highlands did not trust the cat-sìth. They believed that it could steal a person's soul, before it was claimed by the gods, by passing over a corpse before burial; therefore, watches called the Fèill Fhadalach (Late Wake) were performed night and day to keep the cat-sìth away from a corpse before burial. Methods of "distraction" such as games of leaping and wrestling, catnip, riddles, and music would be employed to keep the cat-sìth away from the room in which the corpse lay. In addition, there were no fires where the body lay, as it was said that the cat-sìth was attracted to the warmth.

On Samhain, it was believed that a cat-sìth would bless any house that left a saucer of milk out for it to drink and those houses that did not put out a saucer of milk would be cursed into having all their cows' udders go dry.

SHAPE SHIFTING & ANIMAL WEARING

LARISA

Much of the information on 'witchcraft' from the Nordic side is mixed up in various practices. There is no real concept of a familiar, however there is concepts that some women could 'control' animals. I am unsure if this was the same as how its seen in witchcraft. There are some concepts that gods, giants and other can 'appear' in animal form, but none on the concept that they could do things for you.

On the topic of magic, there is not much other that what I mentioned earlier in terms of them practicing all kinds of magic from good to bad an everything in between. There is a new interest in Trolldom but this seems to be similar to quackery in that a lot of it stems from old wives tales type practices, herbal knowledge etc and does not really seem to be specifically witchcraft, although I supposed you could say it is similar. We plan on diving into magic in a third book of this series.

The concept of familiars is not mentioned, however shapeshifting is. " the hamr is most-often described as a physical garment that can be worn and removed and which in and of itself can be a cause for transformation. A good example of the physicality of the hamr can be found in the prose introduction of the Eddic poem Vǫlundarkviða in which human-looking women are in possession of swan-pelts (álptarhamir) and later leave the narrative's protagonists by flying in the air (Vǫlundarkviða, 2014: 428).4" [Shapeshifting in Old Norse-Icelandic Literature Perabo. L]

Its unclear if this was a literal changing of the person into an animal and more metaphorical or 'changing' the person into a different mental state. There are examples of gods and men changing into a mythiical hero by either doning a 'cloak', transforming into an animal, consuming the parts of an animal in order to gain it's power, transforming gender, acquiring magical powers and the like.

"Tales of supernatural transformations that clearly imitate older indigenous Norse tales as well as new, innovative narrative elements that feature variations on the theme of transforming into various creatures". The gods were not the only ones able to transform. Queen Gunnhildr could apparetnly transform into a bird, in the Völsunga sagats mentioned that two characters can transform into wolves. There is even a story of a dwarf that transformed into a dragon.

The concepts are more or less that one could 'beome' these things by either physically wearing a garment that represented an animal (wearing skins) or mentally putting yourself in the mindset of the animal. In the paper Shapeshifting in Old Norse-Icelandic Literature by Lyonel Perabom the author states, "one could possibly bring up the fact that indigenous mythic-heroical and far-northern narratives might have been based (at least in part) in either actual practices or beliefs most-likely stemming from a pagan worldview and the exercise of magic.

As such, even if such stories of the pagan past (or the pagan other when confronting Sámi sorcery) might have been compiled and transmitted in Medieval Scandinavia to an extent, 13th and 14th-century Christian authors might have been unwilling to present supernatural metamorphoses (and magic in general) in a positive light or as practices honorable heroes could dabble in. This might explain why, in so many romance-inspired sagas, while the hero himself almost never make use of magic (besides, obtaining, at times, some inconspicuous magical items), he is often endowed with a supernatural helper (often a dwarf or a troll) that suffers no such restrictions: Changing one's physical appearance or shape is not necessarily seen as a nefarious per se, but as more rightly belonging to far-away lands and eras, together with the vast array of semi-human pagan monsters associated with such spheres, and not to the gentle hero readers are to identify with."

OTHER MAGIC

SHEAL

THE 'DARKER' KIND

There is no such thing as evil and good magic, and there is no three-fold rule that I subscribe to myself. 'Dark' magic does have its purposes when used in the correct manner. If your intent is malicious there is as many consequences for it as there is if your intent is kind. A lot of Neo-Pagan circles believe in the karmic three-fold back at you rule where what you put out comes back to you three-fold. If you believe in such a rule, that is your predilection, I will never judge another for what they believe in.

It is my stance that everything does have consequences or an opposite and equal reaction to an action, and sometimes karma needs a little push in the right direction. Although, I do believe in ethical and moral practice. What you would not do to someone to their face, don't do behind their back. Respect, ethical practice, and that which is not of your personal moral code should be something you don't condone, even from yourself.

MALEDICTIONS & CURSES

A curse or malediction is a spell that is performed with 'mal-intent'. These kinds of spells are generally performed to cause misery, pain, strife, and/or destruction upon a target. Most are generally just to make someone uncomfortable or to "steer karma in the right direction".

Basic Terminology:
Baneful - causing destruction or serious damage.
Curse - a spell performed with mal-intent.
Hex - used interchangeably with "curse" or "jinx".
Jinx - said to be a lesser form of baneful magic; also used interchangeably with "curse" and "hex".
Mal-intent - "bad" or negative intent.
Target - the person on which you are performing the spell.
Taglock - a personal item belonging to or describing the target (their name written on paper, a poppet designed to represent them, etc.)

Basic "Rules":
- Exhaust all mundane methods of resolving an issue before resorting to cursing.
- Educate yourself on various methods of protection before even thinking about casting a curse.
- Know what you're doing. Research, plan, and set your intentions straight in your mind to prevent any kind of backlash from the curse. This means, be specific. Be sure that your curse is aimed at your target/s, and no one else, including yourself.
- Methods of cursing can include the construction of poppets, jar spells, sachets, effigies, sigil, or pretty much any other type of spell you can come up with.

Disappointments Jars & Crossroads

A disappointments jar is something of a personal creation. It runs along the same lines as maledictions and curses but with a twist. The idea is to take a mason jar, fill it with nauseous substances (herbs that cause bad dreams, irritations, strife for example), adding your intent on paper toward the intended person.

Then adding something of theirs and yours, an old promise ring, a friendship bracelet, gifts from them to you. You seal the jar with wax and bind the jar with twine or string of choice and bury it in the ground. If you wish to cause indecision and difficulties with the direction of their lives, you bury it at a crossroads.

Bindings & Cord Cuttings

Bindings are the most common spell or intent performed. As well as cord cuttings. Bindings can be for protection purposes or for, as with Anamchara, binding two people together. Cord cuttings are used to separate two people from each other and typically are used at the ending of a friendship or relationship that was particularly toxic and a person wants to completely remove themselves from the other person spiritually, emotionally, and psychologically.

Binding Spell/Intention Work

What is needed:
Piece of paper
Pen
Name of person
Twine

What to do: Write person's name on paper, fold paper. With intent of binding either the person or specific behavior of the person, tie the twine around the paper with their name on it. Either bury it or put it in a Ziplock bag with water and toss it in the freezer.

Cord Cutting Spell/Intention Work

What is needed:
Cord, twine, or string
Sharp object to etch names on candles
2 Candles, either black or white or combination
Lighter/matches

What to do:
  ⸙   Etch each candle with each person's name with the intentions you wish to work with.
  ⸙   Loop the twine, string, or cord around each candle near the wicks.
  ⸙   Light both candles and let them burn down to the cord, allow the flame to burn the cord until it separates from itself, releasing each candle from the cord.
  ⸙   You can either allow each candle to burn down completely or put them out and bury them.

MALEDICTION BOXES: THE PUNISHMENT BOX

This intent work or spell work is another personal one. It is meant to "punish" someone for bad behaviors. Especially if those behaviors had a rather harmful effect on the person making the punishment box.

What is needed:
- Paper and pen
- Twine
- An item you care for and must give up to the punishment box
- Personal epitaphs of your spiritual practice (symbols, bind runes, ogham, etc.)
- Something of theirs but is not necessary
- A small box to hold everything together

What to do:

On the paper write the intended person's name you are intent on punishing. Bind that paper with the twine as you would in a binding spell or intent work. Place it in the box. Place your other items in the box with your intents in mind. To take something, you must first give something so remember to place an item you care for and are fully willing to give up for the spell work. Close the box, place under your altar as a symbol of that person being "beneath you". As discussed in the blood magic chapter, you may add blood magic to any intent work or spell work as a bolster to your spells and intents.

THE PHYSICAL PRACTICE [CELTIC]

SHEAL MULLIN-BERUBE

THE HISTORY, THE PERSON, THE MAGIC, AND THE TOOLS COME TOGETHER

THE CIRCLE, THE ALTAR & THE RITUALS

Your altar is as unique as you are. There is no right way or wrong way to setup, cleanup or tear down an altar. The circle and rituals are also as unique as you are. If your instinct guides you to do something differently then follow your instincts. The following are merely suggestions to get you started.

Altar Set Up

From House of Intuition

1. Get a table
Find a sturdy table that doesn't wobble, something with a solid surface that is not too big and not too small. It should be dedicated solely for the practice of magic, so make sure to never use the table for anything else. If you're re-appropriating some furniture for this purpose, just cleanse it with sage, incense, or holy water. Many witches insist on having a sacred cloth to cover the altar, so you may want to get a fabric that suits you. It can be monochrome or patterned. Make sure to cleanse whatever you choose before draping it across your table.

2. Choose your theme
Next, decide the theme of your altar. You have many options here. Most people center their altars around their chosen deity, patron saint or guardian angel. Obtain an image or statue to use as the centerpiece of your altar. The Buddha, Ganesha and the many Catholic saints and Yoruba Orisha are all popular choices. And if you're making an altar for a loved one who is sick or has passed on, you can use their picture.

3. Obtain the Four Elements

Acquire four items representing the four elements: Fire, Water, Air and Earth. For Fire, you can use incense, a candle or tea-light. For Water, you can use a bowl or glass of water.

For added oomph, use holy water or water gathered from sacred rivers or lakes. For Air, you can use a feather and for Earth, try crystals, stones, or sand.

4. Align to the Four Directions

Align your four elemental totems with the four directions. You can use your intuition or adopt a traditional method but know that there is no official right or wrong way to align the elements with the directions. A common alignment is to place Fire in the East for the rising sun, Water in the South, Earth in the West, and Air in the North. Find a system that's meaningful to you.

5. Consecrate sacred tools

Now gather your sacred tools. Practitioners in the Western Magical Traditions will need a ritual cup or goblet; a consecrated sword, knife, or blade of some kind; a plate or shield, usually inscribed with a pentagram symbolizing Earth; and a wand, staff, or stick. All these tools should be cleansed before use. Additional tools include a cauldron, bowls, mortar & pestle, lamp/lantern, candles, incense, sage & feather.

6. Place your Book of Shadows

Lastly, you'll want to reserve a space for your Book of Shadows. Any serious practitioner will keep a book of records documenting their magical workings to keep track of their successes and setbacks. Keep this sacred book on your altar to amplify its power and the altars.

Altar Tear Down

How to Cleanse Your Altar

This is my way of cleansing and charging my altar, so feel free to change it and tailor it to your needs and preferences. I use a combination of smoke and water.

What You'll Need:
1. Smudge bundle or incense
2. Lighter
3. Abalone shell or fireproof container OR incense holder
4. Clean rag
5. Lemon juice OR cleaner of choice

What To Do:
First, take everything off your altar and set it to the side. Next, take your rag and lemon juice/holy water/pledge (cleaning agent) and wipe down your altar in a counter clockwise fashion. The entire time you're visualizing and/or saying out loud that you're cleansing negative energies from your altar and making it as a clean slate for divine energy. Take your rag and clean all your tools/supplies that will be going back onto your altar.

Continually visualizing and stating your intentions. Next, light your incense or smudge bundle and gently blow smoke onto the top of your altar and all around it. The smoke serves to further cleanse your altar of unwanted energies. Visualize the smoke blowing away all negativities. Do the same to your tools and altar supplies (smudge or blow incense smoke to cleanse).

THE CIRCLE: CALLING & DISMISSING OF THE AIRT'S

THE CARDINAL POINTS AND ELEMENTALS

Please know that you can make substitutes to any of the materials used in the following rituals.

OPENING THE CIRCLE

We open the circle by calling on the Airts. What are the Airts? They are the Four Directions, the four elements of creation. When we do ritual work, we call upon the Airts to invite their blessings of our work and to strengthen both us and our ritual work. You always start facing the cardinal direction of the East. East represents the element of air.

The winds of change and time. The air that escapes from the mother's lips when she kisses the foreheads of her children. The breeze that cools our cheeks in the hot summer sun. The next cardinal direction you turn to is South. The South represents the element of fire. The burning fire of change and renewal.

It is the force and power of destruction, the burning ember of knowing. The glow of life after death. After that, you face West. The West represents water. The ocean, our great mother of all things living for we came from the depths of her womb, crawled upon the Earth, and grew from there.

She feeds life. Without water, life cannot sustain itself. Last, but certainly not least. You will face North. The North represents the element of Earth. Earth, the mother of sustenance and provider of food. From the pebble on a riverbank to the granite boulders that form fortresses of protection.

CALLING OF THE AIRTS

East (Air): Greetings, oh Guardians of the Watchtowers of the East, the elemental power of air. We call upon the roaring winds, the hurricanes, tornadoes, and typhoons; we call upon the puff of air from a mother's lips as she kisses her child, the breeze that caresses our cheeks, the spiraling swirl of steam from a hot drink. We ask that you witness this rite and guard this circle. Bless us with your presence, Life-sustaining air!

South (Fire): Greetings, oh Guardians of the Watchtowers of the South, the elemental power of fire. We call upon the shooting flames, the embers, the gentle flicker of candlelight; we call upon the campfire glow and the forest fires' raging holocaust. We ask that you witness this rite and guard this circle. Bless us with your presence, Life-enhancing fire!

West (Water): Greetings, oh Guardians of the Watchtowers of the West, the elemental power of water. We call upon the Ocean, Mother of us all; we call upon the rain that falls from the skies, we call upon the rivers and seas, the dew drops and the mists. We ask that you witness this rite and guard this circle. Bless us with your presence, Life-giving water!

North (Earth): Greetings, oh Guardians of the Watchtowers of the North, the elemental power of the earth. We call upon the granite boulders, the loam of farmer's fields, the gritty sand of beach shores; we call upon the molten lava beneath our feet, and the pebble on a riverbank. We ask that you witness this rite and guard this circle. Bless us with your presence, Life-supporting earth!

Honoring the Three Worlds

Spirits of the high skies that guide us to stretch and grow; gentle lord of the sun, distant stars, ancestral light; cloud folk who paint such art above us; breath of life, soft breeze and chasing winds; feathered folk who know the dance of freedom upon the wing.

Spirits of the dark earth that holds and feeds us; mud of our lands, rich and fertile soil into which we so deeply root; rocks and stones, gems of the earth, you who give us stability underfoot; trees and plants, creatures four-footed and two.

Spirits of the open seas that wash and shape the shores of these lands; meandering rivers, guiding our direction, birthing springs of new life, deep still pools holding us upon our journey; you of the tidal waters, emerging and receding, blood and rain, swimming, diving.

Spirits of this place, the power of nature, who you offer us the breath of life, the fire of passion, the sweet taste of love, the ground upon which we walk, know that you are honored here. Let us feel your presence, let us share the Awen.

Honoring your Ancestors

I call in peace to the ancestors of these sacred lands, you whose feet have walked the fields and forests, the valleys, and hills, those whose hands have worked the earth and touched the waters of the seas, you whose stories lie in the mud and sing in the wind, whose breath we now breathe. I call to you that we may feel your presence here, that you may know you are honored here.

I call in peace to the ancestors of our spiritual heritage, teachers of old who guide us now, whose wisdom whispers in our hearts and minds. I call to you that we may hear your wisdom here, that you may know you are honored here.

I call in peace to the ancestors of our blood, those to whom we are joined through birth and death, heart to heart, womb to womb, whose love and tears, strength, and weaknesses, remain as stories in our bones. I call to you that we may accept the gifts you bring, that you may know you are honored here.

I call in peace to the ancestors of [your family name], those of the bloodline that have lost this their companion. Gathering as the hidden company on this sacred day, joining those who have come to say farewell, guiding the soul of [your family name] and honoring their life, know that you are welcome here in peace.

Those who would join us in peace, be with us within our Circle, consecrated and blessed with beauty and wakefulness. May this rite be blessed by your presence. May we have ears for those who have gone before.

Hail ancestors, hail, and welcome!

Closing the Circle

Before you can leave your sacred space, you must close the Circle by dismissing the Airts. The officiant will do this by using the following below to close the circle and release both your gathered coven, friends and/or family, yourself, and the Airts.

Dismissing the Airts

EAST (Air): Hail to thee, Guardians of the Watchtowers of the East, the powers of the air. We thank you for joining our celebration today. As ye depart to your mighty realms, we bid thee Hail and Farewell, and harm ye none on your way. So, it will be.

SOUTH (Fire): Hail to thee, Guardians of the Watchtowers of the South, the powers of fire. We thank you for joining our celebration today. As ye depart to your mighty realms, we bid thee Hail and Farewell, and harm ye none on your way. So, it will be.

WEST (Water): Hail to thee, Guardians of the Watchtowers of the West, the powers of water. We thank you for joining our celebration today. As ye depart to your mighty realms, we bid thee Hail and Farewell, and harm ye none on your way. So, it will be.

NORTH (Earth): Hail to thee, Guardians of the Watchtowers of the North, the powers of the earth. We thank you for joining our celebration today. As ye depart to your mighty realms, we bid thee Hail and Farewell, and harm ye none on your way. So, it will be.

HEATHEN RITES & BASICS

LARISA

How exactly does a heathen worship? What do we give honour and thanks for? In order to know this, we first need to understand what worship and veneration mean. The act of veneration means "to regard or treat with reverence; revere. From the Latin "venerates", past participle of venerārī to solicit the goodwill of (a God), worship, revere" (Dictionary.com, venerate). In heathenry veneration represents any act in which the Gods are treated with reverence or respect.

This concept could stretch beyond just ritual service and offering, extending to activities such as rune readings, or even giving donations to charities that have associations to a particular God (such as donations to cat rescues for Freyja or marsh land preservation funds for Frigga). It may also include acts involving service oathed to a God. Sometimes people promise to do particular acts like write for a year or work for a charity as a service to the Gods. There are a number of ways for one to revere and honour the Gods. Sometimes a little creativity or finding new ways to do this outside of ritual is all you need to succeed.

When we give an offering to the Gods we're also venerating them. That is we are giving them our honour and respect. Offerings can be physical gifts such as: food, liquid libations in the form of mead; handmade items crafted for the Gods such as wooden carvings, metal work or food offerings such as honey cakes, porridge or other food products.

You can also oath and profess to the Gods as a veneration, however, the ones we'll focus on in this chapter are those that are typically given within acts of worship. The term worship signifies any act in which a person is acting out a form of spiritual devotion. For example, leaving food or drink out for Odin would be a form of worship. The word worship can be defined as: "to render religious reverence and homage, as to a deity" (Dictionary.com Unabridged, n.d.). It is the gesture by which we pay honour to the Gods, the physical act by which we choose to display this honour. Other forms of worship include writing poems or stories for the Gods, praying to them, or meditating.

Veneration, offerings, and worship are important to heathens regardless of what path they follow. These actions provide a way for us to connect to our Gods. By seeing the Gods as holy beings from which we seek out spiritual 'communion' we show them respect. We would not give things to a being for whom we held no reverence or respect. For example, we would not leave out an offering for a slug unless we saw that slug as important. It would be meaningless to leave out offerings without some level of 'importance' being placed on it it. It also tells them that we want to know them and hope that they'll want to know us as well.

I believe that most heathens enjoy rituals, even those who do not necessarily believe that the Gods are real. For me, ritual is the physical expression of the relationship and understanding one has with their spiritual connection. While ritual is almost a separate entity in itself, it is hard to have a chapter on connecting with the Gods without mentioning ritual. Veneration, offerings, and worship work together like this: In heathenism, the drinking horn being shared by the community and then offered is considered a divine act. The horn holds the community's luck, words, and wishes.

The usage of the drinking horn likely became a staple in heathenry because they are mentioned in various sources as being used in ceremony. However there is a secondary reason that the drinking horn is considered appropriate. "It's an incredibly important practice because the Drinking Horn is seen as a sacred vessel. It not only holds the drink for the toast but it is the vibration of your words upon the surface of the liquid that carries your words through all the 9 Worlds" (Dark 2012).

As the words and their power are contained within the horn when it is poured out onto the land, we gift the Gods with our own energy. In this chapter, I'll mention several key parts to rituals that are also acts of veneration. Any act of veneration, whether incorporated into a rite or done separately, is important. These acts show that our devotion to the Gods is a deeper, more heartfelt connection than just the words that are spoken.

All forms of veneration work together to form the 'act' of ritual. This is the moment where all things come together, fusing life and spirituality into one form. Suddenly the mundane slips away and there you are at the foot of the rainbow bridge with the Gods smiling upon you. There are many ways one can venerate, pay tribute, honour, revere, respect and worship. Below are a few of these forms to get you going. Use your creativity to uncover many more ways!

Veneration in Ritual

Heathens have many rituals that support their love for the Gods. The blot, Sumbel, and our rites of passage are the three most common ways we show respect to the Gods. While the rituals described in this section are the most common forms, they are not exclusive to Ásatrú. Many heathens follow these formats.

The consumption of the slaughtered animal would basically be the same as an act of communion as seen in Myth and Religion of the North in which E.O.G Turville-Petre states "that when the flesh of the boar was consumed at the sacrificial banquet, those who partook of it felt that they were consuming the God himself and absorbing his power" (Turville-Petre 1964) ,In blots done today, we offer up liquids like mead, food, hand-made or crafted item, or (on rare occasions) blood. When food is offered it can be either raw or cooked.

WHY SACRIFICE?

We call these offerings "sacrifices" because they are normally items that took effort to create, purchase, or procure. These things are not small but usually given freely by people to the Gods out of respect, love, and reverence. Sometimes offerings are given in order to petition a God or Goddess for help. Sometimes enticing them with things they like provides not only the sense of gifting, which is very important to heathens but also shows the God or Goddess how much thought you put into your request.

The word 'sacrifice' means: "the offering of animal, plant, or human life or of some material possession to a deity, as in propitiation or homage, the person, animal, or thing so offered, the surrender or destruction of something prized or desirable for the sake of something considered as having a higher or more pressing claim" (Dictionary. com Unabridged). In Ásatrú the word 'blot' relates to the concepts of blood being sprinkled onto those gathered for the blot itself. People sacrifice for many purposes: love, respect, reverence, communion, to give thanks, and to increase a community's wyrd/luck.

THE BLOT

Every heathen practices a blot differently, so what goes on in each blot differs. But mostly the following steps are included:

1. Opening the space. Either done with Thors hammer, staff, or just libation. Generally you walk around creating a 'ring' of space, imagining the space becoming 'safe' and sacred.

2. Calling a god/goddess. This is where you can use any poem, written piece or just some general statement to ask one of the gods or more than one, to come into the space. I would say that heathenry has one distinct difference from pagan paths, you have to ask them to come, there is no 'invoking' or demanding presence.

3. Activity, reading or other practice that has something to do with the gathering. This is where you have to be creative, because it involves you thinking about the time of year or reason for gathering, then develop something to do for this.

4. Get your offering ready. Gather the mead or whatever offering you have, and ask via prayer or silent requests for the gods to bless the food/drink that you have.

5. Pass the offering. I always have two offerings, one that goes around to share and one that is passed to 'place' a piece of the offering into by each participant. Basically each person will drink and eat and then pour out and give each offering back to the gods.

6. Either end the ritual with pouring or leaving the offering in a specific place or go onto preform Sumbel.

SUMBEL/SYMBEL

Everyone does this form of ritual differently, but most often the process is a series of rounds drunk by all in attendance. When you gather with others, select a leader. This person ensures that the Sumbel proceeds as planned, keeps an eye out on the alcohol level (if used), and keeps the rounds on topic.

Round 1: A Round to the Gods. Some kindreds/groups do limit this to Gods from the Nordic Pantheon. Some do not allow Loki or any giant to be called. The best thing is to check with the Sumbel organiser before you toast to a God who is not welcome.

Round 2: A Round to the Heroes. They may include: ancestors, historical figures from the sagas, or friends who have died. Round Two can be split to have the heroes/historical figures only.

Round 3: The Open Round. This round is for boasting. Boasting is the act of speaking of an accomplishment of which you are proud. This round can also be used to honor personal ancestors/friends or a God/Goddess who we feel 'significantly' close to.

VENERATING THROUGH GIFTING

Giving gifts as a way to honour relationships has existed since the beginning of time. The Edda has numerous instances where gifts were given to the Gods, including temples full of offerings. Archaeologists have found animal remains, gold, necklaces, and other precious items that were left for the Gods at the base of sacred groves. Gifts can be big or small.

The Gods don't care about the size. What matters is the attitude of the giver. In this method of veneration, respect is paid to the Gods in literal form. Gifts could include mead, beer, wine, fruit juice and or other liquid that is poured out onto the ground, or in a bowl and shared with those assembled.

Gifts could also be tokens like stones or bones. In the blot, words are used to show the deep admiration people have for the Gods. Food at blots also shows our adoration and love for the Gods, for it is in their names we are gathered and for them we make gifts and offerings. Offerings of blood are uncommon, we don't discuss this openly. If they are done it is no more than a drop or two. Blood offerings are usually done when carving rune stones or with finished rune sets in a ritual called 'blooding' the runes.

However, there are some practicing heathens who do engage in animal sacrifice or use of actual blood in rituals. This is all done with the utmost respect and care for the animal in question. It is advisable that people wishing to do actual blood offerings contact or hire someone with experience in proper animal slaughter.

"The concept of one's luck and giving are recurring themes in heathenry. The reason for these themes can be found in the Hávamál. The Hávamál is considered the source where we find counsel on behaviour and wisdom. The giver and the receiver are one, balanced equally. "In ancient times, the giving of a gift was a sign of friendship, trust, respect, and kinship. It not only had a mundane element, but also a magical significance whereas, when one gives a gift to another and a gift is returned (either immediately or shortly after) there is an exchange of might and main or hamingja/luck. To not return a gift means a decrease in one's personal hamingja or luck." (Smith, 2003)

What is unclear is whether or not these gifts have to be objects or if they could they just be gifts of service. The Hávamál does not specifically state that the concept of gifting is the actual exchange of gifts in the form of purchased goods but it seems that many heathens interpret gifting as any exchange that is equal. For example, you could exchange carpentry for grown goods or a service for a service. I participate in a craft exchange group and this is how I gift. I exchange a handmade cloth for something made for me by a fellow crafter.

Again this form of veneration is an example of concepts recorded in the source texts. Thus by performing these acts we show respect for the wisdom and virtues that were important to the heathens before us. We even have a rune for giving. Gebo, the rune for 'gift,' is the most common rune in the connection between divine and human.

We must "differentiate the 'gift for a gift' tradition with our ethics of generosity. In doing so, we will need to use wisdom in determining when they are being liberal and when they are begin[sic] taken advantage of.... but it is important for a balance to be maintained that will elevate the sense of self-worth, for everyone involved... this balance is maintained... with the idea of reciprocal relationships." (Puryear 2006).

Rites

There are so many other rites that could be done in heathenry. I wrote an entire catalog of them and will be publishing all of them for free on our website. Whatever rites are done are not always done in a specific 'sacred' circle or anything like that. In general (again I am speaking for myself) heathens don't need to create a sacred space. '

I myself don't at all. I simply incorprate the gods into my life daily. I like what I found in Natalia Lee's research on heathenry where she states that at some point you just begin 'living' heathen as if its just part of you, a thing you do regardless of any ceremony around it. There is a point I suppose where life becomes an extension of ritual.

Wearing symobls is a ritual, daily prayer is a ritual, even simply when I walk my two dogs and give thanks to the land that I have is a form of ritual. The point of heathenry is to find a way that you can practice that is simple, connective and sacred, however you define that.

Vulture Culture & Bone Tossing

SHEAL

What is 'Vulture Culture'?

Vulture culture is a subculture and form of hobbyist taxidermy based on the collection and preservation of animal remains. It takes its name from the practice of working with animals that have died of natural causes, as opposed to hunting or trapping. Specimens are commonly acquired from roadkill or found in woodland areas.

Practitioners, called "vultures", may choose to preserve an entire animal, body parts, pelts, or bones. Several methods are used to enhance the appearance of pieces; including dying, crystallization, and diaphonization; making jewelry from smaller bones or paws is also popular. In addition to taxidermy, vultures create art featuring skulls and themes of decay. The community largely consists of the sharing and selling of work. Some vultures incorporate the hobby into their spiritual or occult practices.

What does Vulture Culture consist of?

It can be several things from pelts to wet specimens to straight up bones and skulls. My own collection consists of bones, skulls, shells both marine and land, wet specimens, dry specimens and more. I both collect from other collectors and sellers as well as create and sell items, including bone curio pieces and more. Most, if not all my pieces, seeing I live in the bush and in more particular, Northern Ontario Canada, I have several ethically sourced stashes of bone. One that is my favorite to from highway roadkill. At times, I will find bones in the bush while hiking or bush camping. My Vulture Culture focus is dry and wet specimen as well as bones.

As Vulture Culture is heavily based in preserving animal remains, it is a staple activity of the aesthetic. This can be done in a multitude of ways. For bones, dying or painting, using borax to crystallize them, or utilizing them in jewelry are common practices. For whole animal remains; taxidermy or preserving them using the diaphanization processes are usually preferred.

In Canada, the laws for shipping and purchase for bones and specimens, including human remains and ashes are that it is legal to ship anywhere in Canada. I have specimens, including a wet specimen of an octopus, from British Columbia (cavemansdigs on Etsy; https://www.etsy.com/shop/CaveMansDigs?listing_id=1025683335).

I have shipped bear, deer, and moose to another Ontarian as well (magpiesandravens on Etsy; https://www.etsy.com/shop/MagpiesAndRavens). Each province has laws about remains disposal only, including Ontario where I reside, where it is stipulated that the remains or ashes of both animals and humans must be disposed of either in a pet memorial or cemetery, or alternatively, kept in a private home. If you intend on becoming a part of the Vulture Culture community, please look up the laws in your country (or state, province, area) to be sure that you are following all the laws that pertain to remains for both humans and animals.

Some areas may require a taxidermist license to collect, keep and manipulate remains. Please be mindful that if you are American, there are laws that stipulate that remains be transported through the mail across the border in a very specific set of circumstances that the CDC lists out here; https://www.cdc.gov/importation/human-remains.html. Another source of bones, including human ones is The Skull Store (https://www.skullstore.ca/).

Vulture Culture in Witchcraft Practice

For lack of a better term, I will be using the word 'witchcraft' as an all-encompassing term for all forms of magic and spiritual practice. Vulture Culture does not need to be a main staple of anyone's given practice; however, you will see the culture among death workers the most. The two are not symbiotic in any way and Vulture Culture does not necessarily mean the person practices witchcraft for that matter.

Although, those who use bones as a divination tool like bone throwing readings, also known as osteomancy, will lean into the Vulture Culture community as well as the various sub-communities of witchcraft. Myself, I use bone throwing as a tool as much as I do a tarot deck. I also collect curio based of off bones, sell my own bones, curio and creations to other practitioners of both Vulture Culture and witchcraft.

Osteomancy: Reading Bones & Bone Throwing

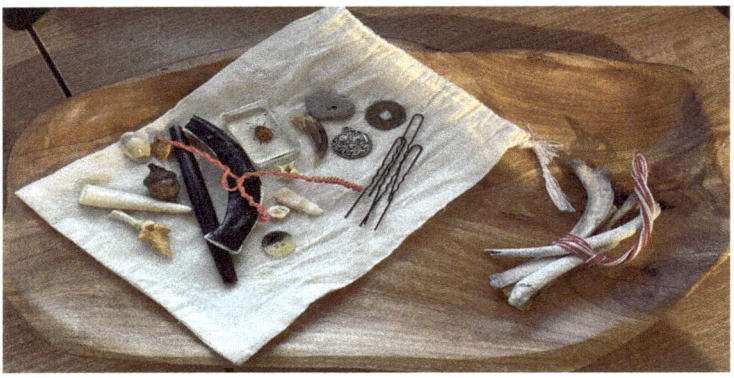

There are two distinct ways to read "bones" in bone throwing readings and two distinct styles of bone reading tools [pictured above]. The one style I am yet to become familiar with and the set and I have not, as the saying may go in some circles, bonded yet. The second style is my preferred style of bone throwing and reading. A simple system of yes or no answers depending on the way the bones land. Some will use four rib bones from a preferred animal that they are in tune with. Mine are of two animal sources, some from bear and deer [pictured on the right]. I use five bones rather than four myself.

Since I am still learning the more complicated style of osteomancy, I will talk only to the simplified osteomancy practice. There are answers that can mean either a soft no, soft yes, a hard no or a hard yes. Typically, the reader will ask the person, much like tarot card reading but less complicated in manner, for a yes or no question. Sometimes this may be "Will I get that new promotion I want at work?" Or something similar. The bone reader will then toss the bones either on a pelt or into a flat, wood plate. Depending on how the bones land it will give you your yes or no answer. What could the typically accepted answers look like as your bones may speak to you differently and you will get to know them?

Hard Yes

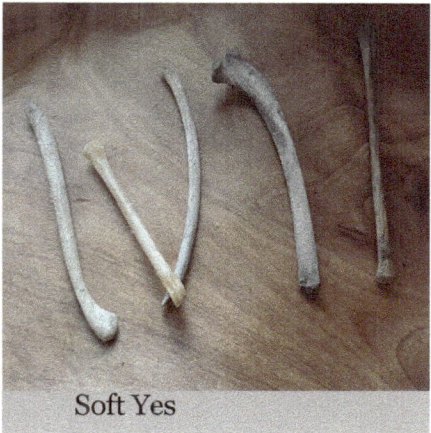

Soft Yes

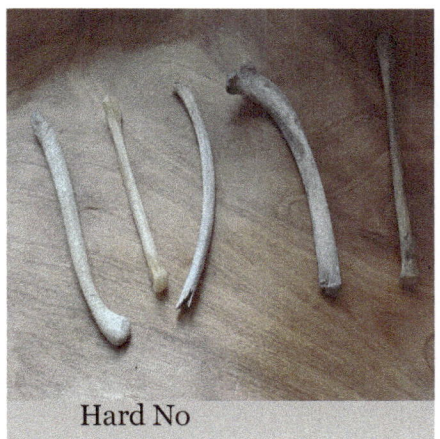

Hard No

Soft No

BONES TOSSING
(Uses for bones, preparation for bones, tossing bones)

LARISA

I personally use randomized objects for casting in some cases. I have always loved the idea of using natural and unnatural materials instead of specifically crafted for the purpose of divination. In doing research for this section, I came across a book called *Throwing Bones, How to Foretell* the future with bones, shells , and nuts by Catherine Yronwode mentioned that bones could also refer to things that are not exactly skeletal, they can also be shells (both animal shells like tortoises and nut shells like walnuts).

She also mentions that there are different types of bone readings and breaks it up into several categories. For the purpose of this piece, I will focus on the completely prepared bone rather than the unprepared bones or bones that could be interpreted through cooking them. **SLAUGHTER BONES** could be cooked and then removed from a cooked state and read through interpreting the clarity of the bone, the remaining 'meat' on the bone, the shape of the meat, any 'apparent' shapes that were revealed through the cooking process.

This would be used more or less with animal bones, however preparation of human bones would be similar, you could boil flesh off bone to use in creating tools like distaff whorls and 'rune' staves (although we don't have any direct evidence that runes in particular, either the Elder or Younger Futhark were used in divination, they did use 'bones' but it's unknown what was etched on them if anything. Yronwode also mentions an extensive list of meanings for each type of bone and shows examples of how to toss them and interpret them.

She does say something that does appear time and time again in heathen sources, there is a connection between bones and a magical force from which is invisible. This concept does come up time and time again, even beads used from a burial site would be 'connected to the wearer'. These objects, as we previously linked in That One Time We Ate Grandma become the person or connected to the person and thus this dead linked object held otherworldly powers.

I see random objects similar to this, because there is a sense of owned power that attaches to an object, by wearing it, by living with it, an object becomes magical in a sense. Although there is no direct evidence for the practice of using bones specifically for divinatory purposes, there is a lot of evidence that bones in particular had meaning throughout the Nordic regions. One curious connection is that of the frequency of sheep bones. Although sheep are quite abundant throughout that region, the fact that there are links to other cultures that had these bones in particular as 'sacred'. If we go a bit outside of the Nordic region and look to Mongolia there is a sense of bones having a practical and magical connection because of the fact of what seems to be common throughout the bronze-iron age, the concept that all things are linked to a animistic magical connection.

An animal that served a useful purpose like providing fiber, milk products, skins and also meat/bone was not only practical for preserving life but also connected to a spiritual sense of universal reciprocation. The sacrificial animal or one offered to feast had connection to the world of the living and dead, it somewhat held both places and so just like human remains the bones served a dual purpose. In this paper "Birtalan, Ágnes. "Ritualistic Use of Livestock Bones in the Mongolian Belief System and Customs. ." Altaica Budapestinensia MMII. Proceedings of the 45th Permanent International Conference Budapest, Hungary, June 23–28, 2002. Ed. Alice Sárközi – Attila Rákos. (2003): n. pag. Print." Which goes into how Mongolian tribes used bone in different seasons as well as ritual use, "The shoulder is the most respectful [bone]. It is said that when you slaughter a sheep and eat its meat, leave the forequarter to the end. Why is it respected? It is connected to the tale of the "Calf-man", I have told you recently, to the preserving of the fore-quarter of the lean lamb. The forequarter of the lean lamb has been preserved, then cooked and its meat filled up a vessel with nine seals. Just imagine it! That is why the forequarter is respected. The shoulder is served for the maternal relatives (naɣc); the shoulder will not be served for the nephews on the maternal side (ze). Besides the maternal relatives, the nephews do not touch the shoulder."

I general buy bones for ritual use, as I don't have a way to gather them myself and the laws where I live are very clear about what to do with remains. We have a continual decaying animal pickup crew that cleans the streets in Hawaii as we have a tremendous feral cat, chicken and dog issue as well as mongoose, geese, ducks, wild pigs/boars, goats, deer and other animals that do occasionally meet a car.

"Bones are heavy enough to hurt with, sharp enough to cut through flesh, and when old and if strung, tinkle like glass. The bones of the living are alive and creatural in themselves;; they constantly renew themselves. A living bone has a curiously soft "skin" to it It appears to have certain powers to regenerate itself. Even as a dry bone, it becomes home for small living creatures." [Women Who Run With The Wolves, Estes, C]

When I use them in any 'readings' I generally do random tossing with them, similar to Sheal, I let them fall where they may and then interpret them. I generally have carved bone runes with futhark symbols etched on. I will turn over the ones that fall face down and turn all of them facing upward and then begin. If I need clarifying answers, I will pull out a fourth or fifth rune to get further answers.

"In the bone trade, saying that a skeleton was sourced ethically can mean many things. Perhaps it was obtained without the organism suffering, or the animal was not killed for the purpose of making a trophy. Maybe it was used in the meat trade, or died of natural causes. "Ethically sourced" can mean so many things, that it becomes vague and unwieldy."JonsBones

It is hard to know for sure if you are getting ethical bones, but try to do some due diligence before purchases. I myself do think its perfectly ok to use medical grade bones from human donors. I would say at best we can just call these 'responsibly sourced' as they are voluntarily donated and we cannot ensure that the person did not suffer before they died.

Its critical that you ensure that the bones are not stolen, they are not; rave-robbed, anthropological, or tribal bones. This is a critical must! I recommend JonsBones or the Bone Room as both ethical and certified human medical bones which are free from any issues in terms of in-proprietary.

https://www.jonsbones.com/blog/human-bone-provenance
https://www.boneroom.com/store/c1/Featured_Products.html

BIBLIOGRAPHY

Abolotion. Feminisim. Now. Angela Y. Davis, Gina Dent, Erica R. Meiners and Beth Ritchie

Arwill-Nordbladh, E. 2016 Viking Age Hair, Internet Archaeology 42. http://dx.doi.org/10.11141/ia.42.6.8https://intarch.ac.uk/journal/issue42/6/8.cfm

Artisson, Robin. The Flaming Circle. Sunland: Pendraig Pubishing, 2008.

Andrews, T. ' Enchantment of the Faerie Realm'

Baba Yaga, The Ambigous Mother and Witch of the Russian Folktale. Jons, Andreas

Baba Yaga's Book of Witchcraft, Slavic Magic from the Witch of the Woods Madame Pamita

Barber, Elizabeth Wayland. The Dancing Goddesses: Folklore, Archaeology, and the Origins of European Dance. United States, W. W. Norton, 2013.

Buckly, J. 'Inspiration and Inebriation' Dissertation.

Child, F. 'The English and Scottish Popular Ballads'. V1, pg 95-6. Dover Publications. 1965

Day, C. 'Ireland'

Davidson, H. 'Gods and Myths of Northern Europe. 1990

Dickson, E and Woodman, M. 'Dancing in the Flames, The Dark Goodess in Transformation of Consciousness': Shambhala Publications, 1997

Dommasness, L. 'Spun on a wheel where women's hearts'. Archaeporess. 2008

Dolfyn. Shamanism ~ Working with Moon Medicin

Dunn, Steven T. "Weaponizing Ordinary Objects: Women, Masculine Performance, and the Anxieties of Men in Medieval Iceland." Master's Thesis (2019): n. pag. Print.

Eriksen, M. (2019). 'Lift Me over Door-Hinges and Lintels': Doorways, Bodies, and Biographies. In Architecture, Society, and Ritual in Viking Age Scandinavia: Doors, Dwellings, and Domestic Space (pp. 145-178). Cambridge: Cambridge University Press. doi:10.1017/9781108667043.010

Feral, H. 'Between the Living and the Dead: A Perspective on Witches, and Seers in the Early Modern Age. Central European University Press. 1999

Gadon, E. ' The Once and Future Goddess'

Gimbutas, Marija. The Living Goddesses. United Kingdom, University of California Press, 2001.

Grimes, R 'Deeply into the Bone: Re-Inventing Rites of Passage'

Grimm, Jacob. 'Deutsche Mythologie'. 1835

Green, M. ' Celtic Goddesses: Warriors, Virgins and Mothers'

Goode, S. 'Icon of the Vulva, A Basis of Civilzation". 2001

Halvardsson, A. 'Blood & Magic, A Microstudy of associations between Viking Age women and their weapons'

Heide, E. 'Spirits Through Respiratory Passages'

Herm, G 'The Celtics: The People Who Came Out of the Darknes'

Kvilhaug, M. 'Burning the Witch!-Initation of the Goddess and the War of Aesir and the Vanir'

Kyngervi Journal: https://www.kyngervi.org/issues/issue2
 Last Ride of the Valyries: To (reinterpret Viking Age Female Figurines According to Gender and Queer Theory by Julia Wihlborg

Baugrýgjar: Old Norse 'Ring Ladies' and Legal Husband-Killing in Ynglinga saga by Ashley Castelino

But, What About the Men? Male Ritual Practices in the Icelandic Sagas by Dan Laurin

LeCoutex, Claude. 'The Tradtion of Household Spirits'.2013

MacCrossan, T ' The Sacred Cauldron'

Matthewes, J. 'Drinking From the Sacred Well'

Marklewicz, K. The Icelandic Völva and the Old Polish Witch. A Comparative Analysis

Maraschi, A. 'Eaten Hears and Supernatural Knowledge In Eiriks Saga Ruda. Abstract

McCoy, E. ' Sabbats ~ A Witch's Approach to Living the Old Ways'

McCoy, E. ' Celtic Women's Spirituality ~ Accessing the Cauldron of Life'

Monogham, P. ' The Red-Haired Girl from the Bog'

Monaghan, Patricia. PhD. Encyclopedia of Goddesses and Heroines. Novato: New World Library. 2014. Print

Myers, Brenden Cathbad. The Mystery of Druidry: Celtic Mysticism, Theory and Practice. Franklin Lake: Career Press, 2006.

Peterson, M: "Hulje: Calendrical rites along a small stream" Electronic Journal of Folklore 2013

Pohl, Ulrike. "Frija, Frea, Frigg." Herdfeuer Ausgabe 47 (2017): n. pag. Print.

Penczak, Christopher. 2012). E—book. Feast of the Morrighan: A grimoire for the Dark Lady of the Emerald Isle. U.S.A.: Copper Cauldron Publishing, 2012

Reynolds, Tara. The Morrigan: Goddess Connections Workbook. 2013.

Rolleston, T. Chapter III: The Irish Invasion Myths. Myths and Legends of the Celtic Race. 1911. Internet sacred text archive. 2011.

» Riddle, J. ' Contraception and Abortion from the Ancient World to the Renaissance'

» Srsic, E. "On Female Witches and Woodcuts". Thesis. Academia. edu

» Telesco, P. ' 365 Goddess ~ A daily guide to the magic and inspiration of the Goddes'

» Virtue, D. 'Archangels & Ascended Masters'

» Weaponizing Ordinary Objects: Women, Masculine Performance, and the Anxieties of Men in Medieval Iceland. Steven T. Dunn, University of Florida, Scholar Commons, Graduate Theses, March 2019

» Waldherr, K. ' The Book of Goddesses : A Celebration of the Feminine Divine'

» Woodfield, Stephanie. Celtic Lore & Spellcraft of the Dark Goddess. Invoking the Morrigan. Woodbury: Llewellyn Publications, 2011.

Online Sources

Https://www.Lifeinnorway.Net/creatures-in-norse-mythology/

Https://www.Academia.Edu/17457422/hulje_calendrical_rites_along_a_small_stream_folklore_electronic_journal_of_folklore_55_2013

Https://www.Academia.Edu/5971504/bl%c3%93t_houses_in_viking_age_farmstead_cult_practices

Https://www.Academia.Edu/41683416/gold_foil_figures_in_focus_synthesis_chapter

https://www.connollycove.com/tuatha-de-danann/

https://www.ragingrootsstudio.com

https://www.cheryl-morgan.com/?p=28606

https://skemman.is/bitstream/1946/22619/1/Final%20Thesis.pdf

https://irishfolklore.wordpress.com/2017/10/13/the-irish-wake-and-its-gender-roles/

https://classicalwisdom.com/people/leaders/becoming-boudica-how-celtic-female-warrior-culture-challenged-rome/

https://tigereyedesigns.blogspot.com/2011/07/celtic-anamchara-ritual-for-best.html

http://penelope.uchicago.edu/Thayer/E/Roman/Texts/Strabo/4D*.html

https://www.britannica.com/topic/Brehon-laws

https://www.ancient-origins.net/history-important-events/anglesey-druids-0016639

https://www.ancient-origins.net

https://www.britannica.com/topic/Scathach

https://www.connollycove.com/scathach/

http://www.historynaked.com/scathach-the-shadow/

https://en.wikipedia.org/wiki/Kellas_cat

https://www.skullstore.ca/

http://www.otherworldlyoracle.com

http://www.hranajanto.com/GoddessGallery/Danù.html

http://en.wikipedia.org/wiki/Danù_(Irish_goddess)

http://www.thaliatook.com/AMGG/Danù.html

http://irelandsown.net/mothergoddess.html

http://www.jmasonart.com/celt/irish2.htm

http://www.fatheroak.com/Celtic_Gods.html

http://www.darkages.com/2002 /community/phi/Chult_Danù.html

http://www.circlesanctuary.org/goddesscircle/Danù

http://www.pantheon.org/articles/d/Danù.html

http://www.care2.com/c2c/share/detail/391339?pid=343025695

Laura Cameron. "Morrigan" and "Raven Spirit" http://www.lauracameron.net/

Olivier Villoingt. "The Soul of War" and "Morrigan" http://vilantares.blogspot.fr/

Yoann Lossel. "La Morrigan" http://yoannlossel.blogspot.com/

*www.goddesswithin.co.uk/apri_rhiannon.htm (ritual)

*www.goddessgift.com/goddess-myths/celtic_goddess_rhiannon.htm

*www.angelfire.com/va/goddesses/rhia.html

*www.answers.com/topic/Rhiannon

*www.en.wikipedia.org/wiki/Rhiannon

www.epona.net/later.html

Goddess of Light quote. Ruth Shaw. http://feminismandreligion.com/2013/07/31/aine-summer-goddess-of-love-light-and-fertility-by-judith-shaw/

Aine Goddess of Love, Fiary Queen...Mary E. Pritchard, Ph.D.

http://awakeningthegoddesswithin.net/featured-goddess-aine/

Hail to thee, thou Sun of the Seasons poem from the Carmina Gadelica. http://www.sacred-texts.com/neu/celt/cg.htm

A Blessing to evoke the Goddess Aine. http://www.voicesfromthedawn.com/wp-content/sites/knockAine/citations/knockAineCitation_6.html

Full Moon Irish/Celtic Love Spell. Hepzibah. Sept 4, 2009. http://hepzibahjames.blogspot.com/2009/09/full-moon-irishceltic-love-spell.html

Aine and Midsummer Incense: The Sanctuary of the Mother Earth. Goddess recipes (n.d.) http://calliope_le_fey.tripod.com/id8.html

Solar Goddess Meditation. (n.d.) (n.a.). Sun Godderss Daily Meditation. Onespiritx. http://onespiritx.tripod.com/medi14.htm

Greenfield, Trevor. Naming the Goddess. Sept 2014. Moon Books. Google Books.

http://www.goddessalive.co.uk/index.php/issues-16-20/issue-19-spring-summer-2011/aine

Aine and Midsummer Incense: The Sanctuary of the Mother Earth. Goddess recipes (n.d.) http://calliope_le_fey.tripod.com/id8.html

https://celtichermit.com/2021/08/25/st-patrick-and-the-druids/

OTHER SOURCES

Jarvis, Jana. Aine: Goddess of Midsummer, Goddess of the People. Issue 19 (Spring/Summer 2011). Goddess Alive. Goddess celebration and research.

SageWoman #63 – The Journey, (A Circle is Cast by Jo Lynne Gianvecchio), Published by Blessed Bee, Inc.

SageWoman #64 – Prayer & Invocation, (Garlands for the Goddess by Carrie D. Cooper, Published by Blessed Bee, Inc. Notes from the Journal of Lavanee, 2004

Skye, Michelle. Midsummer's Eve Invocation and Aine Speaks. Goddess Alive!: Inviting Celtic & Norse Goddesses Into Your Life. July 8, 2007. Llewellyn Publications; 1st Edition.

IMAGES

Where possible credit for all images is located along side the image in place throughout. All sources used in this book were accessed via the commons or through legal licences purchased by The Three Little Sisters.

OTHER

TEA PAIRINGS

FRIGGA

TEAS:
- ⸙ Twingings: Fig & Vanilla Flavored Herbal Tea
- ⸙ Traditional Medicines: Organic Fennel Tea
- ⸙ Tazo: Glazed Lemon Loaf

FOODS: Lavender cookies, shortbread, scones with lemon, dark chocolate

FREYJA

TEAS:
- ⸙ Twinings: Heartea+ or Blackcurrant Breeze
- ⸙ Traditional Medicines: Rose Hips & Hibiscus Tea
- ⸙ Tazo: Passion (hibiscus flowers, orange peel, rose hips, passion fruit flavor and a lively hint of cinnamon spice)
- ⸙ FOODS: Strawberry tarts, apple turnovers, hearty stew.

SIF

TEAS:
- Twinings: Orange & Cinnamon Spice from
- Traditional Medicines: Organic Ginger
- Tazo: Wild Sweet Orange

FOOD: Flax seed bread or any bread with rough oats, a good rye is also a great option.

RAN

TEAS:
- Twinings: Chai Tea with sea salt
- Traditional Medicine: Throat Coat or Gypsy Tea
- Tazo: Cucumber White

FOODS: Any type of fish. If your not a fish or shellfish eater, an alternative could be kelp chips or sea salt infused food.

ANGRBODA

TEA
- Twinings: Darjeeling is a good earthy tea
- Traditional Medicine: Licorice Root Tea
- Tazo: Turmeric Bliss

FOOD: She prefers raw foods or foods cooked only to rare. Meat offerings are good, if you're a vegan, choose an offering that is gathered from the root. Root veggies like turnips, carrots, beets are a great option. I suspect using Beyond burgers or blank based meats would also be a good substitute.

BABA YAGA

TEA

- Twinings: Winter Spice Tea
- Traditional Medicine: Gypsy Tea
- Tazo: Turmeric Bliss or Prickly Pear

FOODS: Any kind of Slavic foods like soap, pirogies etc.

≈

HEL

Tea

Twinings: Comfort Tea with Tumeric
Traditional Medicines: Gypsy Tea
Tazo: Roasted Dandelion Root or Reishi Mushroom with Rooibos & Orange Peal Tea
Foods: She likes dark breads and grains along with dark chocolates like 90% coco or higher.

During the creation of this book, we had an an amazing oppertunity to work with a skilled herbalist named James who owns a little tea company called Tree Fifty Four.

Through many converstations, chats and late night banter we worked together to create a series of teas inspired by our gods. James has lovingly taken our ideas and transformed them into drinks fit for consuption, offering and more.

Having tried all of his teas, I can firmly say, they taste amazing, are profoundly potent and provide a unique way to honor godddess. We encourage readers to check out his complete line and take a bag out for a test drive!--Larisa

https://www.treefiftyfour.com

Biographies

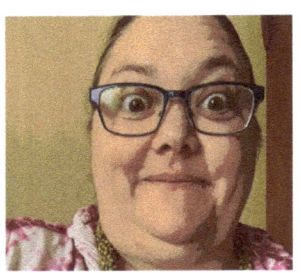

Larisa Hunter: Runs the day to day operations, handles layout and marketing. Larisa has a background in law/writing and publishing and has a Certificate in General Arts & Science from Sheridan College.

Sheal Mullin-Berube: Second in command, Sheal does everything from; covers, editing, marketing, video trailers, video ads, audio/visuals and more. She has over 20+ years of editing experience. She has a BA in Office Systems Management and Document Technology from John Abbott College.

Sarah Strickland: runs creative marketing, ads, themes and helps develop projects for TLS. She also assists in the platform and direction of TLS and our various outlets [Nevermore Podcast and Unicorn Canvas].

The Three Little Sisters

The Three Little Sisters is an indie publisher that puts authors first. We specalize in the strange and unusual. From titles about pagan and heathen spirituality to traditional fiction we bring books to life.

https://the3littlesisters.com